Narratives of Parental Death, Dying and Bereavement

"This pioneering volume brings together eight personal reflections on parental death. It speaks powerfully of the complexities and shifting alignments of parental and familial bonds, care and responsibility, identity, guilt, self-reflection and celebration of a life, all of which combine to create the singular sense of loss and grief brought about by the death of a parent. These remarkable accounts, as unique as the lives and deaths of the individuals they reference, are all the more compelling because they are written by leading authorities in the field of death studies. By focusing on a subject which to an extent has been eclipsed, this moving, instructive and richly textured book makes a significant contribution to the study of death, dying and bereavement."
—Professor Hilary J Grainger OBE, *President of The Association for the Study of Death and Society and Chair of The Cremation Society of Great Britain*

AF075044

Caroline Pearce • Carol Komaromy
Editors

Narratives of Parental Death, Dying and Bereavement

A Kind of Haunting

palgrave
macmillan

Editors
Caroline Pearce
University of Cambridge
Cambridge, UK

Carol Komaromy
The Open University
Milton Keynes, UK

ISBN 978-3-030-70893-1   ISBN 978-3-030-70894-8   (eBook)
https://doi.org/10.1007/978-3-030-70894-8

© The Editor(s) (if applicable) and The Author(s), under exclusive licence to Springer Nature Switzerland AG 2021

This work is subject to copyright. All rights are solely and exclusively licensed by the Publisher, whether the whole or part of the material is concerned, specifically the rights of translation, reprinting, reuse of illustrations, recitation, broadcasting, reproduction on microfilms or in any other physical way, and transmission or information storage and retrieval, electronic adaptation, computer software, or by similar or dissimilar methodology now known or hereafter developed.

The use of general descriptive names, registered names, trademarks, service marks, etc. in this publication does not imply, even in the absence of a specific statement, that such names are exempt from the relevant protective laws and regulations and therefore free for general use.

The publisher, the authors and the editors are safe to assume that the advice and information in this book are believed to be true and accurate at the date of publication. Neither the publisher nor the authors or the editors give a warranty, expressed or implied, with respect to the material contained herein or for any errors or omissions that may have been made. The publisher remains neutral with regard to jurisdictional claims in published maps and institutional affiliations.

Cover illustration: Randomerophotos, iStock.

This Palgrave Macmillan imprint is published by the registered company Springer Nature Switzerland AG.
The registered company address is: Gewerbestrasse 11, 6330 Cham, Switzerland

Foreword

The editors and contributors to *Narratives of Parental Death, Dying and Bereavement: A Kind of Haunting* are academics and professionals in the UK who have provided significant leadership in the field of death, dying and bereavement both nationally and internationally. It's an honour to welcome this anthology that adds to our knowledge of the meaning and experiences of parental death.

Each of the book's chapters focuses on parental death, a universal experience that has for too long received little theoretical, psychosocial and research attention. This volume offers an important contribution to the field of death studies that has more often tended to explore the death of a child or death of a spouse.

In these sensitively wrought chapters, the contributors describe their parent's life and death, as well as share their own personal meaning of this loss. One chapter was written decades ago shortly after a parent's death. Most were composed in 2019–2020 long after the parent's death, in part through the lens of memory and in part through the perspective of the author's academic and professional knowledge of death studies, theory and research.

Although the authors each have recognised expertise in research and academic death studies, they are a heterogeneous group, differing in gender, age at parental death, current age, cultural and class upbringing, family composition, and life-time patterns of emotional and physical closeness to their parents. They each contribute a unique and thoughtful perspective in describing their experience of parental death.

This anthology raises important issues and questions about the interface between the knowledge of academic professional scholars, and their personal private experiences of the death of their own parents. The boundary-transcending nature of this book will make it useful for academics who have undertaken research to study others often without considering their own personal experiences. Gratitude is due to the contributors who have opened a revealing window into the interface of the personal and professional aspects of their lives.

I am particularly pleased that the topic of parental death is the main focus of this collection. Although parent-child relationships have been studied for the first decades of their lives together, child-parent relationships in middle and later life have been under-investigated and often limited to issues of role reversal and caregiving. After decades of professionally researching issues related to middle-aged children and the death of an elderly parent, I believe that understanding the impact of parental death can significantly add to our conceptualisation of the complexity of relationships between middle aged adults and their parents. Once a parent has died, a haunting tie remains, a theme that continually reappears throughout the book. My hope is that many family researchers will read these chapters and find new avenues to explore.

Most authors describe their parent's health, functional capacity, cognitive abilities, and resources available, as well as the choices of care that were available and desired by the parent. Readers will note that the contributors differ in what they share of their personal feelings. Some of the inner thoughts of each author are shared directly (e.g. a daughter's ambivalence toward a new pattern of recovery after her father's very long and deep decline). Many write of their sense of regret after parental death, such as wishing there had been less medical intervention, their lack of intimacy with their parent, regret that they had not spent more time with the parent, and of the impact of not being with the parent at the moment of death.

A noteworthy underlying theme recurring in several chapters is that of family privacy and "sacred-secrecy" (the silences, what is and is not spoken or shared within the family and out of the family). This contrasts with the more openly described ways in which the authors responded to the structures and policies of the outside supporting professionals with whom they interact, whether medical (to diagnose, treat and cure), funeral (designating procedures to be followed), or clergy (setting expectations for family in ritual). These professionals could find that reading this anthology will help them gain insight into better filling their changing roles as they seek to sensitively interact with family members of parents and others regarding the end of life.

Most of the parental deaths discussed in this volume occurred toward the end of the twentieth century or early in the twenty-first century. However several children described the death of both of their parents over a span of decades. This broader temporal perspective allows contributors to highlight societal changes over time in gender roles, the place of death, timing of funerals, and flexibility in rituals of burial. What was fitting when the first parent died sometimes changes when the second parent dies. In any case, the death of the first parent typically increases the bereaved child's sense of responsibility and interaction with the widow/er, while the death of the last parent often generates a sense of 'orphanhood', as well as the loss of a final buffer against death.

Scholars interested in family interactions and relationships will gain insight from these authors' discussion of the degree to which an individual bereaved child shares, or does not share, their experience and meanings of parental death with their siblings and other kin. This is consistent with our group's research which has found that each child's experience can be very different from what a sibling experiences (Moss and Moss 2012–13).

I think that therapists who provide bereavement care will be enriched by this anthology. This volume might also be a useful tool for university students in their introduction to death studies, since it offers rich fuel for thought and discussion.

Finally, I believe that persons who have experienced parental death will find that this anthology speaks to them about their own identity, how they related to their own parent in the past, how their parent had an impact on their own lives, and how their tie with their parent will be maintained or modified in the future. Several authors discuss their thoughts of eventual plans for their own death after reconsidering the end of life and death of their parent.

The experiences shared by each of the authors will inevitably sensitise readers to the multi-dimensionality of this topic. The book makes an important contribution toward expanding our understanding of parental death.

Glenside, PA, USA   Miriam Moss

Reference

Moss, M.S. & Moss, S.Z. (2012–2013). Meaning of the death of an elderly father: Two sisters' perspectives. *Omega: Journal of Death and Dying, 66, 195–213.*

Acknowledgements

This anthology reflects the collaborative reciprocity that exists in the death studies community. It arose from informal and sometimes intimate conversations about personal loss. Like many anthologies, it is intended as a shared offering of personal experiences for people interested in the detail of what it is like to be involved in the dying and death of a parent. More than this, it highlights the difference and diversity in such experiences.

As editors we are grateful to those authors who have shared their experiences and reflected on what it means to them; taking the reader behind the scenes of family life. We also thank the reviewers of an early draft of the manuscript and acknowledge how important peer support is to academia.

Contents

1. **Introduction: Narrating Death** 1
   Caroline Pearce and Carol Komaromy

2. **A Kind of Haunting** 33
   Carol Komaromy

3. **A Death Recalled** 51
   Jenny Hockey

4. **Continuing and Emerging Bonds: Working Through Grief as a Daughter and an Academic** 79
   Kathryn Almack

5. **A Bittersweet Legacy** 101
   Gordon Riches

6	**Two Traumatic Bereavements** *Colin Murray Parkes*	119
7	**Death, Dislocation and Discovery over Five (or Should that Be Six or Even Seven?) Decades** *Rosaline S. Barbour*	129
8	**Bereavement, Sacred-Secrecy and Dreams** *Douglas Davies*	155
9	**Conclusion: Recovering Ghosts** *Caroline Pearce*	177
Index		195

Notes on Contributors

Kathryn Almack is Professor of Health and Family Lives in the School of Health and Social Work at the University of Hertfordshire. She is a sociologist with a particular expertise in the sociology of family lives and relationships of care in people's lives, addressing ethically challenging and sensitive research areas. A key area of her research over the past 15 years has been to explore the palliative and end of life care needs and care environments of our ageing populations. She is interested in bringing sociological perspectives to death, dying and bereavement studies.

Rosaline S. Barbour is Emerita Professor at The Open University. A medical sociologist, her research career has focused on the intersection of the social and the clinical. Examples include a study of the concerns about fertility for young people with a cancer diagnosis. Several projects have also looked at the personal impact for practitioners of taking on new roles and responsibilities, in responding to various clinical developments (such as the emergence of HIV/AIDS in the 1980s and 1990s). Her commitment to qualitative research – and interest in focus groups, in particular – has led to the publication of several books and articles appearing in a range of social science and medical journals.

Douglas Davies, anthropologist and theologian, is Professor in the Study of Religion and Director of The Centre for Death and Life Studies at University of Durham, and was previously at Nottingham University. He works on the interplay of anthropology and theology, especially on the ritual, symbolism and belief of funerary rites. He is also internationally recognised as an expert on Mormonism. A Doctor of Letters of Oxford and an Honorary Doctor of Sweden's Uppsala University, he is also an elected Fellow of the UK Academy of Social Sciences, The Learned Society of Wales, and The British Academy.

Jenny Hockey is Emeritus Professor of Sociology at the University of Sheffield. Trained as an anthropologist, her research encompasses hospice and bereavement care, funerals, cremation, natural burial and exorcism. Key theoretical focuses have been material culture, gender, ageing and the life course. Her recent publications include: *The Matter of Death: Space, Place and Materiality* (Palgrave 2010), co-edited with C. Komaromy and K. Woodthorpe, and *Natural Burial: Landscape, Practice and Experience* (Routledge 2015), co-authored with A. Clayden, T. Green and M. Powell. She was president of the Association for the Study of Death and Society (2009–13) and is a member of the editorial board of the journal Mortality.

Carol Komaromy has worked extensively in both NHS clinical practice as a nurse and midwife and in medical sociology in academia. Her main interest lies in ethnography and death studies which she researched and taught for 20 years at The Open University. Carol served as co-editor of the journal *Mortality* and was a founding member of the Association of Death and Society. Carol worked as Media Fellow at The OU and was awarded a Public Education Award for her contribution to raising public awareness about death and dying. Main publications include: Komaromy, C. and Hockey, J. (2018) *Family Life, Trauma and Loss in the Twentieth Century*, and Earle, S., Komaromy, C. and Bartholomew, C. (Eds.) (2009) *Death and Dying: A Reader*. London: Sage.

Colin Murray Parkes is Consultant Psychiatrist Emeritus at St Christopher's Hospice, Sydenham and President of Cruse Bereavement Care. Aged 92 in 2020, he remains closely involved with the study and management of bereavement, stress and disasters until recent years. Colin is author of numerous influential works on the psychology of bereavement, stress and disasters, including Parkes, C. M. and Prigerson, H. (2010) *Bereavement: Studies of Grief in Adult Life*, 4th Edition. London: Routledge; Parkes, C. M. (2006) *Love and Loss: the roots of Grief and its Complications*. London: Routledge; and Parkes, C. M. (2014) *The Price of Love: Selected Works by Colin Murray Parkes*. London: Routledge.

Caroline Pearce is a Research Fellow at the University of Edinburgh and Visiting Researcher at the University of Cambridge. She has worked previously at King's College London and completed her PhD at The Open University. Trained as a sociologist she focuses on experiences of bereavement, complex forms of grief and notions of recovery. Caroline is currently Editor-in-Chief of *Bereavement Care* and was part of the editorial team for the journal *Mortality* for seven years. She is author of *The Public and Private Management of Grief: Recovering normal* (2019) London: Palgrave.

Gordon Riches was Senior Lecturer in Sociology at the University of Derby and was involved in researching the impact of a child's death on family and marital relationships. Along with Pam Dawson, he published a number of articles and the book *An Intimate Loneliness* (2000, Open University Press). In doing this, he benefited greatly from the support of both The Compassionate Friends (TCF) and Survivors of Bereavement by Suicide (SOBS). Much of his work was based on first-hand accounts of bereaved parents. He retired from post-graduate supervision in 2013.

1

Introduction: Narrating Death

Caroline Pearce and Carol Komaromy

Death is universal and everybody's business, yet much remains hidden about how it feels to experience the death of someone close. This book is designed to stimulate reflection on parental death through accounts of end-of-life, death and disposal experiences told by the children of their deceased parent(s). These narratives of parental death, dying and bereavement are written by key academics in death studies in the United Kingdom and take the reader behind the scenes, so to speak, of academic theory and expertise to highlight how death has impacted their personal lives. The intensely powerful, detailed descriptions give the reader an insight into the feelings and experiences of people who have devoted much of their professional lives trying to make academic sense of death, dying and bereavement. The collection answers questions such as how do

---

C. Pearce (✉)
University of Cambridge, Cambridge, UK
e-mail: cmp89@medschl.cam.ac.uk

C. Komaromy
The Open University, Milton Keynes, UK

© The Author(s), under exclusive license to Springer Nature Switzerland AG 2021
C. Pearce, C. Komaromy (eds.), *Narratives of Parental Death, Dying and Bereavement*,
https://doi.org/10.1007/978-3-030-70894-8_1

people who have sought to provide structure and order to death and dying cope with the death of one or both parents, and what does it mean to be orphaned?

It is assumed and often expected that practitioners and academics in sensitive areas like death and dying should remain distanced, or distance themselves, from patients, research participants or data. Here we seek to disrupt the boundary between the researcher and participant, ethnographer and observed, to journey into the private realm and explore first-hand experiences of deaths that were up close and personal. All authors are experienced researchers in the field of death studies, including sociology, anthropology, theology, and psychology. For these authors, the narratives are of both personal and academic interest. However, some have chosen to relate their account in a deeply personal way with little or no academic interpretation, while others have refracted their experience through an academic lens.

The individual descriptions of death and grief capture the everyday practicalities of managing death and dying, including the difficulties of caring responsibilities, and realities of dealing with occasional tensions and ambiguities in family relationships. Some authors carry a sense of regret about how the death was managed, while others find an intimacy that was absent in their everyday relationship or a deepening of closeness. While sharing the experience of the end of life, the diversity of these accounts reflects the range of emotions authors experienced. However, what they all share is the way in which their discipline within death studies frames the experience and the expression of events, whether or not this is foregrounded. Indeed, their professional lives are part of their identity – but when death is a personal experience, the extent to which that disrupts this identity is explored.

From the perspective of the personal interest of the editors, Caroline Pearce is a researcher in the earlier phases of her career trajectory which has focused on understanding experiences of grief and bereavement. For Caroline it was the personal experience of the death of both parents as a teenager that provoked a personal and then academic enquiry into making sense of death and grief. She explains: 'Growing up with an ill and disabled mother and absent father, loss featured in my personal landscape from a young age. Looking back, I see how I – like many others – was thrown by circumstances beyond my control into a situation for which I was woefully unprepared, and within which I felt completely powerless. What followed was a long process of making sense of grief and finding meaning – what I now recognise as common psychological processes referenced in bereavement literature. Negotiating with the idea of 'recovery' became central to my enquiry, born out of a resistance to the doomed narratives that were associated with being a teenage orphan. The experience of living with loss ultimately became a powerful critical lens to understand what I've described as the other side of recovery: non-recovery. This is a focus on those things that cannot be recovered, to understand how people live with deterioration, where loss is not overcome but a fundamental part of human existence and a reality of social life.'

Carol Komaromy is at the end of a career that has spanned practice and academia over 50 years throughout which her interest in death studies has been central. In particular, she has been committed to good end-of-life care. As she relates, her father died while she was training to be a midwife, but her mother died when she was teaching and researching in death studies. From the perspective of working in acute health care in hospitals for the first half of her career and making academic sense of health and social care in the second half, Carol Komaromy notes how the terrain of death and dying is messy. She explains, 'I have been struck by the way that romanticised notions of death bear little or no relationship to reality. I have witnessed people dying in terrible fear, in pain, in distress, suddenly and unexpectedly and, occasionally, with ease. As a young nurse, it seemed to me that most people were hanging on to life, no matter how awful that life appeared to be to us outsiders. When it was clear that someone was dying, we had a huge investment in being able to predict the moment of death in order to inform family so that they could say goodbye. These were the days when visitors were not allowed to be on the ward without express permission. Moving on to academic work in death studies, I knew the terrain was messy and that trying to impose some theoretical order on it was always going to be difficult. However, I also knew that being able to take people to the detail of that reality was important. What my dear friend and colleague Jenny Hockey called giving the reader a taste of the reality, "take them there and tell them how it feels!"

So, despite the messiness of the terrain, the purpose of this introductory chapter is for us as editors to offer some sort of theoretical frame, drawing on key, relevant literature and interpretation with which to navigate the narratives.

In this first section, we outline the broader societal context concerning the medicalisation and professionalisation of death in western societies. But the context is important to note. The perspectives offered in this book disrupt boundaries around what we reveal about dying, death and bereavement yet in other ways cohere to a dominant perspective. Specifically, the accounts in this book are examples of white British responses to death, a set of experiences which are clearly not representative of all experiences of parental death. What is offered are accounts that speak to British deathways that emerged following the First and Second World Wars. These descriptions of death and dying are situated within a changing society that has become increasingly secular, where knowledge and advancements around medicine have expanded, people are living longer, and death and grief have been seemingly 'sequestered' from public life. Family forms have also shifted with the establishment and now apparent demise of the 'nuclear family', increases in social mobility, and the destabilising of traditional gender roles. As we show, issues of class, intergenerational compacts, and gender, which frame and structure the experiences, are significant divisions in society that persist – both within and outwith considerations of ethnicity. In many ways, the interdisciplinary area of study known as death studies in the UK emerged in this climate of white, British responses, and the authors in the book are among those who developed and shaped this emerging discipline. There remains a glaring absence of Black and minority ethnic experiences of death and dying within this field of study (Gunaratnam 1996), despite the diversity of multicultural Britain; an absence this book cannot make any claim to help rectify. What this book does highlight is how the post-war deathways – sequestration of death, emotional inexpressiveness, and breakdown of shared ritual forms – from the white British perspective are present to varying degrees. The accounts either support these elements and demonstrate the constraints people experienced and how they responded to them, or challenge these criticisms and reveal the availability of other resources within post-war British society.

On an individual level, while the idea of accounting for parental loss carries the danger of appearing to be self-indulgent and potentially a betrayal of the private moments of parents' lives, it is also part of the authors' identity. Many of us in this collection have been privileged to see the final moments of peoples' lives, or to be told the details of such endings. Yet such details may rarely feature explicitly in our academic work. This is despite the fact that the lens through which we, as authors, view the experiences of others in academic study into death, dying and bereavement is altered by these deeply personal events. Here these personal experiences are foregrounded in the belief that drawing out the intersections between the personal and professional can develop our work as researchers and practitioners in end of life and bereavement care and, in accordance with the reflexive turn in the social sciences (see Foley 2002), can ultimately generate deeper understanding and new forms of knowledge. While this is far from claiming that we share the same experiences – clearly each one is unique – we are committed to recognising those differences and trying to put them to one side in order to more accurately portray the experiences others have agreed to share with us in our research. Issues associated with this are discussed further to varying degrees in all chapters.

Death, Dying and Bereavement: A Personal, Clinical and Academic Arena

Any consideration of death, dying and bereavement is of interest to a range of disciplines and there is not one prevailing social view. It is fair to say that death is both historically and socially constructed with great variations across and between cultures and belief systems in any historical moment. General meanings associated with death and dying have changed over time and contemporary attitudes are influenced by representations of death in public media and its visibility in everyday life (see Kellehear 2007; Howarth 2007). Most deaths in UK society take place in older age and are largely hidden from view in that the majority of deaths take place in institutions, mainly hospitals with few occurring at home

(Public Health England 2018). This supports the argument that death is a medicalised event, and one that is largely hidden and unfamiliar. Kellehear has argued that the cost to society of the medicalisation and institutionalisation of death is the deskilling of communities in caring for dying people (2005). Indeed, of the 12 deaths recorded in this anthology – only two took place at home, one of which was a sudden and unexpected death. Clearly, the way in which society manages death and dying influences experiences of death. Further, as the accounts highlight, the way in which people are treated at the end of life and the resources available are not evenly distributed. Many authors here express some degree of regret, mixed with guilt about not securing good quality of end-of-life care, alongside some ambiguity about who should be the caregiver, not least the gendered assumptions underpinning some accounts. And death comes in many forms; even those deaths which were interpreted as timely – at the end of life and following an anticipated trajectory (so well categorised by Glaser and Strauss 1965) – were not necessarily straightforward. It could be argued that like birth (a highly medicalised and controlled event), dying is only defined as straightforward in retrospect. The slow and uneven trajectory to death – even those with a clear diagnosis and prognosis – such as Jim's death from cancer in Chap. 2 can be full of uncertainty. While his illness trajectory over 14 months was progressive in its downward path to death, it was uneven and the moment of death difficult to predict. By contrast the sudden and unexpected death of Colin Murray Parkes' father was disruptive and shocking. In Chaps. 3 and 7, Jenny Hockey and Rose Barbour, respectively, discuss the dilemma of needing to go away and yet being afraid of missing the terminal phase of their parents' life. In Chaps. 4 and 5, for both Gordon Riches and Kathryn Almack, their fathers were not expected to die (nor was Rose Barbour's father in Chap. 7), thus making decisions about end-of-life care more difficult and highlighting the need for a formal diagnosis of dying to trigger access to care, or at least for it to be discussed. This does not mean that it automatically follows that good end-of-life care is offered following a formal marker of dying, but the accounts highlight how the authors reflected on and judged the last stages of life and their role in this. The relative powerlessness of these experienced and articulate children in the face of death and dying that is so close to them is striking. Part of the explanation lies in the western management of death and dying.

A broad overview of death and dying highlights the shift away from death as part of life, with the end of life sequestered in hospitals and care homes, both a medical and professional event (Illich 1976; Armstrong 1983). A medical event because it is a legal requirement for death to be registered as having a medical cause, and professionalised because end-of-life care is often handled by professionals. This is also the case for disposal, even though rituals around different forms of disposal increasingly are being renegotiated, largely, funerals tend to be professional affairs (Hockey et al. 2010). In some accounts the degree to which the deceased person's body was an important part of their involvement in the end of life had to be negotiated. For Colin in Chap. 6, he and his mother were able to hold his father before the General Practitioner arrived with the death certificate, after which his body was taken away. Indeed, in all cases, deceased bodies were handed over after death to a funeral firm. None of the examples describe the body being waked. Although, he died at home and Carol and her sister spent time with their father and secured a lock of his hair, people like Jim, in Chap. 2, had waked his mother and father in Ireland and had been a coffin bearer carrying the coffin to the church for burial. This ritual which continued to be enacted in Ireland, was not offered to Jim. The business of the funeral in all the accounts seem to have been 'typical' and any attempt to do things differently met with some resistance.

Various historians most prominently Ariès (1981) have claimed that death was part of life and 'tamed' in the way it was part of the wider community, a social and public event as well as private and domestic one. Ariès went on to argue that significant changes began in the nineteenth century as the modern family was formed and medical regulation and professionalisation dominated death. While such a monolithic and dominant view is problematic, and many have criticised Ariès' claims (see Elias 1985; Armstrong 1983; Kellehear 2007), it is difficult to deny the extent to which death in society is no longer a 'normal' event. In a care home study into death and dying, Komaromy argued that being resigned to death in old age was interpreted by care home staff as being 'natural' and 'timely' (Komaromy 2010). This differs from debates about what constitutes natural and unnatural death; the definitions of which carry legal requirements (Howarth 2007). Any unnatural death, which is usually sudden and not anticipated, has to be reported to the Coroner. It's interesting to note that Nell's death in Chap. 2 was reported to the Coroner by the GP, even though the Coroner claimed this was unnecessary.

According to McNamara framing death as a normal part of life is difficult when different narratives of secularisation, privatisation and medicalisation are played out against one another (2001). She goes on to argue that tensions and paradoxes of uncertainty and certainty make it difficult for people to know how to behave. The accounts testify to issues of control around the dying person which are played out through various stakeholders. Not only is it the case that dying is not formally diagnosed in every instance, as noted earlier, but also positioning the dying person at the centre of decision making about their end-of-life care wishes created feelings of ambiguity and uncertainty. Since most deaths occurred in old age, when it is usual to assume that death is closer, it is also the case that dying is more likely to be diagnosed in the last few weeks or even days of life (Komaromy 2010). The impact of all of this on the quality of dying is discussed next.

The Quality of Dying: 'Good' and 'Bad' Deaths

The hospice movement of the late twentieth century heralded a reaction to the medicalisation of death and raised concerns that death should be seen as part of life. Its philosophy also promoted a shift from cure to achieving a good death through better end-of-life care; a concern more with the quality rather than the quantity of life. The concept of a 'good death' has a large body of academic and practice literature and remains a prevailing theme in end-of-life care policy. Kellehear argues that it has deep historical roots insofar as awareness and anticipation are continuing features (2007). While ideal deaths have changed over time in terms of how they are socially judged, the contemporary meaning usually refers to the way in which stakeholders are prepared. But, as Kellehear points out, dying has to begin with an awareness – and whatever features make it 'good' will vary according to different customs in the community.

Fundamental to any understanding of what it means is the question, 'good for whom?' and Howarth (2007) describes the extent to which representations of death are culturally prescribed. She draws on Bradbury (1999) to argue that understandings have changed from a focus on the fate of the soul to anxieties about the physical dimension of dying. Following on from McNamara's points above, however death is defined, what is clear is that certain pathways seem to dominate at different times. They are what Foucault would term: historical constructions contained within régimes of truth (1973). This applies to the accepted norms after death – through such things as handling the deceased body and choosing funeral practices. In relation to the form of death, for those who might want to die differently resistance might be judged harshly. For example, refusing life-saving treatment might be frowned upon, and conversely, demanding treatment when it is deemed futile equally so. Regardless of individual treatment expectations and wishes, it would appear that death is increasingly postponed (Clark 2002). Some of the accounts raise tensions about how prepared people were to die – and how family members might not agree on how death should be faced or handled. In Chap. 4, Gordon Riches raises issues of dignity, loss and regret. Regret is a theme for many authors – and Kathryn's account in Chap. 5 details her continuing concern about the quality of care of her father at the end of his life. For Colin Murray Parkes in Chap. 6, his mother's active treatment at the end of her life seemed inappropriate. Both Jenny Hockey on behalf of her father and Carol Komaromy on her mother's behalf had to be clear about resisting rescue treatment which seemed futile. It seemed that the medics were committed to treatment unless told clearly otherwise.

Even assuming that it is possible to define what it means and for whom, delivering a good death is dependent on many factors, not least what resources are available. For example, had Jenny Hockey's father been able to choose where he died, the question remains of how that setting might have been possible. For him, dying in his own home would have been dependent upon carers being available. His death contrasts starkly with Jim's death, who was able to die in his own home and surrounded by people he loved; but he was dependent on his wife providing most of the care, in turn supported by a highly specialised community care team with palliative expertise. Further, as argued above, being diagnosed as dying is crucial and it is unlikely that this care would have been available if Jim did not have a cancer diagnosis, even though the entitlement to good end-of-life care is being extended – rhetorically at least (Clarke 2002). Indeed, those parents who needed palliative care did not necessarily access it, despite the expertise and articulate skills of their children. In Chap. 6, Colin Murray Parkes describes his own feelings about not asking for good palliative care for his mother sooner.

So, the construct of a good death highlights a number of variables. As noted above, Green argues that the main critique of the good death rhetoric is that it serves more of an institutional agenda for the efficient management of dying people and less so for individual patient preferences (2008). In a review of studies in western societies, Meir et al. (2016), while recognising the inherent difficulties in making comparisons between studies with different criteria and emphases, concluded that of the three key stakeholder groups – dying people, families, and health care professionals – patients were more likely to focus on being pain-free, while families were more likely to cite quality of life and health care professionals focused more on pain control and comfort. What the authors make clear, and in general agreement with Kellehear, is that death and the process of dying are imbued with social, cultural and political meanings.

The judgements made in the narratives have included aspects of dying within this triad of interested parties. In some of the accounts there was a degree of negotiation about who played what role. Indeed, the end-of-life period can provide an especially illustrative understanding of how families are 'done' (Borgstrom et al. 2019). As Woodthorpe and Rumble explain (2016), how resources are bequeathed within a network once an individual has died both expose and construct relationships. Practices of inheritance can reveal norms and rules that frame family practices. Bailey (2012) discovered a hierarchy of responsibility over funeral arrangements – who is excluded revealing unspoken assumptions about familial relationships according to long-standing expectations about the constitution of a 'family'.

As the dying parents began to withdraw from life, some of their children – as depicted here – had to make decisions on their behalf. Further, family relationships and roles shifted at the end of their parents' life. For most people the negotiation took place with the surviving parent – who was the most significant decision maker. However, when the surviving parent was dying issues of care and responsibility were prominent. For some, this shift involved ambiguous feelings about duty and power. Some authors were only children and were unable to share responsibility with other siblings – or like Carol Komaromy and Kathryn Almack, were seen by other family members as 'experts' in their parents' end-of-life care. This responsibility in getting it right weighed heavily – and many narratives highlight the extent to which they themselves might have felt ill-equipped. For example, despite her commitment to full disclosure as a basic human right, Carol and her sister did not agree that their father should have been told that he was dying. Kathryn, carried feelings of guilt about not being able to do more for her father in terms of good end-of-life care, even though this was not shared by her brother and sister. For Colin Murray Parkes, his regret about his mother being admitted to hospital and her continued active treatment in the last few days were mitigated to some degree by the outstandingly good quality life that she had until then.

What is interesting to note, given the 'good death' rhetoric in professionalised health and social care, is the extent to which the ten hospital and care home deaths might have been classified as bad deaths. Certainly, for many parents the end of life comprised care that was not 'good enough'. It is not surprising that the need to get things right and feelings of regret should emerge as a significant theme. However, in terms of achieving a good death – the narratives highlight the question of 'good for whom?' which, as discussed, has been an enduring problem with defining the concept of a good death. Further, even the hospice 'good death' was a reintroduction of ritual, as McNamara (2001) has argued. Certainly, institutions through their practices, routines and roles inevitably shape experiences (see Goffman 1961 on total institutions). But however the death is defined, its enactment depends upon what it is possible for the institution to achieve. Factors that affect the achievement of individual wishes are in a dynamic relationship on several levels, individual, institutional and social (Komaromy 2007) and the narratives highlight this reality. Both within and between these levels degrees of power are exercised and have to be negotiated. Not everyone was in a strong emotional position to be able to negotiate effectively, indeed, it is reasonable to argue that everyone personally involved in end-of-life care is vulnerable or, as McNamara (2001) would argue, 'fragile.'

As the narratives illustrate, being able to get it right for the dying person was far from easy, not least because, as some of the narratives explain, the issue of being prepared and anticipating death was not always explored with the dying person. The dimensions of awareness which Glaser and Strauss (1965) identified, crude as they might seem, still pertain. For some, the silence and lack of discussion about the needs of the dying person are striking and seem to rest within topics that were 'off limits.' Not all authors had regrets about not saying 'goodbye', but those who did say farewell seem to have valued that opportunity. As death approached, and its inevitability seemed to be obvious, the accounts relate attempts to be present at the end. Jenny Hockey seemed to find some resolution, a new way of expressing intimacy with her father, while Rose Barbour's description of being a young person and having chicken pox, kept her away from her father's death bed; even though he was considered to be on the road to recovery.

Bereavement and Parental Loss

All bereavements are not experienced equally. Grief is an individual experience but also a social one informed by societal and cultural norms and values around death and dying, establishing what bereavement researchers refer to as a 'hierarchy of grief' (Doka 1989; Robson and Walter 2013). This hierarchy is formed by perceptions of the timeliness of a death and of the significance of a relationship. For instance, bereavement literature may often claim that the death of a child is the 'worst' type of bereavement, whereas the death of an elderly parent is to be expected and part of the natural life course. Whether deaths are considered timely or natural are social constructed notions that rely upon certain assumptions within a given culture or society about who is expected to die and when, as discussed above in reference to 'good' and 'bad' deaths. The grief expressed following a death is then expected to be in proportion to the social importance and significance of the death.

The deaths recounted in this book are mainly deaths of old or elderly parents experienced by children in mid and later adulthood, with two exceptions: Rose Barbour (in Chap. 6) and Caroline Pearce (in Chap. 9) who lost parents in adolescence. Death in old age is considered timely, natural and unproblematic, deemed less worthy of the label 'tragic'. Bereavement research, predominately drawn from psychological perspectives, and its focus directed largely on complicated and prolonged forms of grief and fears of medicalising normal grief, has meant 'ordinary' deaths have been overlooked (Pope 2005). This has led to the suggestion that grief of the death of elderly parents has become disenfranchised (Pope 2005). That is to say that the perception of parental death as a normative event in life course may cause bereaved adult children to feel their grief is less socially acceptable and so should be kept in moderation, which could potentially lead to increased difficulties in grieving (Klapper et al. 1994). In Chap. 5, Gordon Riches notes that by viewing his parents' death as timely he avoided examining their meaning and his own emotions. Evidence of such social norms around death and grieving are apparent in the response to the COVID-19 pandemic, which at time of writing continues to risk the lives of older people and has had a devasting impact on those living in care homes. As discussed above, the medicalisation of death has also constructed the concept of natural death (Illich 1976) which may in turn minimise the social impact of the deaths of older people.

The accounts in this book attest the claim that midlife experiences of parental loss are no exception to the social complexities of grief, and timeliness may be irrelevant to offspring as they face a life transition from an adult with living parents to an adult without (Moss and Moss 1984). Indeed, as those living in western societies increasingly have their first experience of bereavement later in life, people may feel just as unprepared as at any other stage in the life course (McDaniel and Clark 2009). The death of a parent holds its own specific challenges, and for many contemplating when their parents will die may inhabit some type of 'legendary time' (de Beauvoir 1969). Though it is it anticipated and expected, it can be hard to fathom life without the people who have been present in one's life (in varying degrees) since its inception. The death of a parent can present unique existential and ontological dilemmas and questions as it removes the 'buffer against death' (Moss and Moss 1984). Moss and Moss further explain:

> Questions of identity are 'thrust to center stage' as individuals are starkly forced to realise their own finitude as they become the eldest generation in their family and lose a primary anchor to their sense of self and being. The parental loss demands a realisation of one's own mortality as the 'next-in-line' in a constant flux of generational turnover. For midlife adults, the death of a parent may often be considered 'on-time'. It therefore highlights not only the fragility of life as a sudden death might, but also the mortality of the self and inevitability of death in the turnover of time. (Moss and Moss 1984, p. 354)

Becoming the 'next in line' can involve taking on new roles and responsibilities, previously held by the deceased parent, what Petersen and Rafuls (1998) described as 'passing the sceptre'. This experience of transition can be compared to a 'rite of passage' (van Gennep 1960) where bereaved adult children find themselves shifted to the top of the ancestral hierarchy (Pope 2005) bestowed with a new sense of identity, along with duties and obligations. In Chap. 5 Gordon Riches describes feeling 'taken over' by a sense of responsibility to manage the consequence of his father's death, and an obligation to become the 'man of the house'.

In a rite of passage, the death of a parent might signal one's final entrance into adulthood – regardless of whether this comes late in the life course, beyond the point at which adulthood is commonly deemed to begin. Bereaved adult children may experience a sense of loss of their child identity even as an adult as they are thrust into the elder role (Pope 2005). This 'developmental push' (Moss and Moss 1989) might encourage personal growth but also foster ambivalence at feelings of loss and gain. For example, depending on one's relationship with their parents, autonomy from parents could feel liberating. In Chap. 3, Jenny Hockey touches on this feeling describing moments of relief from caring for her dying father, she writes 'I'd felt powerless…Now I'd reclaimed my liberty'. The death of parent can then confront bereaved children with a sense of both ultimate freedom and responsibility. Gaining authorship of one's life can be a gift and a burden, as all bereaved navigate life with an increased sense of groundlessness – or the sense that someone has been removed from 'above' (Pope 2005).

This period of transition might span many years as losing parents is, as Marshall (2004) notes, generally a two-staged process. Chapters in this book reflect this as Carol Komaromy, Gordon Riches, Colin Murray Parkes and Rose Barbour describe and compare the deaths of both their parents. These accounts highlight the differences experienced between first and subsequent loss. Following the loss of one parent, one may feel a sense of responsibility to the surviving parent. In Chaps. 2 and 5, Carol Komaromy and Gordon Riches, respectively, detail the sense of responsibility to care for their mother following their father's death. As a result, one's own grief may be filtered through actions for the surviving parent (Marshall 2004). The impact of the second loss can trigger reflection on the first parent's death as it is then the adult child becomes an orphan, and also perhaps when one can finally 'own' feelings of grief.

By contrast, the death of a parent during childhood and adolescence has received considerable research attention, perhaps precisely because this is a less common experience in contemporary western societies. Reflecting this, two of the 12 deaths described in this book document the experience of parental death in adolescence. As Turner and Almack (2019) describe, research in this area has focused on the harms and negative outcomes of parental loss on young people, drawing on models of risk and resilience. Variables such as depression (McLeod 1991) and the inability to form adult relationships (Hepworth et al. 1984) are used as the lens through which the young people are understood and interpreted. The application of the harm narrative to young people who lose parents neglects the personal subjective meaning of loss and diversity of young people's experiences (Ribbens McCarthy 2006).

The moral tale of a good death is influential in shaping responses to young people's experiences, where bereavement at this age is considered outside the normative life course. Certainly, the impact on young people and their self-identity can be amplified as the transitional stage of youth can increase the sense of powerlessness felt in bereavement, and young people are often isolated from key decisions (Pearce 2011). Adult identities are viewed as far more static, yet the impact of parental death can provoke reflection and transformation, destabilising one's previous sense of self. The enduring influence of conceptions of a good death supports the contention of Barbour et al. (2013) that the differences between losing a parent in childhood and adulthood may be over-stated. Whether as a young person or adult in midlife, the changes in circumstances may be comparable, each framed by overarching social and political narratives concerning a good death, as discussed above, and conceptions of family relationships and identity discussed next.

Family Practices at the End-of-Life and in Bereavement

As Moss and Moss point out, parental death is not just about loss of parent but the loss of family structure (1989). Though often overlooked in end-of-life and bereavement care theory and practice, individual deaths occur in a relational and familial context (Borgstrom et al. 2019; Towers 2019; Woodthorpe and Rumble 2016). Parental death can impact on surviving family members and their relationships with one another, for instance increasing and decreasing closeness with one's siblings (Khodyakov and Carr 2009). Impacts on family relationships and roles can also be far more complex both at the end of life and in bereavement, as death may transform or reinforce particular roles, for instance who gets an opportunity to participate in funeral rituals might have gendered overtones, as described by Kathryn Almack in Chap. 4 and Rose Barbour in Chap. 7.

The accounts in this book portray examples of family life being 'done' – how responsibilities are shared and negotiated between siblings and family members, revealing assumptions that might be rooted in gendered values or influenced by social class norms. These narratives are set within a backdrop of social and cultural shifts in what is considered a 'family' within western societies. Such narratives include the demise of 'traditional' practices, the rise and current demise of the nuclear family, and changing perceptions of marriage, all of which frame perceptions of loss. For example, growing up accustomed to a family structure that contains parents and children, the death of a parent might produce feelings of being robbed not only of parent but the concept of family. Sociologists have described these changes in the conceptual reconfiguration of 'the family' from a social institution into a set of practices (Morgan 2011), which focuses on how people remain embedded in webs of interdependent relationships despite social and demographic changes. This refers to how practices can be both dynamic and reflexive but also rooted in institutional norms that govern western secular perceptions of what family constitutes, particularly as it became defined in the post-war period.

The relational nature of the narratives presented in this book is evident in Carol Komaromy's and Kathryn Almack's chapters as they include the perspectives of family members in narrating the experience of death and bereavement. As Nadeau (1998) argued, making sense of death is something undertaken not just by individuals but within family contexts. Families possess their own norms, values, and beliefs including around death, dying and bereavement that deeply bind the family together and inform individual family members' identities and worldviews (Baddeley and Singer 2010). Walter (1995) illustrated the decisive role of families and social relations in sustaining the memories of a deceased family member arguing that bereavement stimulates a 'biographical imperative'. This is often motivated by the many questions that arise following the death of someone close. Walter gives voice to these ambiguities by demonstrating how individuals and families collectively construct a postmortem biography in which stories and memories of the deceased can be repeated and tensions effectively resolved.

Walter's theory aligns with dominant discourse in bereavement theory and practice that states people need to speak about grief, experiences, memories in order to recover. Alternatively, Baddeley and Singer (2009) looked at silences and 'unspoken memory' and how they inform identities in family contexts. Further, Smart (2011) has argued for the significance of family secrets in illuminating the complexities of how families work, explaining that secrets reveal: 'how they [families] present themselves to the world, how they manage their weaker members, how they control knowledge, and how they construct their heritage and aura' (p. 551). Across the chapters, authors refer to moments where things were not said or kept silent, revealing how families can act to sustain or erase particular memories. For example, in Chaps. 2, 4 and 5 the impact of experiences of war are present and yet often not articulated, in turn the bereaved children inhabit a legacy of war. Selecting and speaking about memories help families sustain a particular narrative of their collective past forming what Misztal (2003) describes as a 'mnemonic communities' that socialise its members into what they remember and what they forget. Collecting photographs, making videos, keeping heirlooms and mementos, are all part of a process of creating a mythical 'family we live by' (Gillis 1996) and on occasions like funerals the need to present the ideal mythical family is emphasised. In bereavement such practices are used to continue bonds with the deceased person, which Klass et al. (1996) identify as the means by which individuals and families hold on to the deceased person. Indeed, death rituals also reaffirm a sense of continuity with the past and with the practices of previous generations, in turn reinforcing or constituting collective norms around both death and family practices.

Individual stories draw upon those of previous generations in order to perpetuate or silence certain family myths, denials and secrets. In this way memories are transmitted through generations (Kuhn 1995). Scott and Scott (2000) discussed the role their mother's stories had in shaping their identity, to uncover their 'autobiographical inheritance'. They identified their mother's life as a 'precursor', seeing their own lives build on the pre-history of her life, exploring the ways in which they had learnt from their mother's stories. Similarly, the authors of this book seek to understand who their parents were and how they shaped their own sense of identity. For Scott and Scott, such stories were heavily embedded in notions of gender and class, particularly the presence of social mobility. The role of social class is likewise present here as authors describe the experience of returning home to help parents at the end of life which raises specific issues about being out of place. For example, several authors articulated the shift into a different social class through their education which left them feeling 'out of place' with the family. For some, the transition is foregrounded and plays a significant role in framing the experience of witnessing parental death. Rose Barbour, Gordon Riches and Kathryn Almack in Chaps. 4, 5 and 7 are clear about this transition. But what does it mean to grow beyond one's family at the time of death?

So far, we have discussed relevant literature pertaining to the thematic areas raised in these narratives. In the following sections we seek to clarify the epistemological context for this book, as well as draw attention to the process of writing, and making sense of autobiographical accounts and narratives.

Experience and Knowledge

Scholars of death, dying and bereavement may have become accustomed to a curious, or perhaps even negative, response to what they do. Some struggle to understand why one would choose to spend time thinking about death. Hockey (2007) describes the implicit accusation when asked why death and dying is one's chosen topic of study, the implication being: surely it is depressing. Certainly, personal experiences of death and dying can spark an interest in studying the experience through an academic analytical lens; a curiosity to seek understanding through theory or to better the experiences of others. Yet as Hockey points out, wider social trends have also contributed to the development of an interdisciplinary study of death, dying and bereavement known as death studies. These include trends we have discussed above, such as the sequestration of death through the professionalisation of death care.

Also, some might assume that if engaged in end-of-life and bereavement research and practice, when death enters your own life you are expertly equipped to manage the emotional, physical and social impacts that may occur. Troyer (2020) described feeling 'completely unprepared' for his sister's death, despite his lived experience and academic credentials on human mortality. This struggle to balance what one professionally knows and recognises versus one's personal emotions and experiences is described by Kathryn Almack in Chap. 4. She writes feeling that working as an academic in the field of dying, death and bereavement may have 'complicated' rather than eased her grief. Knowing too much can present its own problems. The knowledge of what makes a 'good death' could present an impossible measure, increasing feelings of anxiety about getting things 'right'. Thus the narratives demonstrate how the personal intersects with professional in ways that are not necessarily so clear cut, reflecting on how lived experiences of death, dying and bereavement might stimulate inquiry into self-identity, subjectivity and meaning.

Understanding the intersection between personal issues and social processes is a task not unique to research on death (Davidman 1997), yet it seems to have special resonance for topics considered sensitive. To some extent, the growing literature on reflexively researching death and dying is an acknowledgement of this. Further, alongside any emotional impact this turn draws attention to the role of the researcher, and how, as a consequence, they might reflect on their own mortality (Komaromy 2020; Pearce 2010; Woodthorpe 2009). Studies of practitioners' experiences of providing bereavement and palliative care suggest that knowledge and skills alone may be insufficient to cope with the existential and emotional demands in 'death work' (Chan and Tin 2012). This corresponds with a dominant discourse among those who provide bereavement care in the voluntary sector which suggests that bereavement can only be fully understood if one has been through it (Pearce 2018). In health research and practice, the 'experiential knowledge' of patients and services users has become recognised as a significant resource in the construction of medical knowledge (McKevitt 2013). The term 'experiential knowledge' as well as another increasingly commonplace descriptor 'expert by experience' imply that experience leads to expertise, and thus to knowledge.

In these contexts, 'experience' is often utilised instrumentally and uncritically, with the personal account consumed as 'fact', a true record of events. However, here we interrogate the connections between 'knowledge' and 'experience'. In presenting (or re-presenting) the experiences of intimate death we acknowledge the constructed nature of experience, and of narrative, remaining vigilant to claims to 'truth'. In this argument we borrow from Foucault (1984) to recognise that 'truth' is not absolute but multiple. Rather than seeing objects or identities as singular, they can comprise multiple 'truths' – often produced at the intersections of different discourses. Foucault disregarded any universal notion of truth, arguing that universal understandings are historicised, and by examining how they are constructed and emerge out of a particular historical context reveals this 'truth' fallacy. Put simply, as highlighted earlier, truth is historically located and socially constructed. This characterised Foucault's largely 'genealogical' approach to research, which involved building a 'critical history' of an object or phenomenon. For Foucault things didn't just exist 'out there' but emerged as identifiable objects through various social structures – including language. For him, the task is to examine how things come to be seen as truth; to critically engage with all claims to truth.

Autobiography and Memory

In applying this perspective to the autobiographical accounts in this book we refer to feminist work and the development of autobiography as a method. As Scott (1991) argued, when analysing accounts of experiences, one needs to acknowledge experience is constructed, relational and historically situated:

> Experience is at once always already an interpretation and something that needs to be interpreted. What counts as experience is neither self-evident nor straightforward: it is always contested, and always therefore political. (p. 797)

By centring the experiencing subject, it follows that the basis of knowledge-claims in autobiographical writing should be made available for analytical scrutiny (Stanley 1993). However, influenced by feminist epistemology we also seek to contribute to understanding the ways in which *all* knowledge, however much the experiential basis of knowledge is denied or silenced, 'is rooted in the knowledge production processes engaged in by inquiring and experiencing and therefore knowing subjects' (Stanley 1993, p. 214).

Stanley analysed entries from her research diary that documented the illness and eventual death of her mother. Her recollections were not only (ontological) insights into the workings of her own individual mind or of her personal and social relations, but an epistemological claim on the very grounding of how knowledge is formed. For Stanley, the lived experience enabled insights that could not be grasped through academic study:

> I came to think about, and write about, the complexities of the self, its entwined fragility and indomitability, not through reading academic feminist texts, but through living and experiencing the illness, dissolution and death of people close to me. (1993, p. 213)

Responding to the claim that autobiographical accounts are naively referential and essentialist, Stanley argued that experiential claims are no less, but certainly no more, problematic than other kinds of knowledge claims. In her view, the written accounts of the past we produce certainly trade on and are typically structured by means of referential assumptions and claims, but writers and readers are aware that these are historiographies and not history itself. Stivers (1993) further expands on this argument proposing that accepting the impossibility of removing the observer from the knowledge acquisition process – in other words the impossibility of objectivity – means that subjective knowledge, such as that found in personal narratives, can be considered an equally respectable way of knowing.

Stivers highlights the difficulties in drawing a hard and fast line between 'fact' and 'interpretation' that is implied by the distinctions between history and literature. For example, in Chap. 7 Rose Barbour refers to the process of being aware of one's role as narrator in constructing knowledge as she writes of 'being careful not to impute, without good reason, thoughts and insights to my former self/selves.' As editors and authors, we recognise the process of writing involves remembering, re-constructing and layering on meaning and memory. In accounting for past experiences, the authors here are not writing the past 'as it was', for the past as experienced is inaccessible. As hooks describes: 'the act of writing one's autobiography is a way to find again that aspect of self and experience that may no longer be an actual part of one's life but is a living memory shaping and informing the present' (1989, p. 158). This description echoes the psychoanalytic notion that the past continues to shape the present, and what one consciously remembers and what remains unconscious can play powerful role in shaping one's internal world (Kuhn 1995). Komaromy (2018) has argued how through the process of psychoanalysis she became aware of realising how the motives we attribute to actions are often retrospective justifications and how unconscious drives are not rational.

At a psychodynamic level, the filters through which we explain actions and memories that might serve to protect us from harsh realities are far from obvious – if accessible at all. We acknowledge then that there is an unavoidable gap between experiencing an event and remembering it, though it is in this gap that memory lies (Misztal 2003). Memory is a creative interpretation of the past; it is reflexive, unavoidably partial, fragmentary, and selective, and is continually retold in light of experiences. Therefore, how people re-member and re-narrate such experiences and create different versions of their lives/selves depend not least on the setting, who they are telling and their position in the life course (Kehily 1995). Reflecting this, the chapters here contain different levels of recall. For example, in Chap. 3 Jenny Hockey explains her chapter was written entirely within a month of her dad's death. In Chaps. 2 and 6 Carol Komaromy and Colin Murray Parkes include excerpts from diaries written at the time to relay the detail of events. These unfiltered extracts serve to give credence to the immediacy of their emotions and actions at that time.

Narrating Death

Finding the words to tell one's story has a central role in the politics of, and recovery from, trauma and following death and bereavement the healing properties of narrative are often proposed, where constructing a narrative is seen to repair disrupted identities (Bury 2001; Frank 2001). Dying and bereavement are increasingly popular topics in bestselling memoirs indicating the significance of narrative for authors and readers alike to help make sense of death and bereavement. For example, titles such as Rachel Clarke's (2020) *Dear Life* and Atul Gawande's (2014) *Being Mortal* draw on professional experience as clinicians to explore how death and dying are managed in contemporary society, with the death of a parent framing their narrative. They are deeply personal accounts that serve as illustrative 'parable-like' stories of how to help dying people to achieve the sort of death they want.

For some, to write about the experience of grief may be both a way to express the 'unsayable' of death and to make public what is felt to be private. When the understanding that grief is a 'taboo' persists, then writing openly about an experience like bereavement enables people to connect with otherwise hidden and silenced stories. In an analysis of bereavement memoirs, Dennis (2008) described how the autobiographical account acts to provide a map for others in their navigation through the liminal space of grief, arguably offering some form of consolation in learning that someone else has also endured a similar sense of pain. Making sense of grief and establishing one's narratives is also deeply tied to the psychological notion that in bereavement one has to 'work through' one's grief in order to 'recover' (Pearce 2019). Thus, life histories do not just emerge automatically but are heavily constructed by the culture in which they are situated (Tilly 1999; Goody 2006). Narratives are constructed and composed through interactions with others: what Goffman described as 'performances' in which individuals express their sense of self and create a specific impression of reality (1959). In this way individual narratives make identity a self-conscious construction according to Giddens (1991); it is not just given but something that is routinely created and sustained in the reflexive activities of the individual.

As discussed above there will always be a gap between the embodied experience and the writing of it. In Chap. 8, Douglas Davies questions what is lost in narrating a story challenging the notion that one can ever 'reveal all'. Inevitably all attempts to express suffering will in a sense fall short because of the lack in language to convey its meaning (Struhkamp 2005). Aligned with this view, Douglas Davies suggests some personal experiences are sacred and should remain secret. This contrasts with feminist approaches which embraced life writing and personal narratives as a political statement – making the personal public was revolutionary. Baddeley and Singer (2009) make a case for the significance of silences, particularly silences about the deceased and how they may play an important function in stabilising individual and family identity. Yet, as hooks (1989) has persuasively articulated, it remains crucial to talk about the points where the public and private meet. Reflecting on the process of writing her own autobiography hooks described feeling blocked from telling one's story: 'Secrecy and silence – these were central issues' (p. 156).

Silence here was acting as a means of oppression, whereas speaking publicly about private issues could enable healing and recovery, not an individual basis only but to remedy hurts caused by domination and exploitation. The split between public and private selves is therefore deeply connected to ongoing practices of domination including racism, sexism, and class exploitation. Indeed, as hooks points out, not everyone has the luxury of choosing what to tell or not; telling one's story can be a matter of survival. Thus, the ability to tell one's story but also the ability to remain silent is enabled by different levels of privilege.

Our Own Positioning

As editors we believe it is important to reflect on our own positioning, and privilege, in collating this collection of narratives. At the time of writing, different groups of people across the world are facing struggles – whether along class, race, gender divides – to have their stories represented and to make their voices heard, a struggle that seems perhaps more contentious than ever. Who can tell or listen to a story remains a pressing question, encouraging one to reflect on who has 'narrative privilege' (Adams 2008). The authors including us as editors might be safely considered privileged to tell their stories – but what of the many stories not included in this anthology? This privilege includes representing those who cannot respond or are unable to tell their stories for whatever reason – notably for this book, those who are dead.

The relationships between parent and child documented across these chapters describe feelings of love, affection and admiration but also mixed emotions of ambivalence as the authors seek to convey an image of their parents that remains truthful from their own perspective, even if perhaps it may not have been how the deceased parent would want to be remembered. Scarre (2013) puts forward a moral argument against speaking ill of the dead arguing that to 'slander' a deceased person is morally offensive as they cannot speak for and defend themselves. Within the current socio-political climate such arguments are increasingly contested and politically messy as Scarre himself notes, permitting that there are times when revealing uncomfortable truths about a deceased person is necessary even if it will damage the reputation they upheld while alive. How to respect the equality of the dead while also ensuring that the dead do not simply remain in reverence for the sake of it? Scarre's argument seems to ignore how usually it is only the privileged and powerful who can preserve their reputation and keep their secrets. Returning to hooks' (1989) argument – silences can conceal experiences of oppression and exploitation. On a smaller scale, keeping silent about the at times ambivalent or difficult relationships documented in this book would serve to convey an inaccurate reality of parental and family relationships.

In terms of ethical considerations, as authors we are telling *our* stories of how *we* experienced parental death. The embodiment of parents into our identity suggests that the stories belong to us; we are writing about the experience of parental death. At its simplest level, we are telling our own stories. We have no way of knowing what story our parents might have told. Some of us have gained consent from research participants as part of ethical practice to tell the story of people's death and dying. More specifically, Carol Komaromy interviewed children and partners of deceased people who had died in care homes in order to reconstruct the circumstances of their death. These people were considered to be the owners of the accounts and many accounts involved intimate detail.

In the end we might ask whose story is it to tell? The subtitle of this book – a kind of haunting – refers to the profound impact parental relationships can have on our lives, both in life and death. Parents and what we inherit from them are deeply intertwined into who we are and what we become – whether our parents are present or absent. Our story is their story and vice versa.

Outline of the Book

In Chap. 2, Carol Komaromy draws on vivid memories of events and some written recordings at the time, to provide an ethnography of two very different deaths (her mother and her father) which involves starkly contrasting relationships. Jenny Hockey in Chap. 3 uses her detailed diaries of the end of her father's life as field notes to recount his dying and death. In an account of her father's death, Kathryn Almack in Chap. 4

describes the personal conflicts she felt about the hospital setting of his death, despite problematising place of death in her professional life. In Chap. 5 Gordon Riches delves into childhood memories as he reflects on his parents' deaths and re-examines his own emotions, that at the time were eclipsed by family and work commitments, and his defences of denial and avoidance. Differences between deaths are highlighted by Colin Murray Parkes in Chap. 6 who draws on diary extracts to detail his father's sudden and unanticipated death, contrasted with the slow and uneven trajectory of that of his mother. Reconstructing the events of her parent's deaths in Chap. 7, Rose Barbour grounds her experiences in sociological theory to understand how deaths are situated in wider societal changes and cultural shifts, particularly through the lens of social class. This theoretical reflection is expanded in Chap. 8 by Douglas Davies who undergoes a deeper exploration of the process of narrating and speaking about one's biography and how secrecy and opacity intersect into understandings of personhood. Finally, in Chap. 9 Caroline Pearce connects the themes described across the narratives through the lens of her own experiences of early parental death, questioning how experiences of death, dying and bereavement inform and construct our multiple 'selves'.

References

Adams, T. E. (2008). A Review of Narrative Ethics. *Qualitative Inquiry*, *14*(2), 175–194.

Ariès, P. (1981). *The Hour of Our Death*. London: Allen Lane.

Armstrong, D. (1983). *Political Anatomy of the Body: Medical Knowledge in Britain in the Twentieth Century*. Cambridge: Cambridge University Press.

Baddeley, J. and Singer, J. A. (2010). A loss in the family: silence, memory, and narrative identity after bereavement. *Memory*, 18(2), 198–207.

Bailey, T. (2012). Going to funerals in contemporary Britain: The individual, the family and the meeting with death. PhD thesis, University of Bath, Bath, England.

Barbour, R. S., Komaromy, C., Morgan-Brett, B. and Barbour, M. (2013). Re-conceptualising adult orphans: a scoping literature review. Presented at the British Sociological Association Death, Dying and Bereavement conference, 15th November 2013.

Borgstrom, E., Ellis, J. and Woodthorpe, K. (2019). 'We don't want to go and be idle ducks': family practices at the end of life. *Sociology*, 53(6): 1127–1142.

Bradbury, M. (1999). *Representations of Death*. London: Routledge.

Bury, M. (2001). Illness narratives: fact or fiction? *Sociology of Health and Illness*, 23(3), 263–285.

Chan, W. C. H., and Tin, A. F. (2012). Beyond knowledge and skills: Self-competence in working with death, dying, and bereavement. *Death Studies*, 36(10), 899–913.

Clark, D. (2002) Between hope and acceptance: the medicalisation of dying, *British Medical Journal*, 324, 905–7.

Clarke, R. (2020). *Dear Life*. London: Little, Brown.

Davidman, L. (1997). The Personal, The Sociological and the Intersection of the Two, *Qualitative Sociology*, 20(4), 507–515.

De Beauvoir, S. (1969). *A Very Easy Death*. Harmondsworth: Penguin Books.

Dennis, M. R. (2008). The grief account: Dimensions of a contemporary bereavement Genre. *Death Studies*, 32(9), 801–836.

Doka, K. J. (ed.) (1989). *Disenfranchised grief: Recognising hidden sorrow*, Lexington, Mass: Lexington Books.

Elias, N. (1985). *The Loneliness of Dying*. Oxford: Blackwell.

Foley, D. E. (2002). Critical ethnography: the reflexive turn. *Qualitative Studies in Education*, 15, (5), 460–490.

Foucault, M. (1973). *The Birth of the Clinic: An archaeology of medical perception*, London: Routledge.

Foucault, M. (1984). Preface to The History of Sexuality Volume II. In Rabinow, P. (ed.) *The Foucault Reader: An introduction to Foucault's thought* (pp. 333–339). London: Penguin.

Frank, A. W. (2001). Can we research suffering? *Qualitative Health Research*, 11(3), 353–362.

Giddens, A. (1991). *Modernity and self-identity: Self and Society in the Late Modern Age*. Cambridge: Polity Press.

Gillis, J. R. (1996). *A World of their own making: A history of myth and ritual in family life*. Oxford: Oxford University Press.

Glaser, B.G. and Strauss, A. L. (1965). *Awareness of Dying*. New York: Aldine.

Goffman, E. (1959). *The presentation of self in everyday life*. London: Penguin.

Goffman, E. (1961). *Asylums*. London: Penguin Books.

Goody, J. (2006). From oral to written: An anthropological breakthrough in Storytelling. In Moretti, F. (ed.) *The Novel Volume 1* (pp. 3–36). Princeton, New Jersey: Princeton University Press.

Green, J. (2008). *Beyond the good death: The anthropology of modern dying*. Philadelphia: University of Pennsylvania Press.

Gunaratnam, Y. (1996). Culture is not enough: a critique of multi-culturalism in palliative care. In Field, D., Hockey, J. and Small, N. (eds.) *Death, gender, and ethnicity* (pp. 166–186). London: Routledge.

Hepworth, J., Ryder, R. G., Dreyer, A. S. (1984). The effects of parental loss on the formation of intimate relationships. *Journal of Marital and Family Therapy*, 10(1), 73–82.

hooks, b. (1989). *Talking Back: Thinking feminist, thinking Black*. Boston, MA: South End Press.

Hockey, J. (2007). Closing in on death? Reflections on research and researchers in the field of death and dying. *Health Sociology Review*, 16(5), 436–446.

Hockey, J., Komaromy, C. and Woodthorpe, K. (Eds.) (2010). *The Matter of Death: Space, Place and Materiality*. Hampshire: Palgrave Macmillan.

Howarth, G. (2007). *Death and Dying: A sociological introduction*. Cambridge: Polity Press.

Illich, I. (1976). *Limits to Medicine – Medical Nemesis: The Expropriation of Health*. New York: Pantheon.

Kehily, M- J. (1995). Self-narration, Autobiography and Identity Construction. *Gender and Education*, 7(1), 23–31.

Kellehear, A. (2007). *A Social History of Dying*. Cambridge: Cambridge University Press.

Kellehear, A. (2005). *Compassionate Cities: Public health and end-of-life care*. Oxfordshire: Routledge.

Klapper, K., Moss, S., Moss, M. and Rubinstein, R. L. (1994). The social context of grief among adult daughters who have lost a parent, *Journal of Aging Studies*, 8(1), 29–43.

Klass, D, Silverman, PR, Nickman, SL (Eds.) (1996). *Continuing Bonds: New Understandings of Grief*. London: Taylor & Francis.

Komaromy, C. (2020). The performance of researching sensitive issues. *Mortality*, 25(3), 364–377.

Komaromy, C. (2018). *Family Life, Trauma and Loss in the Twentieth Century*. Hampshire: Palgrave Macmillan.

Komaromy, C. (2010). Dying Spaces in Dying Places. In Hockey, J., Komaromy, C. and Woodthorpe, K. (Eds.) *The Matter of Death: Space, Place and Materiality* (pp. 52–68). Hampshire: Palgrave Macmillan.

Komaromy, C. (2007). 'Concepts and Contexts', *Communication, Relationships and Care*. Buckingham: The Open University.

Khodyakov, D. and Carr, D. (2009). The impact of late-life parental death in adult sibling relationships: do parents' advance directives help or hurt? *Research on Aging*, 31(5), 495–519.

Kuhn, A. (1995). *Family Secrets: Acts of Memory and Imagination*. London: Verso.

McDaniel, J. G. and Clark, P. G. (2009). The new adult orphan: issues and considerations for health care professionals. *Journal of Gerontological Nursing*, 35(12), 44–49.

McLeod, J. D. (1991). 'Childhood parental loss and adult depression'. *Journal of Health and Social Behavior*, 32(3), 205–20.

McKevitt, C. (2013). Experience, knowledge and evidence: a comparison of research relations in health and anthropology. *Evidence and Policy* 9(1), 113–130.

McNamara, B. (2001). *Fragile Lives: Death, dying and care*. Buckingham: Open University Press.

Marshall, H. (2004). Midlife loss of parents: The transition from adult child to orphan. *Ageing International* 29, 351–367.

Meir, E.A.,Galleos, J.V., Montross Thomas, L.P., Depp, C.A., Irwin, S.A., and Jeste, D.V. (2016). Defining a Good Death (Successful Dying): Literature review and a call for research and public dialogue. *American Journal of Geriatric Psychiatry*, 24(4), 261–271.

Misztal, B. (2003). *Theories of social remembering*. Maidenhead: Open University Press.

Morgan, D. H. J. (2011). *Rethinking family practices*. London: Palgrave.

Moss, M., & Moss, S (1984). The impact of parental death on middle aged children. *Omega* 14(1), 65–75.

Moss, M. S. and Moss, S. Z., The Death of a Parent, in Midlife Loss, Kalish, R. A. (ed.), Sage, Newbury Park, California, 1989. pp. 89–114.

Nadeau, J. W. (1998). *Families Making Sense of Death*. London: Sage.

Pearce, C. (2010). The crises and freedoms of researching your own life. *Journal of Research Practice*, 6(1), M2.

Pearce, C. (2011). Girl Interrupted: An exploration into the experience of grief following the death of a mother in young women's narratives. *Mortality*, 16(1), 35–53.

Pearce, C. (2018). Negotiating recovery in bereavement care practice in England: a qualitative study. *Bereavement Care*, 37(1), 6–16.

Pearce, C. (2019). *The public and private management of grief: recovering normal*. London: Palgrave Macmillan.

Petersen, S. and Rafuls, S. E. (1998). Receiving the sceptre: the generational transition and impact of parent death on adults. *Death studies*, 22(6), 493–524.

Pope, A. (2005). Personal transformation in midlife orphanhood: an empirical phenomenological study. *Omega*, 51(2), 107–123.

Public Health England (2018). Statistical commentary: End of Life Care Profiles, February 2018 update. https://www.gov.uk/government/publications/end-of-life-care-profiles-february-2018-update/statistical-commentary-end-of-life-care-profiles-february-2018-update. Accessed 8 September 2020.

Ribbens McCarthy, J. (2006). *Young people's experience of loss and bereavement: Towards an interdisciplinary approach*. Maidenhead: Open University Press.

Robson, P. and Walter, T. (2013). Hierarchies of loss: A critique of disenfranchised Grief. *Omega* 66(2), 97–119.

Scarre, G. (2013). Speaking of the dead: a postscript. *Mortality*, 18(3), 313–318.

Scott, J. W. (1991) The evidence of experience. *Critical Inquiry* 17(4), 773–797.

Scott, S. and Scott, S. (2000). Our Mother's Daughters: Autobiographical inheritance through stories of gender and class. In Cosslett, T., Lury, C. and Summerfield, P. (Eds.) *Feminism and Autobiography: Texts, Theories, Methods* (pp 128–140). London: Routledge.

Smart, C. (2011). Families, secrets, memories. *Sociology*, 45(4), 539–553.

Stanley, L. (1993). The knowing because experiencing subject: Narratives, Lives, Autobiography. *Women's Studies International Forum*, 16(3), 205–215.

Stivers, C. (1993). Reflections on the Role of Personal Narrative in Social Science. *Signs*, 18(2), 408–425.

Struhkamp, R. (2005). Wordless pain: Dealing with suffering in physical rehabilitation. *Cultural Studies*, 19(6), 701–718.

Tilly, C. (1999). The trouble with stories. In Pescosolido, B. A. and Aminzade, R. (Eds.) *The social worlds of higher education: Handbook for teaching in a new century* (pp. 256–270). London: Sage.

Towers, L. (2019). *Life after death: Experiences of sibling bereavement over the life course*. PhD thesis, University of Sheffield.

Troyer, J. (2020) 'I was completely unprepared': confronting my sister's death, *The Guardian*, 24 March 2020. https://www.theguardian.com/society/2020/mar/24/growing-up-in-a-funeral-home-couldnt-prepare-me-for-my-sisters-death. Accessed 6 October 2020.

Turner, N. and Almack, K. (2019). Troubling meanings of family and competing moral imperatives in the family lives of young people with a parent who is at the end of life. *Children's Geographies*, 17(5), 527–38.

van Gennep, A. (1960). *The rites of passage*. London: Routledge & Kegan Paul.

Walter, T. (1995). A new model of grief: bereavement and biography. *Mortality*, 1(1), 7–25.
Woodthorpe, K. (2009). Reflecting on death: The emotionality of the research encounter. *Mortality*, 14(1), 70–86.
Woodthorpe, K. and Rumble, H, (2016). Funerals and families: locating death as a relational issue. *The British Journal of Sociology*, 67(2), 242–259.

2

A Kind of Haunting

Carol Komaromy

In her account of A Very Easy Death written in 1964, Simone de Beauvoir details the four-week dying period of her mother; but contrary to the book's title, her mother's dying and death was far from easy. The book provides a compelling read in its intimacy and compassion. In relation to the account that follows, the difference in levels of disclosure and end-of-life care contrast with that of my father's dying; however, his death was not easy either. It was hard for him and the people who loved him, and the subsequent grief was enormous and still persists. While we had the freedom of what Glaser and Strauss called 'open awareness'(Glaser and Strauss 1965), unlike de Beauvoir I'm not convinced that the lack of deception made the acceptance of his end of life any easier. In what follows, I explore how being intimately involved in my father's dying affected my experience of coping with his slow deterioration. However, I share the sentiments of de Beauvoir in not finding any consolation in other forms of immortality, as she writes about forms of commiseration she was offered by well-intentioned readers:

C. Komaromy (✉)
The Open University, Milton Keynes, UK

© The Author(s), under exclusive license to Springer Nature Switzerland AG 2021
C. Pearce, C. Komaromy (eds.), *Narratives of Parental Death, Dying and Bereavement*,
https://doi.org/10.1007/978-3-030-70894-8_2

'Disappearing is not of the least importance: your works will remain.' And inwardly I told them all that they were wrong. Religion could do no more for my mother than the hope of a posthumous success could do for me. Whatever you think of it as heavenly or earthly, if you love life immortality is no consolation for death. (1969, 81)

In this chapter, I contrast Dad's death with that of my mother's whose deterioration followed a less even trajectory – and whose identity was compromised by her dementia and with whom my relationship was deeply problematic.

My father died in 1991 at the age of 70 and his dying took 14 long months. He was diagnosed with terminal cancer in October 1989 following admission to hospital for elective surgery to have a tumour removed from his bowel. I remember vividly how I felt when the surgical consultant, Mr Murphy, told Mom and I the bad news. We were surprised to be given an appointment to see him about the result of Dad's surgery and realised it did not bode well. Getting straight to the point, Mr Murphy shook his bowed head and said, 'Metastases spread across his peritoneum like grains of sand. I've never seen anything like it in my long career. An open and shut case of inoperable cancer.' I don't remember what else he said as the terrible news hit us. I do remember he offered us the chance to tell Dad before he did by asking, 'Do you want to tell him or shall I?' The consultation lasted ten minutes at the most and it felt quite stark and brutal. Indeed, our world changed in just those few minutes. Apart from reeling with shock and in the turmoil, I remember noting that there was no negotiation about him *not* being told.

As we walked to the ward, I felt relieved that we had been trusted to tell Dad – after all I had experience in breaking bad news and ran some training courses. When we entered the ward, I went to fetch a chair to sit with Dad desperately working out how to tell him as gently as I could, but when I got to the bedside, I could see my mother was already telling him. Not in words but with a grim expression and a shake of her head in answer to my dad's question, 'What did he say?' *He* was the consultant. I can still see my dad's face as he tried to make sense of the news. The feeling of hopelessness weighted us all down and seemed to render us silent. On reflection, I also felt helpless and I *so* wanted to help him.

A few minutes later Mr Murphy appeared on the ward. He came straight to us gathering up the ward sister en route, sat on the side of Dad's bed and asked, 'Do you have any questions?' My dad pleaded, 'Is there *nothing* you can do?' He then took my dad's hand and said, 'I'm sorry.' I experienced this as an act of compassion – but I later found out that my dad did not. Dad was offered the chance to go home and he decided he wanted to go immediately; but while we sat in my car waiting for Mom to get his medications, Dad looked at the outpatient's appointment card and declared, '*He's* only given me an appointment for three months because he knows I'll be dead by then!' This amused and puzzled me in equal measure – what possible motive could the consultant have for doing that? It was clearly an expression of perceived hatred on Dad's part, I suspect, deeply rooted in his indoctrinated mistrust of Catholics. Perhaps passing a death sentence on Dad – and the rest of us who would have to manage life without him – was what he considered to be typical behaviour of Irish Catholics when dealing with a Protestant Irish man like Dad. Further, perhaps the 'why me?' question that often follows a terminal diagnosis was simply being answered by Dad's own prejudice. Not that Dad would have thought that the consultant caused his cancer, but rather, his apparent refusal to treat Dad on the basis that it would be futile Dad took personally and to him meant that he was not worth saving.

At the time of these events, my parents lived in a council house in a village between Stafford and Wolverhampton. They had lived in the west Midlands since the Second World War, apart from a few years in Northern Ireland, where Dad was born and spent his childhood and early adulthood until he joined the Royal Air Force (RAF) in 1943. My parents' hopes and dreams were overshadowed by two key issues, poverty and Mom's mental fragility. Mom had suffered from undiagnosed post-natal psychosis, which she described as 'having turns', following the birth of my sister in 1944, when Dad was in Europe fighting with the RAF. They moved to Ireland when Dad returned from the war in 1946, and when she became pregnant with me in 1947, unemployment in Northern Ireland forced their return to England. For the first few years in England they struggled to find accommodation – even being homeless for a while and Mom and I going into the Poor House; Mom into one of the large female wings, and me into the 24-bedded nursery. For most of their married life, money remained a central concern and cause of insecurity and anxiety. In the late 1980s, Dad had taken early retirement due to ill-health in the form of angina but they enjoyed their life together and had some savings boosted by a small win on the football pools. This windfall of just £8000 meant they felt rich and the later years of their life could be described as comfortable. They had a small group of close friends, a good social life and most weekends went ballroom dancing. They even took a few holidays abroad with friends. The quality of this new life was ended dramatically by the diagnosis of terminal cancer.

I was very close to my dad and in the months that followed, I tried to spend as much time with him as possible. In practical terms, it was not easy as I lived over two hours' drive away and had family responsibilities. My children were aged 16 and 18, my partner and I shared two dogs who needed walking three times a day and I worked 30 hours per week in the NHS while studying part-time for a degree.

Mr Murphy had referred Dad to the local hospice for pain and symptom management, after all he still had a partial bowel obstruction. My memory is that he attended Compton Hospice in Wolverhampton soon after discharge from hospital where he had his pain and symptoms assessed and a syringe driver fitted and was started immediately on a small dose of morphine and other symptom-relieving drugs. While everything was being done to relieve Dad's physical pain and to reduce his anxiety, I don't think his emotional distress was ever relieved. Fundamentally, Dad did not want to die. While he recognised and commented from time to time that he'd nearly had his three score years and ten and that many children and young people were dying who 'should not', he still told me that he just wanted to be able to potter about. I noted this plea in a diary I kept intermittently:

> 'I just want to be able to get up and potter about, it's not too much to ask is it?' A question which I found impossible to answer. He looked me in the eye with his piercing blue eyes. This is someone who gave so much and who was so totally unselfish. Later, on the way home, I sobbed as I thought about this heart-breaking plea.

Everyone close to Dad – his immediate family and his friends – were devastated by the news that he had terminal cancer. A wide group of people adored him. He was so special – kind, generous and funny but most significantly, he never realised how special he was. My sister, whose life was limited by a degenerative long-term condition (systemic lupus erythematosus – SLE), was furious that Mom and I had agreed to tell Dad that he was dying. She thought we had removed all hope for him. At the time, I believed firmly that Dad deserved to know and that this was his right. I remember remonstrating with Pauline about it, imagining myself to hold the moral high ground. Anyway, arguing with my older sister was a significant and routine part of our relationship, although since her SLE diagnosis we had become much closer and less antagonistic. I was fiercely committed to the principles of the Hospice Movement – and also believed in respecting people's autonomy. I have wondered since about whether or not he could have been told in a way that might have mitigated some of the emotional pain, but I know that he would have seen through any attempt to soften the blow with partial truths. I imagine that if he had been diagnosed now, he would have been offered a myriad of curative treatments. Perhaps, his period of dying could have been extended – perhaps he might have achieved a remission? It's impossible to know what the outcomes might have been. I suspect it would have been just as awful to see him going through aggressive treatments as it was to witness him dying.

During his period of dying some aspects stand out clearly. The trajectory was not straightforward and although overall he declined, there were peaks and troughs. Some days were better than others but his overall physical decline was marked by weight loss, increasing weakness and breakthrough pain. The latter meant he needed to have regular reviews, including a residential period in Compton Hospice (where a friend of mine, Jane, with whom I had done some cancer counselling training worked full time as a social worker). Dad told me that one day he was asked to sit with a very young woman who was dying and feeling lonely. Seeing someone so young who was dying upset him a lot – but it also seemed to help him to make some sort of sense of the comparative timeliness of his own death.

About ten months into his illness in the summer of 1991, in an attempt to reduce his abdominal pain, Dad was given radiotherapy – which resulted in complete loss of appetite; intermittent, intense pain; and terrible diarrhoea. Mom called me and I went to help her to look after him because we both thought that he might die. I recorded the detail at the time in my diary:

> This brutal treatment had caused much more pain and torture than the cancer. He very nearly died on Thursday and it was almost peaceful. 'Not bad', I thought. He was asleep and I was sitting with him – Mom watering the garden. She walked into the bedroom quietly – his eyelids fluttered, then he opened his eyes with a supreme effort, and said, clearing his throat as he always did before he spoke, 'I haven't done the Pools!' We laughed. He always made us laugh, then we helped him to do the pools. He gave us a number every few minutes – it took ages. He went back to sleep and Mom and I went downstairs and discussed the funeral because we decided that he would not live through the night. The GP had been twice that day to give him pain relief and she had said, 'I've been wrong before, but I really think this is it.' The district nurses had agreed that this was his last week, we thought so too and so we discussed the funeral. Then he had an angina attack and Mom got really scared. He took tablets which relieved it and into the long night we went.
>
> Friday heralded a recovery. Sitting up in bed and wanting his tea to be hotter and eating toast. Then up to the bathroom to wash himself unaided. 'You've decided not to die then Dad?' I said. 'Well I was a bit dodgy yesterday!' But dying wasn't on his agenda yet. And that is when we made a deal. 'I really do have to go to Bath Dad, but you will tell me if you're going to die won't you?' He replied, 'Yes, if I can, but I'll be alright – you go and I'll be up again.'

I rang every day from Bath and a speedy improvement followed – frustrating my mother who thought that after about ten months of dying, it might have come to an end. I can sympathise with her as being his full-time carer clearly was taking its toll, but I was delighted to keep him for longer. When I went to visit him a week later, I went into the bedroom and he was getting up ready for my visit, albeit very unsteadily. As he was putting on his dressing gown, I could see his face in the wardrobe mirror and he was grinning from ear to ear – clearly delighted to have survived enough to get out of bed again and come downstairs. It was a grin of pride, and I was proud of him!

I have written a lot about Dad's emotional state when he was dying and how his war-time memories returned to haunt him (see Komaromy and Hockey 2018), especially the sights and smells of Belsen. With the help of my partner, Peter, we found a Belsen survivor called Mala Tribich, who agreed to visit him so that he could see that it was possible to survive the nightmarish hell and live a full life. Along with the traumatising memories of what he saw as one of the first visitors to the camp before the medical corps arrived – he told me he still saw those dreadful images every time he closed his eyes and that they haunted him. Also, that he felt guilty that he and his mate who had volunteered to take water and flour into the camp, could not take anyone with them, despite their pleas. He was very concerned about what happened to the people he saw and those like them in other camps. Overall, he could not understand how human beings could be capable of committing such horrific crimes.

On the day that Mala visited him – she and her husband Maurice drove from London and had lunch with Peter and I before driving to Mom and Dad's house. We had tea with them and made polite conversation – Mala and Maurice talked about their life in England and their children. I remember feeling frustrated that Belsen was not mentioned. However, as we were leaving, Mala took my dad's hand and said, 'Thank you, Jim.' My memory is that he dismissed this saying something like, 'I did nothing.' I know he was embarrassed to be thanked – but also he was pleased to meet Mala who had been a child of 14 and very ill with typhus when Belsen was liberated. After that, they wrote to each other. I still have these letters. I like to think that some of his emotional pain was eased by this visit.

On an entirely practical level, being able to spend time with Dad during this period of dying meant managing my annual leave was difficult – I didn't really know when I might need to spend more time with him. Therefore, I had to try to balance the practicalities of his dying with making predictions about when he might die. As the late autumn approached, the community nursing team came in twice a day and for the last few weeks, a volunteer night sitter came. Mom continued to sleep with

Dad – so the night sitter sat downstairs – but her presence seemed to offer reassurance to Mom in case anything happened at night. As the end of his life drew nearer and as Dad grew weaker, there were several false alarms when he seemed to deteriorate only to bounce back again.

As winter approached, it was clear that the end was near. By now, 14 months into his illness, Dad was on 7000 mgs of morphine a day via his syringe driver along with a cocktail of other drugs but he remained compos mentis. Near the end on Sunday, 1st December 1991, I have a vivid memory of getting up at 5.30 am. Peter, my partner, asked me what I was doing and I said, 'Going to see Dad, he's going to die today.' Declaring that he hadn't heard the phone, I told him it hadn't rung – but that I knew because Dad 'told' me. Dad and I sometimes communicated in times of distress, but not always physically. We'd made a deal and somehow he had let me know. As I was leaving home, the phone rang and my mom told me that Dad had asked permission to die the night before. She told me how he had said, 'Is it alright if I go now, Nell? Will it be alright with Carol and with Pauline?' to which she had answered 'Yes' both times. Then she told me he had toasted us all in turn with a glass of water.

When I got to my parents' house Dad was sitting up in bed. He tried to talk to me but I could not decipher what he was saying and that remains painful. Over the following hours I said just two of the things I wanted to say to him. I sat on the bed beside him, and held him and said through tears, 'I've come to say good-bye, Dad'. A while later, I told him I loved him. We were not a family given to open declarations of love and it might have been the first time I had said this. Later that day, I told him I did not want him to die but I wanted his dying to end. My children came to visit. We had moved from St Albans to Kenilworth and so were closer to Penkridge in Staffordshire, where my parents lived. My daughter Debbie was 18 and had stayed in St Albans when we moved, the same town her father, Stuart, lived in. He brought her to the house and stayed to see my dad and to say goodbye – he was extremely fond of Dad. Peter, my partner, brought my 16-year-old son, Nick, and our two retrievers to the house. Shortly after arriving, I had phoned Pauline and insisted that she should come. Pauline was very reluctant and thought we were being too pessimistic; however, she and her husband, Michael, came at lunch-time. I tried to stay with Dad most of the day, going downstairs now and again to help Mom with refreshments. My children were very upset. They adored their granddad. Nick decided to go home and not stay for the end; however, Debbie wanted to stay and did so.

My nephews, who were at university, had been to visit Dad the weekend before. In the following email extract, Anthony describes vividly the last visit they shared with him:

> I am sure I did not want to see him die and felt some (guilt-fused) relief that I avoided the final scene. I don't think I properly said 'goodbye' to Granddad, never wanting to accede to hopelessness. I think this was a complicit denial. He could not help but protect us. The last time I saw him, he was actually more alert than some previous visits when I would often have to stare intently at his face (now a premonition of a skull) to recover him at all. We watched the results come in at 4.40 pm on his portable TV and he checked his coupon. I remember the first two picks were score draws and there was a flicker of old mischief in his eyes (like when he'd rub his hands together and say something like, 'Here we go...24 points...get down the travel agent, Nell'). Come Arbroath and East Fife, when all was lost, he let the coupon fall from his right hand on to the bedside table where a glass of water rested and the morphine driver droned.

Anthony's memory profoundly captures the essence of Dad and represents the loss all four of his grandchildren felt.

As the evening drew on, the Methodist minister came to visit and told Dad that while we did not want to lose him, it was alright for him to go. He also told Dad that God would look after him. All this time Dad had stayed wide awake – mostly I sat on the bed and held him. At ten past eight, he snatched his hand from mine, ground his teeth noisily, contracted into a convulsive-like movement and died. I was to relive this scene regularly for over a year and each night I resurrected him in my dreams – waking each morning to think it had all been a terrible mistake – but as realisation dawned I had to face the terrible truth again. The most significant person in my life had gone! I was 43 years old and I had never known life without him.

Despite it being Sunday evening, the GP came and certified Dad's death and we called the funeral director. I remember feeling in desperate need of keeping part of him and Pauline and I each cut a lock of his hair. When the funeral directors came I supervised his removal from the house as a way of ensuring that he was treated with dignity. I remember feeling very protective towards him. I knew that he had gone, but this was still my dad. While my sister and mother were able to console themselves with meeting up again in an afterlife, I did not share this belief and therefore took no comfort from such ideas.

I have no memory of the rest of the evening. I think I must have stayed the night. I remember Mom being focused on the practical arrangements. For example, before Dad died I had bought him a navy-blue jacket on which to wear his RAF badge, having recently joined the RAF Association. He had seen the blazer in the village clothes shop when he was still able to visit the village and I had bought it for him. Indeed, I was thrilled to be able to do give him something he wanted. I have vague memories of him wearing it a few times – but when he lost weight he became too embarrassed to do so. Mom and I decided that he should be buried in the jacket and with the RAF badge on the lapel. He and Mom had agreed to be cremated, but when he was very ill, he allowed me to persuade him otherwise, 'Dad, I don't want you to be burned.' And he replied, 'That's okay Carol, I'll be buried if that's what you want.'

I said goodbye to him in the coffin and he looked good in his outfit – but it was clear that he had 'gone.' I'm not sure I was able to make any sense of where he might be, but his regular appearances in my dreams, where he clearly told me there had been a mistake and he was still alive, suggested that the reality was really too hard for me to accept.

I remember having a slight disagreement with the local minister who came to discuss the funeral arrangements because I wanted to speak at the service and he was clearly not very keen, unless it was to do a religious reading. The minister's main focus (not the same person who attended Dad's death) was on how we would fit in with his funeral programme and how long I would take, which I experienced as horrendously controlling. I remember buying an outfit for the funeral from Rackhams department store in Leamington Spa and becoming overwhelmed and unable to choose anything. A wonderful shop assistant saw my distress and came to my rescue; she told me to sit down and she chose an outfit for me that seemed just right. In those moments of being lost, such small acts of kindness are enormously significant.

Dad was buried on 10th December. On the day itself, I have a memory of Mom, Pauline and I being in the chief mourner's car following the coffin. For the last part of the journey to the chapel, the funeral director walked in front of the hearse. We agreed that Dad would have been impressed. The church was full. When I spoke and looked up into the congregation I noted lots of very young people crying. I spoke my tribute to him and retained composure – struggling only when I read the lines from T.S. Eliot's *Four Quartets*, '… (T)he end of all our exploring will be to arrive where we started and know the place for the first time.'

In the extract that follows, Anthony shared this memory on looking around the congregation:

> I remember being alarmed by the tear-bred ruddiness and fear now alive in familiar faces. Debbie's is the most vivid of these. I did not have much comparative measure of my own grief but the thought that Granddad Jim's insoluble love and oblique humour would remain absent for the remainder of time felt unbearable. I know it should not therefore be a thought entertained for too long.

I have no memory of the burial itself but in correspondence with Anthony he remembered how:

> The graveside was shaded and it had started to rain. The damp and cold felt permanent. The lowering of the coffin triggered the most communal peak of crying and unquiet and I felt a fear for the feelings of others…and I kept an eye on Mum and Graham….possibly as a displacement activity as the burial is where ritual succumbs to the horror of wet mud and worms and eternal decay.

At the funeral tea, I noted that Mom was 'enjoying' the company and being the focus of attention. I realised that in future, I would have to cope with visiting the house without him there and did not look forward to that.

As the first anniversary of Dad's death approached I wrote in my diary to him, echoing Anthony's feelings about life without him:

> It is now eleven months since you died and I don't cry every day suddenly and unexpectedly, neither do I relive your death every night. But, I feel worse, carrying a horrible heaviness, a sinking sensation, a slow seeping awful knowledge that I will never see you again.

A Death of Contrasts: Mom's Death

What is clear in recounting my dad's death and dying is how much I did not want him to die – indeed, I had hoped to be able to look after him as he aged and welcome him into my home to live with us. By comparison, my relationship with my mother was less easy. Indeed, it was very difficult – mainly marred by her long-term mental illness which was only diagnosed near the end of her life. The voices she heard telling her to harm me as an infant and the paranoia she experienced that meant she thought that friends and family were turning against her and persecuting her, was only formally diagnosed when she was assessed for dementia in her 80s. I was an adult when Mom told me about the voices she heard after my birth that persisted for several years. She was not a monster but sometimes she did monstrous things – and the most difficult aspect was that she was unpredictable, fluctuating between love and laughter one moment to anger and martyrdom the next. Perhaps that unpredictability was the worst thing. So no wonder my father became a hero to me when not only was he constantly loving and kind but he mitigated some of the fear of and damage from my mother.

Therefore, being left with my mother who outlived my father and sister was a challenge to me. However, as Mom aged she mellowed and became more loving and showed huge gratitude for my visits and care. Of course, I remained cautious of her and on guard for any change in mood. Later in her life, Mom became a Jehovah's witness and this offered her the security, company and love that she craved. 'Like being in a family again' she told me. Mom was referring to the large family she had grown up in with seven siblings, but of course, the lack of more immediate family did not escape me. I visited her about every four to six weeks and occasionally invited her to our home.

My mother's period of dying was not heralded by a formal diagnosis as with Dad, but a series of small illnesses and the beginning of dementia. It seemed to be a sequence of physical and mental losses that accumulated into more significant disability. Each acute episode involved me in accompanying her to various hospital appointments and suffering the minor embarrassments that were part of these. For example, one day in the out-patients' waiting room, she looked around and quite audibly declared with lots of tutting how old everyone was and how it might be best to put people to sleep at a certain age. Each consultant she saw she offered a copy of her advance directive – which was met with a mixture of amusement and degrees of humiliation at its inappropriateness. Increasingly unable to manage her three-bedroomed Housing Association house, she moved into sheltered accommodation, but complained a lot about the 'useless' warden and the woman upstairs who hoovered her flat at 'unsuitable' hours.

As Mom slowly deteriorated and became confused, frequent admissions to hospital, often with severe urine infections and 'falls', highlighted her deterioration and eventually her loss of independence. Latterly, about two years before she died, she rang me from the hospital ward, where she told me in a loud whisper that 'they' were trying to kill her. This was quite alarming in terms of knowing how to respond. No longer in need of physical nursing and clinical care, I was invited to meet with her social worker to discuss Mom's longer-term care needs. It seemed that the time had come when she could no longer go back to her home but she no longer needed a hospital bed. Yet again, I explained that I was not her carer – and I was not going to give up my job – nor take her to live with me. Of course, I felt bad about not loving her – or liking her – enough to do this. On another level my feminist side was outraged at being expected to do so.

Following the social work assessment, and combined with the psychiatric diagnosis of dementia and paranoid psychosis, Mom was transferred from the hospital to one of the last remaining Local Authority Residential homes. This gave us six weeks of respite care in which to find a permanent home. Because Mom was a Jehovah's witness, it was possible for her to go to one of their Jah-Jireh homes, although the nearest to her was a few hours away in Lancashire. She and I had discussed this possibility some time before her decline and she liked the idea of being able to take part in daily services and being with like-minded people whom she called her family. Getting her a place involved an enormous amount of bureaucracy, key to which was the strength of her belief and commitment to the faith. But with much support from the Jehovah Elders, arrangements were made and the difference in funding agreed – which I would pay from her savings. When she was discharged, Peter and I took her from the Local Authority home to a Jah-Jireh residential home. I was horrified to note that she was uncertain about where she was going and I reminded her about going to a home that had religion at its heart and I remember feeling a sense of panic when she asked, 'Oh, what religion am I?'

There were other practical tasks to complete associated with this change in circumstances. Fortunately, a few years before the various hospital admissions, Mom asked me to take over the care of her finances – she said she could not cope and we had set up Power of Attorney. We handed over her sheltered accommodation flat and I arranged for it to be cleared. Some of her possessions went to friends but most were removed, presumably to be sold or given away. I was struck by the reality of how little there was of material worth. On one level, I found it to be a sad reflection of my parents' lives.

Mom seemed to be quite happy in the care home. Indeed, I was surprised at how easily she relaxed into being cared for and amused at how she thought everything was 'free', despite me telling her that we were paying a supplement beyond state benefit. The care staff were incredibly kind and demonstrated what I would call, 'unconditional love.' However, it was shocking to see the extent to which she had deteriorated at each visit and, although she seemed to recognise me, she gradually lost touch with who she was and her past life. One day she asked me if she had ever been married. In my ignorance, I thought it was good practice to reinforce reality and would spend time looking at the photo album with her and reminding her of the detail of her life. As time progressed, she got very frustrated with me and sometimes flew into a rage especially when I said I had to go home. I began to dread the visits and felt guilt and resentment in equal measure.

Mom had been in the home for about six months when in late January, 2009, she became acutely ill and was transferred to hospital. She was dehydrated and had a urinary tract infection but also, she was refusing to eat. When my daughter, Debbie, and I visited her in hospital we were horrified to note that they had inserted a naso-gastric feeding tube, something that must have upset Mom and to which she would not have consented. She had an intense dislike of anything near her throat and could barely tolerate dental visits and having to cope with the sensation of choking. We made an appointment to see the medical team the next day and stayed overnight in a local hotel. At the team meeting, we were told that she had removed the tube herself that morning. I told them that Mom would not have wanted this intervention and reminded them of her advance directive. I knew from Mom's decline into dementia that the quality of life was poor and that her refusal to eat was probably her way of expressing a wish to die. The team were obviously relieved and clearly agreed that any aggressive intervention was futile. As we left, Sister told us that relatives usually request more intervention, despite its futility.

The care home head decided that Mom could not return to residential care and needed nursing care and so Mom was transferred to Jah-Jireh Nursing Home in Wigan. This was near the end of January 2009. On Saturday, 14th February 2009, we received a call from the head of the nursing home to say that Mom had deteriorated and was 'very poorly.' I knew from my research into end-of-life care in care homes that this was a euphemism for 'dying' and asked, 'Do you mean I need to come straight away because she is dying?' 'Yes', she replied.

We cancelled our planned meal with friends, booked a room in a local hotel, rang her four grandchildren and travelled to the home, arriving early evening. My children were not able to visit but my two nephews, Anthony and Graham, wanted to see her and we met in the nursing home. Mom was unconscious and the staff were concerned that she might die that night. We went to our respective overnight stays, leaving contact numbers and agreed to meet at the home the next day.

When we got there, Mom seemed to be much the same – she was clearly dying, very pyrexial (high temperature) but her breathing was not laboured. Our death-bed vigil continued throughout the Sunday. Peter had a hospital appointment on Monday and I discussed with the Head of

Home the dilemma of having to leave that day. I remember her words clearly, 'You go home. Don't worry. We will hold her when the time comes. She is safe with us.' This was a huge relief and at this we all decided to leave and phone the next day.

Close friends who lived opposite offered to take Peter to hospital for his appointment and I rang the home at 9 am. The person who answered the phone told me to hang on and then the Head of Home told me that Mom had just died and that they were 'holding her when she passed'. I rang a few hours later to arrange to collect the death certificate and I was horrified to hear that the GP had refused to sign it on the basis that she was not confident about the cause of death and had referred the death to the Coroner. The head of home gave me the Coroner's number – and when I spoke to the Coroner, she told me she was very annoyed that this death had been reported (she used the word 'ridiculous') and had instructed the GP to issue a death certificate. The cause of death was recorded as: 1 (a) Old age.

My partner was not well enough to accompany me and so Debbie agreed to go with me to Wigan to collect the certificate from the nursing home, choose clothes for Mom to be buried in, register the death and travel to the funeral director in Penkridge, where Mom wanted to be buried with Dad. This was quite a complex quest with many miles to travel and deadlines to meet. There were moments of dark humour, not least deciding we had to buy Mom shoes that she would want to be buried in (or seen dead in) – all she had in her wardrobe comprised 'sensible' shoes, many with Velcro fastenings. This meant we had to buy new shoes on the way to register the death – realising too late that we would arrive at the Registrar's office carrying a huge bright red Debenhams's sale bag. It did not help that the Registrar sounded like the comedian Peter Kay. Clutching several certificates, we dashed off to the Co-op funeral director in Penkridge where we were due to arrive by 4.30 pm. Mom had pre-paid her funeral plan – something she reminded me of many times before she became confused. We arranged the funeral and gave Gail, the Director, the clothes for Mom to be dressed in when she arrived from the Wigan Mortuary. We wanted to delay the funeral to accommodate Debbie's booked holiday and Gail was quite resistant, but eventually agreed. Fortunately, Gail was quite willing to negotiate with the Jehovah Elders and the Vicar about them conducting a service at the graveyard; a challenge she seemed to relish. Mom was to have a funeral service at the Kingdom Hall in Safford before the interment in the graveyard in Penkridge. I had to be clear about the Jehovah refusal to allow any form of embalming, and Gail later advised me it was not a good idea to view Mom's body before the funeral. Again, I had to insist that I needed to see her before she was buried. When I did visit the undertakers before the funeral, I noted how dim the lights were in the viewing room and struggled to be able to recognise Mom. She appeared very small, I did not remember her being so small, and, – I think because of the very heavy make-up – I relied on the identifying scar she had at the side of her eye to satisfy myself it was her.

My daughter spoke at Mom's funeral about her memories of her as a grandmother, especially the time that we had lived there when my marriage ended. The interment was relatively brief – with one of the Elders conducting the ceremony. I had arranged for a lunch at the local pub and a room had been set aside and a fabulous buffet laid on. Friends had helped me to set up three photo boards of Mom's life which I entitled, The Early Years, The Middle Years and The Later Years and this served as a focus for discussions of people's memories of Mom. It was also a way of bringing back her identity from that lost to her dementia and the ugliness of dying. Mom was always really careful about her appearance and managed to remain glamorous until the last few weeks of her life and the photographs highlighted this. It is something that always mattered to her and an important part of her identity. The funeral lunch seemed to be a success and I felt that I had discharged my duties as her remaining daughter. It was good to see my cousins again, many of whom I had not seen since my sister Pauline's funeral – or even that of my dad.

I felt anxious that the absence of any deep sense of loss might be because I was suppressing my feelings and that the grief would catch up with me, as if there was a price to be paid for not mourning my mother's death as much as I should. The contrast with the loss of my father (and then my sister) was striking. Writing this over a decade later, I realise that delayed grief is unlikely. The relationship was complex and her death brought me a kind of release from the feelings of fear that endured throughout childhood and remained deep within me into adulthood. We had some good times together, and I can appreciate the gifts she gave me, such as a love of opera. Indeed, I have come to understand that she must have had a terrible struggle to manage her feelings when she was suffering from auditory hallucinations and paranoid delusions after my birth and possibly until her death.

When I had my first child, I was very affected by no longer being the baby of the family and I experienced that as a profound loss. When my mother died, similar feelings returned as I realised that I was next in the line of succession to the grave – according to the 'natural' order of things. Of course my parents might not be physically present any longer, but they continue to influence who I am and who I have become and in that sense they haunt me. Most significantly in terms of this Anthology, they will influence my own demise and how I would like to think that I can retain my own dignity at the end and part of this is accepting when it is time to go.

References

De Beauvoir, S. (1969). *A Very Easy Death*. Harmondsworth: Penguin Books.
Eliot, T. S. (1943). *Four Quartets*. New York City: Harcourt.
Glaser, B. and Strauss, A. (1965). *Awareness of Dying*. Chicago: Aldine.
Komaromy, C. and Hockey, J. (2018). *Family Life, Trauma and Loss in the Twentieth Century. The Legacy of War*. London: Palgrave Macmillan.

3

A Death Recalled

Jenny Hockey

This chapter was written 24 years ago, in 1996, a month after my father died. It describes the three months immediately beforehand and, apart from minor edits, it is as I wrote it then. Until 2019 only Bob, my partner, had read it. In fact, as a psychologist, Bob prompted me to write it because, although my father's manner remained unchanged, what he said began to depart wildly from the truth. Intriguing for a psychologist, but also for me, as a sociologist who worked on questions of identity (see Hockey and James 2002). Now, on reflection, confusion about who my father actually was during this period made it even more difficult.

As the chapter describes, my father was a private man, not given to spontaneous emotional expression and very much in charge of himself. What killed him was a fistula, or opening, that developed between his intestine and bladder and led to his slow poisoning. Confabulation, the unintended telling of untruths, can be an outcome of anticholinergic toxidrome – a dangerous level of toxins that he undoubtedly had in his

J. Hockey (✉)
University of Sheffield, Sheffield, UK
e-mail: j.hockey@sheffield.ac.uk

© The Author(s), under exclusive license to Springer Nature Switzerland AG 2021
C. Pearce, C. Komaromy (eds.), *Narratives of Parental Death, Dying and Bereavement*,
https://doi.org/10.1007/978-3-030-70894-8_3

body. So not only might he talk nonsense – yet sound exactly as he always had – but his body was betraying him dramatically as thick, foul-smelling liquid escaped from it in ways he seemed unaware of.

One thing is clear, as sociologist Erving Goffman argued in his book *Stigma* (1963), my father's identity was 'spoiled'. In other words, he developed a deeply discrediting, stigmatising personal attribute. Added to this, his confabulation created a kind of split identity within a single, increasingly chaotic body. Issues around identity help explain why I kept my account of Dad's death private for so long. Certainly, in 1996 and already established within death studies, I imagined my account would somehow feed into my academic work. Yet the prospect of revealing Dad's spoiled identity made me uncomfortable. Plus, I was ashamed of some of my responses, particularly the self-interest apparent in my account. In the end though, after Carol Komaromy and I had co-authored a family history (Komaromy and Hockey 2018) and I had listened to her training vignettes about the conflict between the needs of a woman's dying father and those of her family and job, I shook the dust off my account and sent it to Carol. Sufficient time had passed. And Carol's vignettes showed me others experiencing what I had (See Komaromy 2012). But now, before the account begins, some background.

My dad died on 11 October 1996. He was 81 and I was 50. He lived alone in his two-up, two-down semi in Cambridge, widowed for nearly 30 years. I lived in East Yorkshire and was establishing my career as a senior academic at the University of Hull. I was Dad's only immediate relative.

I wrote most of my account on a train journey from Hull to Exeter and back. It describes how Dad rapidly became dependent on our decision-making and the care we secured for him. A still-independent man, his life at the time played out within walking and retirement groups, rather than intimate friendships. His conversations with me were rarely personal, revolving mainly around his latest walking itineraries.

Dad was four when he lost his own father, Bert, killed in action on one of the last days of the First World War. His mother, Ella, was left to run the high-class drapers she and Bert established in Topsham, South Devon. Ella sent my father, David, and his elder brother, Arthur, to be educated at the Drapers School in Croydon, London. Later, the Second World

War brought Dad together with Mum, in Cambridge where they married in 1942. The following year Arthur, Dad's only sibling, was killed in action in Italy. The death was confirmed on the day his mother, Ella, died of pneumonia. The words 'What a day that was' are all I can remember Dad saying about that dreadful double bereavement. That and a shake of his head.

Painful feelings were invariably downplayed in the home where I grew up as an only child with my parents and my maternal granddad. Outright rows were unheard of, though occasionally Mum stayed in their bedroom all day. 'Lorna suffers with her nerves', they said of her. She died of cancer in 1967, aged fifty-two, the year Bob and I began married life in a Cambridge flat. I was twenty-one and for the rest of Dad's life felt responsible for him, ill-equipped though I was to provide the two meals I invited him to every week – or indeed to run the home Bob and I had set up. Two years later we moved to Durham where Bob took up his first academic post and I looked after Jo, our baby daughter. From then on, Dad would drive up to stay with us every month or so – in Durham, Sheffield and finally Beverley, near Hull.

Post Mortem: Early Warnings

It wasn't really a shock when Dad's walking friend Neville phoned us in Beverley to say that my father looked very unwell. Even so, it was only later that we found the dates of Dad's illnesses in his diaries. Certainly there had been a cumulative process which led me to see him as permanently with minor health problems. When my friend Tony said he *expected* his 80-year-old father to have such problems I found this reassuring. From then on I accepted Dad's symptoms sympathetically, rather than feeling threatened by the possibility of his dependency. Previously this caused me resentment and I'd suggest solutions to his difficulties, most of which he resisted: taking vitamins, always walking a little, changing his doctor.

When Dad visited that spring he didn't want to go out walking, our usual shared activity. Instead, he and I drove to Burton Agnes Hall where he enjoyed the paintings but didn't want to walk in the grounds. On the

Sunday he took a walking stick when we strolled on the Westwood pastureland – but only as far as the golf course beyond the Black Mill. He'd never used a walking stick before, but he quoted a walking magazine that recommended them for *all* walkers. We ate lunch in the garden afterwards, drinking red wine in the sunshine. Bob was away. I later learnt that Dad went on to have a bad attack of gastro-enteritis that May. He didn't let me know as he didn't want to worry me. But he said his friend Irene almost phoned me herself as she was so concerned about him.

About a month after his spring visit I felt that we owed him another invitation before our July holiday. However, all our intervening weekends were booked up. I phoned him to suggest late August, after our holiday, and he agreed. I was relieved, but aware that he didn't grasp the length of the gap as he usually would have.

Bob had a conference in Cambridge on 6 July and visited Dad. He said he was OK, just withdrawn and possibly depressed. Bob persuaded him to take his chair out in the sun and encouraged him to follow a walking schedule. When Bob returned from the corner shop, Dad had taken his chair inside and closed the patio doors.

On Sunday 28 July, Bob took the call from Neville, who said that Dad's jacket was hanging off him and he was becoming confused. I felt alarmed, overhearing the call, guessing it was about Dad, hoping it wasn't. I phoned Jack, Dad's neighbour, who confirmed what we'd heard from Neville. Next morning, I phoned Dad's General Practitioner (GP), who said he too was worried about him. He suspected a malignancy and had arranged two appointments with a consultant at Addenbrookes Hospital, but Dad had attended neither. I remembered a strange phone conversation with Dad about an appointment on 3 June. When I rang him on the day to ask how he'd got on, he just said, 'Now where have I been?'. When prompted he said, 'they just talked to me'. I was very suspicious, thinking he'd either become very forgetful but had gone to the appointment; or that he'd chosen not to go but was pretending he had. Now I wish I'd phoned his GP immediately but *then* it seemed too intrusive. It never occurred to me to interfere in his relationship with his GP.

On Monday 29 July, we went on holiday. Dad's GP had agreed to arrange a new appointment, with hospital transport provided. He sounded embarrassed that he hadn't done this before. He also agreed to arrange for a geriatric psychiatrist to visit my dad at home on account of the 'dementia'. Just previously I'd begun to unwind from work into an easier holiday state. I'd been feeling very flat and sometimes depressed during July, something I felt was caused by overworking. I'd been hanging on for a holiday. So I felt very threatened by Dad's apparent illness, a sense of no justice, that life could go on making demands which were costly to meet and there was no-one to say when you were due for a break. Anything could be required of me or taken away from me. I rang lots of friends for advice, some more able to empathise than others.

I became very anxious on the Hull-Zeebrugge ferry and rushed to the bar for cigarettes and a gin and tonic. Watching the shore recede I felt the holiday was madness. Why was I going so far away from someone likely to leave me altogether in the near future? In Holland I took hold of the idea that 'life must go on', that one person's problems don't put a brake on other people's pleasure. We met with Dutch friends who were very concerned when we told them about Dad. Why didn't we carry a mobile phone? This pitched me back into anxiety. We shouldn't have gone so far away, so removed from contact. France, when we arrived, was wonderful and I let go, though still feeling subdued. Approaching our gîte in Burgundy one week later, anxiety returned. We'd left the gîte owner's phone number with Neville. Now we could be approaching news of Dad's death. Later I discovered we'd left the wrong number. Whenever I walked up to the phone box in the village square to call Neville or Dad, I became intensely anxious. Over the phone, Dad said the doctor told him he'd had a call from me after I'd been alerted to his health problems by one of Dad's friends. He sounded cross and exasperated but said he didn't know who the friend was. We went out to a meal in Rully, me feeling heavy hearted. Now, with hindsight, it seems I was being very cautious and could have told Dad how worried I was.

Homecoming

The rest of the holiday was fine. We phoned Gareth, our son. Again, I could have asked him to call Dad frequently to check. When we finally got off the ferry in Hull, my anxiety flooded back and we drove slowly up

Sutton Road, stop-starting in the traffic, fearing the worst. At home, next doors' jolly builders welcomed us back. I felt I must use my day well if I was not going to work – wash all the clothes and so on. Bob went off to buy garden furniture and made a French-style lunch. No sense of pressure for him. I put off phoning Dad as I wanted to hear from his GP first. Early afternoon the Cambridge police rang. I thought Dad must have been in an accident with his car but the officer told me he'd been giving large sums of money to a bogus builder. He was sure my father would appreciate a call from me; he looked frail, as if he hadn't been eating much.

I later found out that Dad had paid the builders at least £13,000, and the police suspected he'd been intimidated. He made three cash withdrawals on approximately 18, 20 and 22 July. Bank staff were concerned about his frail appearance and the size of the withdrawals. On the final visit the bank manager took him aside and told him he'd no money left. He'd been trying to make the transfer with the wrong form. Bob went to see the bank manager later on and he was anxious to tell Bob how worried he'd been about Dad, how he'd even driven up to the house to check on the gardening work he was supposedly paying for. Bank policy forbade him from contacting the police but eventually he'd leaked it. The NatWest may now review their policy on the strength of this case.

The call from the police panicked me terribly. I remember washing clothes and being surprised that Bob planned to come down to Cambridge with me. I thought the problem lay in my department. I made lots of phone calls. Dad's GP had no news, though Dad had been seen by a consultant. The GP hadn't arranged for him to be seen by a psychiatrist as he'd found him 'fairly rational' when he'd last seen him. I contacted Cambridge Social Services, saying we needed to arrange for his care and asking if someone could come out to advise us straightaway. I was very worried that we'd find him in a state of collapse and be stuck in Cambridge indefinitely, trying to find a solution. The social worker agreed to come out the day we arrived and said we could put something in place within the week. It felt very hard, just back from three weeks' holiday, but not going into work. The fact that I would be on long-awaited study leave that semester made it even worse as there were no teaching pressures to offset the demands of Dad's situation. I paid lots of bills and remember phoning my friend Allison.

No Longer Dad

Next morning, we left for Cambridge, calling in to work to collect mail and tell admin staff how I could be contacted. We left there at about 10 am and I felt anxious about the tasks surfacing in my mail, my failure to keep a copy of my reply to an important visiting speaker. I was hot in the car and worried about arriving late. I'd told Dad it would be lunch-time and anticipated his disapproval and impatience – 1.30 pm wouldn't count as lunch-time. Dad had sounded husky and faint on the phone, clearing his throat and only gradually getting involved in the conversation. I was preparing to see a thin, gaunt face and body and wondered how Bob would cope with this. He probably hadn't seen as many people in this condition.

We found Dad vastly changed, not the same man at all. He was very thin, unshaven and frightened looking. His hair needed cutting and, as I realised later, he was not wearing his teeth. Only certain characteristic expressions re-assured us that this was the man we knew. We all three sat down and he looked anxious and ill at ease. None of us knew what to say. I felt he must be embarrassed by his appearance. As we came through the front door I saw him push a pair of pants into the hall cupboard. He wasn't at all forthcoming about his health and when Bob asked about the builders and he said the police had it in hand, the builders were just trying to steal some bricks. I decided to go along with whatever line Dad took and told him about our journey and other things that were trivial in comparison with what was happening to him. Bob went to Tesco, returning with vodka and cranberry and lots of food. I began cleaning the kitchen, determined to banish all dirt and stains. The fridge was inches deep in water, afloat with old vegetables and ham. We spent the next twenty-four hours slowly removing a massive ice block from the freezing tray. I was up in the night, chipping at it, worried that Dad would find his kitchen awry and be annoyed.

Next day, the district nurse called to organise special liquid that Dad needed to take in preparation for a CT scan that had been booked. She returned later with incontinence pads. Bronwen, another of Dad's walking friends, had been popping in to look after him – and he referred to visits from 'some charming ladies'. I felt that other people had undertaken what I should have been doing. Now I was back, belatedly, and the onus was on me to untangle the mess. The district nurse returned as a social worker arrived. Dad told them both he was managing fine, able to get up, get washed, wash his clothes, shop and cook. The social worker said he wouldn't stay long since there were so many people in the house. In the hall, he said Dad was doing well and it would be an intrusion to have someone come in and look after him. Briefly I half-believed him, persisting in my view that this was what being in your 80s was like. I shouldn't impose a normalising set of expectations upon him. It was OK to be ill-looking and a bit muddled. The district nurse got up to leave and, again in the hall, asked if I was the only relative – 'so you've got it all to deal with', she said. I was half-surprised to receive sympathy, more open to veiled reproaches, such as 'it must be hard to understand what's happening at a distance. It's difficult the way families live today, different priorities'. But she didn't say this.

When we had arrived, there was a meal in front of Dad on his folding table. I thought he'd cooked it himself, roast meat and potatoes. Only later I discovered that Neville had organised meals-on-wheels. Dad left most of it and then cleared up after himself, wheeling his folding table over the rug edges with painful, painstaking slowness, food spilling from his mouth as he leant forward. He seemed like a hunted, haunted man – not Dad. When Bob made tea, Dad wanted to sit up at the small dining table, trapping the three of us in awkward proximity. Bob had thrown himself into making a special meal but Dad seemed unable to eat it. He just sat up very straight immediately opposite me with embarrassed, staring eyes and sunken cheeks. Only then did he tell us that he hadn't got his teeth in and couldn't chew easily. Bob eventually persuaded him to eat in his easy chair, not make the unnecessary effort to sit up at the table. I was massively relieved when he moved away. He drank vodka and cranberry enthusiastically and went to bed early, maybe by 8.30 pm. I felt a surge of relief, realising that he wouldn't be awake and with us every minute of the day. Like discovering that babies sleep as well as cry.

Earlier I'd asked Dad if he had any pain and he said no. I asked him if he was worried about his health and he said no, 'it just gets you down' and looked frightened. I had no idea what to make of this situation or what I should do. He asked how long we were staying, what was happening. I slept very little, up in the night to chip at the ice block in the fridge. Much, much later, the dismantling of that wretchedly dirty and outdated parental kitchen was a task I relished, a compulsion I again rose early to pursue. *Then*, Dad went past on his way to bed, grimacing at the disorder of the de-frosting fridge.

He lay in next morning and again we struggled to decide what to do. I rang Bronwen who I felt could give us the best overview. I asked if I could come round and talk to her since all our phone calls were audible throughout the house. Dad didn't ever seem to hear though, despite his proximity. Bronwen panicked at my request, thinking I would ask her to take on his care. Again I felt that she must resent my previous absence and disapprove of my lack of care. She asked me what we were going to do and I said I didn't know. She said she thought this was my area of academic expertise – and that I'd have to take him back with me. I said we couldn't look after him as we were both in full-time work. 'Then he'll have to go into a home', she said, 'he shouldn't be on his own. He can't look after himself. It's sad but the time has come'. She was emphatic and I felt ready to be convinced by her certainty. It was an answer to our indecision. I made up my mind at that point, having previously considered staying in the house to look after him or having him come and stay with us.

Making Decisions

When would I tell him about my decision to put him into a home? Bob was very anxious about this. In the end I told him just before tea that day. I said that we couldn't leave him there while he was ill, that we wanted to take him up with us and arrange for him to be looked after in a nursing home. He asked if he could just stay with us. He'd be alright in the house while we were at work. His friends had told him we'd take him up to stay with us. I said that would ideally be the best arrangement but not with him being ill and me out all day. His eyes grew bigger still and he set his mouth set in a tight line, saying nothing. Just nodding.

Afterwards I watched a TV vet's programme about a blind but healthy fox cub that had to be put down because it wouldn't be able to fend for itself. I felt swamped by tearful sadness, seeing cruelty inflicted on a creature unable to function without constant help. We had to repeat our plan to Dad several times in the next few days. He kept asking what was happening. We'd arrived on Wednesday, 21 August, and Bob stayed until Sunday, 25. Getting the fridge beautifully clean was wonderful. Bob mended the door of the ice tray. Dad slept in, sometimes until midday. He ate almost nothing and went to bed early, sometimes straight after tea. The phone rang all the time. Bob began discussions about Dad's finances. Since Dad didn't want to go into a nursing home, how would we get him to pay for it? Bob brought a form back from Dad's bank which he had to sign, mandating us to organise his money. Again there was an anxious build-up to telling him about this, fearing he'd object, feeling like threatening figures. Dad signed the mandate without a murmur.

In the early mornings, before he was up, we'd stretch the phone cord into the living room and began calling Beverley nursing homes. My own GP agreed to take Dad on as a patient and was surprisingly reassuring, giving us the names of two nursing homes. I remember how hard it was to speak to the matrons initially, to get the words out and explain what we wanted. I felt I was betraying Dad, an acknowledgement that his ordinary life was over. The matrons said they could well have beds available as there were poorly residents. But we had to ring every day as there were no waiting lists. They didn't ever say that someone had to die for us to get a bed. I was worried as to whether they'd accept him. Was he bad enough? Or too bad? Or too confused? I wasn't worried about what the home would be like, just that they'd take him. And soon.

I had a bag of mail from work but only gradually began to look at it. I had no work as such with me. I couldn't face demands from an additional source. At night I imagined Dad dying in his sleep and longed for the relief that would bring, the evaporation of our problems. In the morning he'd be awake, lying on his side, big eyes watching the door he always wanted left open. When we arrived I'd realised he had no clean pants. Every pair was in the hall cupboard, stained with brown urine, along with pyjamas and sheets with shit on them. I used Dad's rubber gloves and put everything into a pail with lots of biological detergent. I pulled his washing machine out from under the stairs but couldn't find the connecting hose. I kept feeling overwhelmed and tearful. Neither Bob nor I could think straight or ever complete a task successfully. Bob phoned a laundry that took all the dirty washing and returned it, ironed, the next day. Dad couldn't understand why we hadn't used the washing machine. Even the telly wouldn't work. I longed for telly, vodka and sleep after the evening meal but we'd dislodged the lead in the corner by the table. When I adjusted Dad's long sliding calendar I noticed that the day marker carried on sliding down of its own accord. 'It's no wonder he gets confused', I said. Bob picked up the joke and imagined Dad waking up after a ten-minute nap on a Tuesday to find it was already Thursday. We fell about in wild hysteria, laughing uncontrollably at the lunacy of it all. Afterwards we kept recalling the pleasure of those moments of abandonment.

There was an awful smell in the bathroom and around Dad himself. His urine was dark brown and stinking. He collected it overnight in a plastic bottle and spattered the whole toilet area with it during the day. I was always watching his trousers for leaks and I found it hard both to get hold of incontinence pads from the doctor and have Dad use them systematically. When I phoned Bronwen she asked if I'd found his teeth. I realised that it was not through choice that he wasn't wearing them. She'd hunted everywhere for them. Bob found an old set in the bathroom cabinet, long after I'd given up. We rang round for a dentist to make a new set as Dad couldn't remember his own dentist's name. It would take six weeks, they said, so he used the old set for the rest of his life. All the time Dad spoke rationally, giving serious emphasis to what he was saying, using all his old phrases and speech patterns. Yet he'd forgotten so much and couldn't supply his friends' names for us to phone. He never had the radio on and just held the newspaper in his lap. Telly did seem to interest him if we were watching. But mostly though he slept in his new armchair.

On Saturday 24 August I got up early and went round to the doctor's surgery at 8.15 am. I put on my floppy black skirt, white tucked blouse, make-up and earrings – to look like someone to take seriously. It was wonderful to walk round there in the sun, feeling slim and well-dressed – still the holiday tan. The doctor's was shut and I prowled the nearby chemist, hunting for incontinence pads and any useful items. The human body was laid out on the pharmacy shelves, aids and remedies for every one of its parts. They didn't sell pads but I bought rubber gloves and disinfectant. When the surgery opened I glimpsed an old, surly doctor I knew must be Dad's GP. Another doctor, an attractive woman who looked as if she belonged to my own world, was also there in reception. I took my chance to see her and gave up on the obvious choice of Dad's own GP. She didn't know Dad but listened unhurriedly and told me I was doing the right thing, that he probably had pancreatic cancer, that he'd just fade away painlessly, just needing my support. I left her feeling hugely relieved and deeply comforted, the first time I'd felt OK about Dad for months. I resolved to write and thank her, and after he died I did.

Bob and I went into town that Saturday afternoon. He said the break would do me good. We walked across Midsummer Common, going in Robert Sayles, where Dad had worked, to buy a timer for the lamp. In Marks and Spencer we realised Bob didn't have his wallet. We had a drink in the Fort St George on the way back and I thought how nice it was, dark wood and rainy greenery on either side. The university boat houses opposite reminded me of the 'men' I'd looked up to as a teenager. They're the kids I teach now. When we got home it was clear that Bob's wallet wasn't in the house. Dad said he'd left it on the stairs. He'd called out after us but we'd already left. He couldn't explain why it wasn't there now. He said all this with complete conviction, the knowing parental voice exasperated by his scatty children. It was the same when Bronwen visited. She asked him where he'd found his teeth and he said he'd gone to a social services 'do' and everyone had been allowed to help themselves to a set of teeth. Amazingly he'd picked out a set which fitted perfectly. All this was said with total confidence, the old story-telling expression on his face, the humour and the emphases intact. It was all nonsense. Asleep or awake, there was no real contact to be made with him. Along with Bronwen, several of Dad's friends came round to say goodbye to him before his journey up to Beverley. They knew it was a last goodbye, yet they all said it like dumb soldiers, restrained and inexpressive. I felt for them terribly yet had no comfort to offer.

Bob took Dad's car up to Beverley on Sunday 25 August, Dad only half understanding what was happening. I spent the day working in the garden to make it look tidier, mainly for security reasons. All week, neighbours had been discussing the bogus builders who offered to do garden work and demanded money. They'd threatened one elderly neighbour, saying they'd strip the tiles from her roof if she didn't pay up. She was constantly on the look-out for a ladder up the front of the house. I felt nervous. The police thought Dad had been intimidated and Dad's friend, Irene, said he looked frightened. While gardening I found Dad's shed full of old equipment, the previous pedal-bin, the last mop but one. During this period in Cambridge, my anger over the past 30 years crystallised, now that Dad's credibility had gone, and his remoteness intensified. I saw how inauthentic he'd always been, never given of himself – just a bland, inoffensive exterior, a type-cast pattern of stereotyped behaviour. For all my married life, I'd been responsible for someone who'd held himself aloof from me since childhood, who'd withheld spontaneous warmth, honesty, gifts and the willingness to accommodate to me. The man I felt I now had to care for was isolated within a banal exterior, effectively cut off from any threats those around might make towards him. They're all the same, I thought, the whole sodding family, and I'm one of them.

I enjoyed doing the garden and Dad was pleased. He said he'd have to have me down more often to do jobs for him. I popped in and out to make sure he didn't feel abandoned, organised for him to watch TV, the nun's programme on art. I came in eventually in bare feet and skidded across the kitchen floor in a pool of urine, giving a shout of alarm. He was irritated by the sudden noise and I said crossly that I'd nearly fallen over in a wet patch. Did he know what it was? No, nothing to do with him, he said. On the Monday afternoon we went to visit his friends in a nearby village. I asked Dad for a map, worried neither of us would know the way. He was cross. Of course he knew the way, he'd been going there for years. I discretely found a map but he directed me confidently, telling me firmly which lane to take. I stopped for petrol in a garage he never normally used. After that he got confused. When I asked him if this was still the right way, he said crossly that it wasn't the way he usually went, implying that I'd taken him off-route. Signs led us to the village eventually but he had no idea where his friends lived. My mobile, bought to help me drive him around, didn't help. I couldn't remember how to use it. I ran down the road to a call box, leaving Dad in the car. The car alarm went off but he had no idea how to silence it. His friends did live close by, in a welcoming bungalow with cakes and tea ready. 'I'm a poor old man', he told them as he got out of the car and trotted into what was obviously a familiar seat in the conservatory. Like Bronwen, the friends looked embarrassed and troubled. Did I think the doctor had done enough? They understood that I'd got to go back to work. It was a shame. As ever the questions about when I had to start back were difficult. They all thought vacation time equalled holiday and my study leave had to be concealed from them. Dad ate and drank with gusto but said little, a vacant figure drooping into his chair.

Last Night in Cambridge

Next morning, we were due to leave for Beverley, Dad and I. He was up before me. I'd prayed hard the night before, frightened about spending this last night alone in my parents' former bed, perhaps the last night we'd be in the house as anything like a family. Would Mum appear to terrorise me? I prayed with a passion and fell into a deep, peaceful sleep from which Dad disturbed me at about 7 am. I found him bringing the remnants of his Teasmade up the stairs, then lying beside the machine in the hope of a cup of tea. But he got up and ate Weetabix and toast, full of life in anticipation of his trip to Beverley and escape from the house. My heart sank at the prospect of him improving, the possibility of a recovery of some sort and a protracted period in the nursing home at Beverley. We went up to Addenbrookes for the blood tests and chest x-rays he should have had the previous week. *Then* he'd sent the hospital taxi away, saying he knew nothing of the appointment and his nephew was coming down for him. As we drove to the hospital for the appointment, he kept telling me I was just dropping off his cards before our journey. He'd stay in the car while I popped in. I told him repeatedly that he had appointments for tests. Once inside the hospital he walked from clinic to clinic with a steady tread. He was thin, wasted and scruffy, big eyes, an over-large hat. Only his heavy shoes seemed to keep him upright.

We drove to Beverley, stopping at a service station for a silent, embarrassed cup of tea. I'd packed what I considered his valuables and a selection of his most familiar objects. Some of this we'd done together and he'd enjoyed going through his drawers. 'Interesting', he said. Other things, destined to decorate his room in the nursing home, I packed more discretely, not wanting him to see his home being dismantled. As we neared Beverley he asked where Bob was, where we were meeting him, where was he going to stay, where was I staying, would he just be there at night, how would he get home without any money. Repeatedly I explained the plan to him. When we got to our house he went into the front room and fell asleep on the settee straightaway, uncharacteristically keeping his shoes on. Bob and I made a meal and he burst through into the back room, eager for food and wine. Every sign of energy filled me with dread. He wasn't going to die as soon as I thought.

He stayed with us from Tuesday 27 August until Wednesday 4 September. We took turns to go to work. Dad had a place promised at Carling House and the assistant matron visited him at our house. My GP visited too, and Bob eavesdropped to hear Dad say there was very little wrong with him. Afterwards Bob spoke to the GP who said he could see Dad wasn't well but was surprised as older people usually spent their time telling him what *was* wrong with them. Dad continued to get up late and I helped him dress. On Sunday we gave him a bath and only got him out of it with difficulty. Bob shaved him, which he enjoyed. He got up one morning while I was at work and Bob phoned me to say the brown urine had poured down the front of his trousers and onto the carpet in his bedroom. He seemed entirely unaware when Bob caught him on the landing and said, 'Trouble with your waterworks?' Now I wonder why we didn't impress on him what was happening. When Bob told him he had no money in his account because he'd given it all to the builders he said, 'So they tell me', as if the bank manager was trying to pull a fast one. We said nothing and he understood very little during his whole period with us.

I bought a plastic sheet and lots of toilet spray, air freshener and rubber gloves. The whole house smelled of his foul urine and he would shuffle through the kitchen to the downstairs toilet at top speed, opening his trousers and dribbling piss across the floor. I'd tell him to use his pad and not worry but he often seemed unsure as to whether he was wearing one or not. Bob found the smell very hard and retreated to our bedroom saying it was the only unpolluted room left in the house. On the Sunday we'd planned to take him to the nursing home for a visit and I ironed all day, fearful of his response to it. I hadn't visited it, though Bob had – and liked it. Once again, my fears were unfounded. Dad was taken over by a nurse and afterwards said he was pleased; he hadn't looked forward to going. He'd dreamt that everyone in the nursing home was speaking German. It was awful.

Carling House

I took him in on the Wednesday, having ironed labels onto his clothes for hours the night before. No-one was there to welcome him when we arrived and his bed wasn't made up. Despite the burgundy wallpaper, swagged curtains, old prints and stencilled patterns on the walls, his room seemed bleak, looking out on a plain wooden fence and an untended bird table. Dad sat in a plastic armchair while I unpacked. He'd agreed to take some of Mum and Grandad's paintings from our Beverley walls. I set out the whole room, showing him where all his clothes were. He looked miserable and said I'd better bring him in some books. I said I didn't think he was interested in reading at the moment and he said, well he'd better have something to do if he was just going to be left sitting there. I went in and out, looking for someone to come and talk to him and make him feel looked after. Everyone was busy and eventually I went off to work, feeling terrible.

He continued to look angry and fed up whenever we visited him – tight lipped. He always said 'nothing' when we asked what he'd been doing. I felt angry with him. Why didn't he try? Why didn't he appreciate our efforts? Back home it was great to have him out of the house and I threw away everything associated with the smell of his urine. I got dressed up and we went for a meal at Rustico. I was determined to refuse his anger and enjoy life away from illness and bad smells. He stayed in Carling House for over three weeks. There were some trips out; I took him to Welton and down to the pub below the Humber Bridge. He always looked scruffy and pitiful, spoke little and had no interest in lunch. Bob and I also took him to the Hull Bridge pub one unexpectedly warm Saturday afternoon. It was like a blessing after the grey days of early September. We sat by the river and Dad clearly relished a half of beer. He was getting weaker though, unable to walk without a supporting arm. The home reported explosive diarrhoea and many remedies were attempted. It was a pleasure to know something of the mess and smell the home's staff were facing and be spared it myself. In that first week in Cambridge, and even before my holiday, I'd felt powerless, dumped upon by everyone, one of the people without choices. Now I'd reclaimed my liberty.

Dad slept more and more, barely able to stay awake to hear the end of a sentence. In time he did acquiesce to the home, liked the 'charming young lady' who bathed him. When the doctor came to ask him about his diarrhoea, he said he didn't know he had a problem but his key worker told him that he did. Why didn't he know what was happening to his body? Was it confusion or denial? If we didn't visit immediately after work, he'd be asleep in bed and wake up cross or exasperated at being visited 'in the middle of the night'. When I came back from a conference Bob said he was sleeping most of the time and I felt a spasm of alarm. It sounded like a serious portent. The following weekend I was due to go to Greece for another conference. My GP and the matron re-assured me that 'nothing was likely to happen', though they couldn't promise.

Flying into Athens and the day I spent there was a wonderful escape. But on the Sunday morning Bob phoned to say Dad had been admitted to hospital with dehydration. He was very unwilling to tell me to come back and there were phone calls all morning. I felt upset and my friend and colleague Glennys Howarth fretted over me, obviously thinking I should go back and worried as to how I'd manage the trip. I decided to go home and left the conference group as they headed for Delphi. I felt vulnerable, even in the taxi speeding across the city and out to the airport. No tickets were available. I sat for hours outside the Virgin booth, hoping for a standby ticket, aware of the many others with the same need. My rucksack felt impossibly heavy. Tears welled up whenever someone was kind to me, a contrast with the tight, grim feeling which predominated. I found it hard to tell airport staff how desperate my situation was. My words sounded hollow. An old friend from Durham appeared out of the blue, in a queue leaving via Amsterdam. I considered flying via Paris but feared being stranded somewhere – anywhere – in the entire world. I couldn't respond to our friend. If he couldn't help me, he meant nothing, just a teasing glimpse of a familiar but inaccessible world of home. Then British Airways came up with a £500 business class ticket. I don't know whether I asked a different question, went to a different booth or presented my problem with more force. It just happened and I was thrilled to find myself airborne within an hour.

Castle Hill Hospital

Bob met me in Doncaster at 9 pm and we went straight to Ward 22 at Castle Hill Hospital. It was dark, after 10 pm, and Bob said we may have to knock to get in. The ward area was dimly lit and Dad was in a room alone, beside the nurses' station, the whole hospital in darkness, staff solicitous and offering tea. We sat on either side of Dad's bed. Clearly he wasn't going to talk to us and for the first time I gingerly took his hand. When we left I kissed him and he responded quite eagerly. I even kissed him on the mouth which I usually avoided. During that week I often stroked the top of his head as I left. It was about then that Bob warned me that 'I think you've seen the best of your dad now'. Yet, unable to speak, he seemed accessible in a way he never had before.

I visited him every day for the next 13 days. He always looked very poorly, a lost soul. In the nursing home he'd been like himself, but thinner – sad, angry, tired. He wore the same clothes as usual and made the same gestures, went through many of his familiar sequences of behaviour. Here in the hospital he lay propped adrift on a large pile of pillows, often naked since so much fluid was leaving him that any clothing would get wet immediately. He never failed to recognise us but often seemed miles away. The staff's forceful style, 'Hello, David!' and 'Good morning, David!' – was often more effective. They took him by surprise and he'd respond with a very open smile. Since I'd left the conference before it even began, I felt unwilling to go to work – and anyway I had come back because of Dad. For the next two weeks I felt uncertain where I should be at any point in time. I went back to the hospital on the Monday and sat with Dad for about five hours, holding his hand and reading my book, looking at him, talking to him, trying to understand what he was saying. I saw the senior house officer responsible for him on a day-to-day basis. She said they were trying to re-hydrate him which meant giving the right balance of salts etc. They were waiting for information about his diagnosis from Cambridge. She said he was very poorly and asked if I wanted him resuscitated if he had a cardiac arrest. I felt a sudden rush of tears at this very direct reference to him dying – even though this was what I'd returned from Greece to witness. I couldn't say yes or no directly but instead referred back to a discussion with Bob where we'd agreed we wouldn't want him resuscitated.

I went to lunch alone in the canteen, seeing people I knew from work. I felt very down and, by the time I left the hospital, very, very drained. Was Dad taking strength from me? Across that first week and into the second he kept recovering – from the chest infection, high blood pressure, kidney malfunction. I felt as if a cork at my ankle had been unplugged and everything was draining from me. After a couple of days, a brief report and a scan picture were faxed through from Cambridge. My GP said they were inconclusive. There was something in the sigmoid colon. A tumour? Compacted faeces? It would need a colonoscopy to find out what, but the doctor said he was too weak for that. One night, midweek, a tiny Japanese doctor was in with him while he was being changed and said she suspected a fistula since what was coming out of his back passage smelled like urine. Eventually they managed to get an ultrasound picture which confirmed that a connection had formed between his bowel and his bladder. This explained the 'explosive diarrhoea'. It was urine being released anally. It also explained the terrible smell of his urine and why I sometimes found his pads thickly and evenly coated with something of more substance than just discoloured urine. The only solution was an operation but the doctor said she wouldn't release him for surgery, given how weak he was. Urine in the bowel, however, was throwing his entire metabolism out of balance and would not remedy itself as long as the fistula remained.

On Saturday our daughter, Jo and I visited him. She arrived on the Friday after daily discussions as to whether or not he was dying. I'd also told Gareth, our son, that his condition was serious. The thought of anything other than his death seemed very threatening – an extended life of dependency that would dominate mine. Yet I was unwilling to say directly that he was dying – or discuss his funeral. Privately I'd decided to have it in Cambridge and inter his ashes in Topsham churchyard. I'd discussed how to organise a funeral at a distance with Glennys whose recent research had focused on funeral directors. I also asked her about embalming, thinking that it would be necessary if they transported his body to Cambridge. She said embalming was brutal, something she wouldn't want done to someone she loved – a large syringe rammed into the lower abdomen. None of this I discussed with anyone in the family. Jo and I had a wonderful shopping trip to Hull after visiting Dad. Wearing a brand new, brilliant pair of cream jeans, I prepared for a visit from friends for a meal on Saturday night. Glennys phoned with word about the Greek conference and then the hospital called to say Dad was deteriorating, on a blood drip with a special nurse to watch him. All this happened as our friends were arriving. I flew off, sandwiches and a book in my basket, frightened, excited. Something was happening. Bob was cross that I hadn't accepted the friends' offer to go straight home to Leeds. I felt burdened by his problems with it all. Why couldn't he just let me go?

I stayed all night at the hospital, sleeping on a recliner in Dad's room. He didn't die. I woke in the grey, empty hours at the start of the next day and went all down the corridors for some air at the main doors. It was clouded and anonymous out there, an unspoken-for Sunday morning. I thought about the idea of a world which no longer had Dad in it. The previous night I'd met a patient in the day room, a very easy and attractive older man. There, with Dad on the point of death, I felt excited by the allure of this man and our strange, late-night intimacy in the darkened day room. Gareth and Sally, his girlfriend, visited Dad on the Sunday. Like Jo, they always came in with widened, nervous eyes. I always did most of the talking, in the silence of Dad and the children. I chatted inconsequentially but positively; no response from Dad, but me released from the weight of any censorship or disapproval on his part. I learnt to raise and lower his bed bars and would check up on his tubes. These shifted from the back of his hand to a clutch of them taped into the side of his neck. He wore an oxygen mask over his face, occasionally replaced by vapour from a nebuliser. This was later replaced by a green catheter tube into his nose and laced over his ears. The big ears were really useful here. All the time he shook and trembled and twitched.

During the second week his condition seemed to improve. He never lost his good colour, his open-air complexion, and he began attempting to talk. He would often frown with a question and then his lips and tongue would shakily try to give shape to the sound he was making. He asked where he was and where he was going to sleep. He wondered when they were going to treat his 'queer voice'. He told the nurse he felt 'rough'. On the second Thursday he said, more clearly, that he felt better and he thought he was 'ready to go back'. When I asked him 'where?' he smiled self-mockingly and shook his head. He didn't know where he was and couldn't retain the information. But the question kept forming. We had several 'alarm calls' during this period but he kept going. One night during the second week I called in to see him on my way to have a drink with a friend. I found him with his head slumped to one side and an expression of unutterable sadness on his face. I saw in him a man who'd suddenly realised that all his plans had come to nothing, for whom there was no hope. It was the most intense emotion I'd read on his face throughout this period and it moved me to tears more rapidly than anything previously. I phoned my friend from the Day Room to cancel the drink but could hardly speak. She was taken aback by my distress, but wondered later why she hadn't realised how upsetting it all was. I knew why though – because Dad had shown little feeling and I, in turn, had expressed little myself.

Dad's main nurse was Patrick, a gay man of what Bob called 'the old school'. He was fussy and forceful, compelling as a presence. The first time I met him he said, 'I bet your dad was a lovely man, very gentle'. He referred frequently to Dad's big eyes and indeed, without his glasses, his eyes were alive and active whenever he was fully awake. I felt moved by the sight of Dad cared for so lovingly, appreciated by a man who knew how to love other men. I don't really understand my reaction. Maybe it was the lowering of another barrier, an indication that love could come and be received in previously unthinkable ways. 'You and I have been through a lot together, haven't we David', said Patrick and I liked to think of them sharing a bodily intensity that resonated with sexual intimacies elsewhere. Or maybe I was just in thrall to the undoubted force of Patrick's personality. His warmth and openness with Dad were echoed by all the staff – they were tender and gentle; they were forcefully jokey. I saw Dad nested in their love, losing ground fast. Afterwards Linda, a friend who walked our dogs, laughed and said, 'Oh, Castle Hill. It's like a hotel. I've never known a hospital like it'. Clearly we'd fallen very lucky with Dad's place of death, the care that was the hallmark of the hospital.

A key memory of that period is Dad sitting propped up in bed, shaking, vital, all tubed up, and his eyes riveted to the top of the wall opposite his bed. They were watching, moving, sometimes sweeping across the room. He was rapt, taken by surprise, trying to speak. I love to think that spirits were there, in the bodies of all the people he's loved – his mother, his father, his brother, my mother. I love to think that he was being welcomed, that I was seeing delight on his face. He was often a small child in that last week – here gazing up at some amazing picture show, in seventh heaven. I love to think it's true. I wish I could believe that I've handed him over to them all – that he's young and open to love again. And I don't want my writing down this thought to bring any ghostly visitors in the night!

It all makes me think about his mother. In the weeks before he died we looked into his strong box more carefully and found his mother's diary with details of her height, weight and shoe size. She sprang from the page, embodied. Later I found photos of her when she was older and recognised the woman who had appeared mysteriously, a ghost or a dream, at my bedside in 1992. I had a sense of taking up his care from her directly. Her hands were the last ones to look after him in a state of dependency and I could see them resting on his shoulder in his early family photographs. I even recognised the bracelet she was wearing as a young mother. It was among the jewellery in Dad's house and I like to wear it now.

In the middle of his second week in hospital, Dad's consultant, Mr McCleod, asked me what I wanted to do. Surgery was Dad's only chance but it was a long shot. Since the possibility was nonetheless raised and since the house officer confirmed that Dad has surprised them all by overcoming his infections, I asked to talk to the surgeon. Bob and I met up with a consultant, a young Scottish guy, still in theatre clothes. He looked at his notes, spoke to Patrick, looked at Dad lying bleakly stretched out in bed and then talked to us in the Day Room. He said it would be very risky. Dad could die during the operation which might well be lengthy. It was unlikely that the problem was confined to the fistula but more probable that the whole bowel was in a mess. Dad could well require a colostomy and possible repeat operations, infections, pain and so on.

He and Patrick stressed what a difficult decision it was for me, but at the time it seemed entirely clear. I really didn't want him to survive indefinitely in a dependent state. It terrified me. I wanted it all to end. But it was that night that he looked brighter and said that he felt better. His chest was almost clear. It was then that he said he thought he was ready to go back. The decision to say no to the operation was no longer clear. Dad was very much alive and his strong constitution was holding out. I felt bowed down by it all. I knew he shouldn't have the operation but no longer felt the choice was straightforward and positive, instead a muddied betrayal. After work on the Thursday I phoned to say definitely that we didn't want the operation. Jo left her cooking and came and leant on my knees when she overheard this. About this time, I got out Dad's wartime love letters to my mother that I had brought from his house. I read one and found the first page full of endearments. Throughout this period, Tennyson's lines came to my mind over and over again – 'And in a little while our lips are dumb', '… Our sons inherit us: our looks are strange …'.

We visited that night and he was weaker, his mouth no longer open but set in a tight line, his forearms clenched so I couldn't pull out a hand. I forced myself to sit out the 30 minutes I'd planned to spend with him. Next time I saw him he was dead, empty, entirely gone. They rang me at 3.10 am on the Friday morning to say he was deteriorating. Again the panicky scramble to the car. When I got there his door was closed and the nurse at the desk had nothing to say until the more senior one came out of the female patients' area. 'I'm afraid he's just died,' she said. 'Do you want to see him?' I was disappointed. All week I'd hoped to be there when he died, to see if anything special happened, if anything visible would leave his body. The nurse took me into his dimly lit room. He was covered up, his head back, his eyes shut, mouth open. A glimmer of eye shone under one eyelid. She shut the door and I felt very frightened of his body, this macabre thing. I kept thinking, 'he's gone, he's gone' and began to cry. She heard me and came back in, put her arm round me and I held her hand. She was worried about me driving home 'in that state'. I sat there for about an hour. I thought about touching him but didn't want to. Then I made myself kiss him on the forehead and did so again later. He was warm, though not so well-coloured any more. I didn't know what to do or why I was there, but I didn't want to go away. I felt very grateful to him for what he had done in being my parent, for bringing me up. I had the insight that he'd achieved his parenting within the constraints and contingencies of his life and that was the way it was – and that is the way all human lives are lived, imperfectly, within limits. It defines us and our humanity. And that is true of my life too. None of this would have come to me, were it not for the way he'd been in those 13 days and the way he was cared for.

One of the Bereaved

When I got home I sensed the life in Bob's body very tangibly. First a dead man and now a large, living one. I could see life in the people around me as well during the following days, its intensity or faintness. That night, Bob and I sat on the settee and I told him all about it, wanting to hang on to the intensity and quietness of being with Dad. We took the cats to bed and I dreamt horribly that I was shouting at Jo for not holding on to my dad while I dressed him – and, frighteningly, that Patrick had got me alone and grabbed me. All the sources of love seemed to be turned on their heads in these dreams. Coming back from the hospital, driving Dad's car, I'd been frightened that he was in the back, coming home with me, set free now to be in our house. I remembered that people throughout the world fear the dead like this, immediately after they've gone.

Lots happened after Dad died. Jo hugged me on the stairs when I told her. I found the envelope the hospital had given me and was shocked to find it addressed to 'The Bereaved' – that was me? I got dressed very carefully, wanting to wear nice jewellery. A feeling of festivity? I wanted to resist the bureaucracy and retain the intimacy of the hospital atmosphere. I planned to spend more time there, sitting with Dad. By mid-morning though I was fraught, tired, hungry and bad-tempered. We went to register his death in Cottingham, me gawping at the registrar's large breasts peeping out of the front of her blouse. We went to Stephenson's, the funeral directors, where a woman in a big, lilac T-shirt and black and white scarf made the arrangements for us. Her husband, in overalls, popped in and out from coffin-making, full of jokey stories about long-distance arrangements that had gone awry. We chose everything for the funeral and I was relieved to hear that they 'didn't believe in embalming'. I felt so cared for, comfortable and relieved in this homely, practical setting. The feeling persists whenever I go down that road and past the funeral directors. Bob, Jo and I went for tea in the corner shop in Wednesday Market and I began to feel better, OK, ordinary.

On the Saturday I took chocolates to Ward 22 and to the nursing home. I felt out-of-place in the hospital, someone else already in Dad's room, staff busy, sorry, rather at a loss. Patrick said he assumed Dad had either gone for surgery or to 'what I call the incorruptible world'. I've no good feelings about the nursing home. Jo and I packed up his things quickly and left. Again, staff looked faintly embarrassed. A pile of letters and cards were on his bed table, the ones I'd waited for so long and now arrived too late. Only later did I feel angry that the home hadn't bothered to forward them to us so we could have read them to Dad. Jo and I went to Cambridge on the Monday and I went straight to meet Lilian Dalton, the vicar at Dad's church in Cambridge, who planned the funeral with me. I love to think of these two women, Mrs Stephenson and Lilian, along with Patrick and me, holding the reins at the end of Dad's life. The four of us in charge. Arriving at Dad's house I felt desperately tired and bad-tempered, no patience at all, angry with everything. 'Oh, she was awful', said Jo later. I'd been like this intermittently ever since Dad died. A friend and I laughed later about me finding myself alone in the house on Sunday morning, the family driven out by my irritability.

A Cambridge Funeral

In Cambridge it was a great week, Jo and I systematically emptying and sorting everything in Dad's house. I enjoyed deciding the fate of all my parents' belongings, dumping them, keeping them, giving them to charity. It was compulsive and invigorating, so much old, old stuff. Now I was in sole charge. This was how I felt about the funeral too, having Dad lifted from the hearse and borne in by Gareth and Bob and the expert men from Beverley. I'd chosen the coffin, the flowers, the music, the readings. The whole thing was my doing. I'd put the words into Lilian Dalton's mouth for the address; I'd chosen 'Take a pair of sparkling eyes' and so brought Dad's intimate time at Castle Hill into this public space. And I knew this wasn't what he wanted. I knew he'd grunt with exasperation if he saw where he'd landed – like a treat I'd organised for him that wasn't to his liking. Being in a coffin on a fabulous October day was not part of his plan and he'd be desolated to realise that this was what had become of him. He should have been walking.

Outside were a great crowd of people – old friends from Dad's days at work in Robert Sayles, relatives I hadn't seen for decades. I felt very much in control, elegant in my black jacket, my mother's big brooch, his mother's bracelet and – provocatively – black trousers instead of a skirt. But we had to leave them all before we'd even begun talking. Bob and I felt a sense of real waste, so many warm and friendly people, so many links to trace. Dad's immediate walking group did come to the crematorium. I cried after the service, reading the cards pinned to flowers – 'we'll never ever forget you', 'thanks for the memories'. Jo stroked my back and my cousin's wife gave me a hanky. Tea back at Dad's house was fine. Again I was at ease, everyone playing their part, full of warm and funny comments. Jo and Gareth served most of the food and I felt confident in their grip on things. We went for a tense, tired meal at Café Rouge that night and then finished packing and left on Friday evening.

We'd been busy every moment since Dad died. I never got back to sit with him at the hospital; the whole weekend was taken up. On the Monday I planned to sit with him at the funeral director's but Jo and I went to the hairdresser's and then packed for our journey. In the event I called in at the funeral director's on our way to Cambridge. Mrs Stephenson took me down to the 'chapel' where Dad's coffin was; a small cubicle, one of four, dimly lit. I can't remember the décor but the coffin was on a fairly rough metal support and Dad was dressed in something blue and frilly which seemed to connect directly to the coffin sides – a sort of coverlet posing as a garment. Again I felt frightened of his body and wanted to lurch towards the door when Mrs Stephenson closed it on me. Again I just held on. Dad looked more dead, more dried up. His mouth seemed to have been sewn together, but with a corner gaping open slightly, giving him an unpleasant, smirking look. I held my hand in front of my face to mask his mouth and looked at his eyes. The eyebrows and the bone structure beneath them had become so familiar in the two previous weeks, so like his father's. What pleased me were his hands, lying on the coverlet. They hadn't been visible in the hospital after he'd died, but here they were again, absolutely familiar, the red marks of the tubes on their backs. We'd held them for so many hours. 'That's how we loved him' was the thought which made me cry as I stood there. I said goodbye and left after a few minutes – again the feeling of not knowing how long to stay, why or what for, but hanging in and finding myself inspired to insights and to tears. I told Mrs Stephenson it had been nice to see his hands and she looked at me with concern, saying how often people told her that. I'm very grateful to her and her husband. I want to be part of their strange, large-bodied family, to pop in and out and sit around and chat. That's what they seem to do.

Dad's ashes came back from the Cambridge crematorium. Bob and Gareth picked them up, just in time, before they drove the van with his belongings back to Beverley. 'We've got him', said Gareth as he phoned from the mobile. Jo and I drove up separately, the car crammed with additional items from Dad's home. We left his house empty, locked and in the hands of estate agents. Back in Beverley I picked up the urn holding Dad's ashes and found it heavy, unlabelled and non-spooky – the frightening dead body reduced and sanitised. I shook it to feel the ashes moving about and Bob weighed it. I left it in my study, in its cardboard box, and Bob went away for about a week. The planned interment of the ashes in Topsham, Dad's birthplace, had to be delayed for months while work was completed on the churchyard. But I still sent them down to a Devon funeral director after a week or so. I was so tired and unable to respond to everyday life. The ashes didn't seem to be helping. More than that, I felt they were listening in when I spoke about Dad's death to friends on the phone. We sent them off by Securicor Omega Express and I enjoyed the joke.

Back to Work

Dad's dying took me right out of everyday life, absolved me from all external demands and commitments. I enjoyed telling people my appointments and plans were all provisional. Going to the hairdresser's just after he'd died was like coming out of a cocoon – or seeming to. Going back to work a week later was dreadful, a dark, burdensome re-entry which made me want to hide from everyone and not receive their condolences. 'I bet this is the hardest thing you've had to do, come in and have everyone say they're sorry about your dad', said the departmental secretary. Insightful woman, briskly making sure I was in touch with what was happening to me. I felt terribly sad and very tired for the next two weeks – no appetite for life or work. Lots of beautiful condolence cards arrived. I kept Neville's wreath for a while, unable to leave it at the crem on its own – left behind because it was a wreath and not suitable for a hospital. Later on I phoned Tony, the friend with a father also in his 80s. He too had died, within a week of mine.

It's now Friday 8 November 1996, four weeks almost to the hour since Dad died, 15 weeks since Neville first phoned about Dad's condition. The whole period of Dad's illness, for me, lasted less than three months. Now I feel relieved and satisfied, my energy and appetite for life returning. I don't know how I feel about Dad – that I loved him and lost him, had him briefly and let him slip through my fingers. I wish the man all the best, whatever he went through and whatever may have become of him. 'God rest his soul' still works very well, whoever she is?

References

Goffman, E. (1963). *Stigma. Notes on the management of a spoiled identity.* New York: Simon and Schuster Inc.

Hockey, J. and James, A. (2002). *Social Identities across the Life Course.* Basingstoke: Palgrave Macmillan.

Komaromy, C. (2012). Family Matters: a drama. K235, Dementia Care. The Open University.

Komaromy, C. and Hockey, J. (2018). *Family Life, Trauma and Loss in the Twentieth Century. The Legacy of War.* London: Palgrave Macmillan.

4

Continuing and Emerging Bonds: Working Through Grief as a Daughter and an Academic

Kathryn Almack

Dad was 89 when he died on 11 September 2011. This was at the end of nearly seven weeks in hospital. First, an emergency admission by ambulance to a surgical ward in a National Health Service District General Hospital. He stayed there for about five to six weeks until he was moved to a local Community Hospital, where he died. While thinking about and planning this chapter, I listened to several podcasts about death, dying and bereavement, which I follow. *You, Me & The Big C* and *On the Marie Curie Couch* are favourites for my two-plus hour commute to work. Greg Wise and Alison Steadman have been on *On the Marie Curie Couch*: Greg talking about his sister's death and caring for her at home for the last three months of her life; Alison talking about her mother's death, and the great care she received in a hospice setting. Listening to them made me feel so sad to think of Dad spending those last weeks in hospital. Jess Mills, daughter of Baroness Tessa Jowell, who died from an

---

K. Almack (✉)
Centre for Research in Public Health and Community Care (CRIPACC), School of Health and Social Work, University of Hertfordshire, Hatfield, UK
e-mail: k.almack@herts.ac.uk

aggressive brain tumour, appeared on *You, Me & The Big C*. She spoke movingly of her devastating grief which nevertheless, over time, she feels has offered up such gifts. She articulated thoughts that resonated with mine about continuity; death is not an end but a beginning of a whole new way of life within which you live your relationship with your loved one.

Before I focus on the last few weeks of Dad's life, I will describe some of the slow but progressive functional decline that Dad experienced. He was in pretty good health well into his 80s. Most of his working life he had been a self-employed plumber and well into his 70s, he continued to do small jobs for his old clients. In his 80s, he continued to be active, but he had an increasing number of hospital admissions (planned and unplanned) mainly due to episodes of polymyalgia (an inflammatory disease of muscle associated with old age) and low blood pressure. The low blood pressure caused him to faint which led to a few unplanned admissions to hospital. He'd be back home in a day or two and initially we thought the admission in July 2011 would follow this pattern. At some point, the General Practitioner (GP) informed Dad that he also had heart disease; Dad preferred to believe he must be mistaken. Then, at the age 87, after months of diarrhoea and indigestion problems plus several visits to see his GP, Dad was finally diagnosed with bowel cancer. He had an operation to remove the tumour. This was really the first experience of coming face-to-face with Dad being mortal. I went with him and Mum to a follow up appointment. I remember he was embarrassed to pull down the waistband of his trousers in front of me when the nurse wanted to check the site of the operation. I looked away to protect his dignity; he was always a very private individual.

I still have the diagram and notes that the nurse gave me from that meeting. It was a seven centimetre tumour, moderately differentiated. Meaning that the cells and tissue were somewhat abnormal; somewhere between a low- or high-grade cancer, where a low-grade is considered likely to grow more slowly and is less likely to spread than a high-grade cancer. Writing this, I referred back to the Bowel Cancer UK site to remind myself what the letters and numbers meant that the nurse had scribbled down on a diagram – which refer to the 'TNM system'. T4 – which meant the tumour had grown through the outer lining of the bowel wall; N2 – which meant that cancer cells were found in four or more nearby lymph nodes (six in my Dad's case). Classified as Stage 3. At the time (March 2009) I contacted Bowel Cancer UK for more information to understand what the options were. They were so helpful, much more so than any staff at the hospital. To be fair, it was also easier for me to ask blunt questions by email; I wasn't sure how much information Dad wanted to be given when I attended meetings with him. Even though I was working in a research centre of palliative and end-of-life care studies, it was difficult to open up conversations with my parents about such things as advance care planning. I'd take leaflets when I visited but I suspect they ended up in the waste-paper box! Only now, nearly nine years after Dad's death and at the age of 92, has Mum been willing to talk about her funeral plans. I know she has an absolute fear of ending up in hospital and I have promised her I will do everything in my power to get her home and take unpaid leave to care for her if I must. That is, in part, informed by not achieving that for Dad and wishing I had argued more for alternatives.

But, getting ahead of myself again. Back to the person I corresponded with at Bowel Cancer UK. She explained Dad would probably require adjuvant chemotherapy. At the next hospital appointment, I asked about this and we were told that chemotherapy was not necessarily a good option for anyone over the age of 70. There had been no trials for older age groups to assess whether it would prevent the cancer coming back. This was enough information for Dad to decide absolutely against chemotherapy. His view was that if the cancer came back, it came back; he'd had a good life. About a year after his bowel surgery, Dad was back in hospital for a cystoscopy to check for bladder cancer. I don't know how this came about or what symptoms Dad was experiencing. Apparently, cystoscopies were then scheduled every six months to check for bladder abnormalities. However, Dad felt ill for weeks and experienced such pain after the first cystoscopy that he didn't want further procedures. He did consent to one about nine months later and I was with him when he was admitted onto the ward and emphasised the need for good pain relief. The nurse said he was in for prostate cancer, which I hadn't heard mentioned before.

Increasingly, I tried to attend hospital appointments with my parents because it was hard to get detail from them about what the appointments were about, who they saw, what was said or what they asked. If I wasn't with them, I could never be sure if they'd fully understood or whether I was getting a full picture about what had been said. Given the confusion about the cystoscopies – and lack of clarity about whether Dad had bladder cancer or prostate cancer – I wanted to know what was going on. Taking on this role wasn't something discussed between myself and my siblings; although in writing this chapter, I decided to ask them both what they recalled about this. Their recollections are vague, but they report that they didn't feel the same need as me to attend appointments or to get more information; they also thought if anyone was attending appointments with our parents, I was the right sibling to do so. My sister, Jill (two years older) says she and my (twin) brother, Andrew, probably accept things at face value and they see me as the 'academic' in the family, always asking questions. I have a familial reputation as the one who asks 'difficult' or 'awkward' questions (and in some situations being told not to!). Additionally, I had a bit more flexibility in my job; Jill ran a pub which was open lunchtimes and evenings and Andrew worked abroad for long stretches of time. I also worried about how stressful it was for Mum to drive to the hospital, drop Dad off at the entrance, find somewhere to park and then head into the hospital to find Dad. When I could attend, I drove and dropped them both off and then joined them once parked. We got Dad a disabled badge to make things easier. But at the same time, Mum, in particular, didn't want to bother me. I lived over 100 miles away, had a full-time job and was/am my daughter's sole parent. So, sometimes they (Mum – who was in charge of such things) didn't tell me about appointments. On one occasion when I was visiting them, I found out about an appointment coming up. I had something in my diary on that date – maybe a conference presentation that was going to be difficult to move. Andrew was home for a couple of weeks, so I asked him if he could go with them instead. Mum thought this was a lot of fuss and wasn't sure how this could be helpful. When she thought I was out of earshot, she suggested Dad phone Andrew and tell him not to bother. I was so cross! I had a difficult conversation with Mum, challenging her in a way that ordinarily wasn't 'done' in our family. We were both upset and

Mum admitted they didn't like to ask for help, they had always managed. I have written more about this elsewhere, describing how, in hindsight, this was a pivotal moment; a reconfiguring of intergenerational caring responsibilities with some role reversal negotiated (Almack forthcoming, 2022).

Over the last few years of Dad's life – probably from his mid-80s onwards – I noticed on visits that he was becoming less active and he spent more and more time sitting in his armchair. He was also losing weight. Nevertheless, he was still active in that he went out for a short walk around the village each day and did jobs around the house. He and Mum stayed with Jill, every weekend. Jill and her husband ran a village pub in North Yorkshire, about an hour's drive from our parents' home. Our parents 'helped out' with a busy Sunday lunch service. As they got into their 80s, they started to stay over at Jill's on Saturday nights rather than driving there and back on a Sunday. My visits to see my parents became less frequent than I would have liked. Their weekend commitment made it difficult for me and my daughter, Eva, to fit in seeing them. My parents never suggested staying home for a weekend for us to be able to visit. I have felt a range of emotion about that over the years: hurt, sad, resentful, pleased my parents kept occupied (and they did seem to enjoy their weekends). I never spoke of those feelings, possibly adhering to the implicit norm in our family that feelings were not really spoken about, especially difficult or challenging feelings. It is only recently that conversations in my family have opened up more, and I have felt able to speak about and acknowledge these feelings. This recent opening up of conversations has been instigated by me, influenced by the writing I have been doing about Dad. This writing has raised questions for me on which I wanted to get other family perspectives. Jill and Andrew both call these 'deep conversations' and agree these are not something in which we ordinarily engage. However, they have been happy to have these conversations with me. And they have been willing to be open and honest in their reflections, albeit sometimes puzzled by my questions about aspects of Dad's dying and death, which would otherwise have never occurred to them to mull over. In retrospect, for me, the complex mix of emotions I refer to above connected with a general feeling through much of my adult life of an emotional distance from my family of origin. I was always labelled 'different'. I was the first to 'leave' home and I moved to a job in London. My siblings followed a more traditional working-class trajectory of only 'leaving' home when they got married and both starting out married life living just a couple of miles from our parents. I'll return to this point, related to class trajectories later.

Given that my parents were not at home at weekends, I had to make plans for myself and Eva to see them mid-week during Easter, summer and Christmas school holidays when we would stay over for one or two nights. Sometimes it was hard to fit in visits during the school half-term and it meant juggling taking annual leave from work with other plans Eva might have with her friends or father. Our visits involved a mixture of emotions. Mum and Dad were always pleased to see me and Eva and vice versa. But I think we disrupted Dad's routines in particular. Additionally, their routines, such as a main meal at midday, were very different from our (mine and Eva's) usual everyday family life which tended to be less scheduled. I remember Mum remarking once that it was a wonder we came to visit after some grumpiness of my dad's. Further, the house was always very warm; sometimes uncomfortably so. Eva and I would wander in and out of the front room in the evenings to cool down or try and leave the front room door open, all of which Dad found irritating. Sometimes we laughed or chatted too loudly and he would frown and turn the TV up even louder or take his hearing aid out. I could get grumpy too, but always on leaving, I would be overcome with a mixture of feelings of love for him alongside guilt for not staying longer and relief at going home and sometimes I would feel tearful. Dad had a habit of directing me out of their driveway, waving me out when there were no cars coming. It used to infuriate me, as if I was an incompetent driver! This amused Eva, my wise girl who would comment it was a gesture of love from my Dad, nothing more.

Two years after his diagnosis of cancer and on my Dad's 89th birthday at the end of February 2011, he remarked that if he was around to see in his 90th birthday he would consider himself a lucky man. I acknowledge that this might seem to be a good age to which to live, but it made me mentally add up the number of times I had seen him in the past year. I realised that if he only lived another year, I wouldn't see much more of him. I resolved to find ways to spend more time with him (and Mum) and to 'pop up' for the day more often by myself. I managed to fit in short visits while up north on work visits to Harrogate, Leeds and Preston.

This same year, Jill's husband, Derrick, had a serious stroke in early January 2011 and died on February 16. Derrick was 67 when he died, 17 years older than Jill. At that point, Jill and I didn't have a close relationship but I began to phone her more often in the weeks between Derrick's stroke and his death, six weeks later. She and I met for lunch at Betty's in Harrogate one day about a month after her husband's death; I'm not sure that the two of us had ever met alone as adults. I had hoped Jill would come to the Turkish Baths with me but she pulled out of that part of the day. Still, from that point on, and later after Dad died and Mum moved next door to Jill's pub, Jill and I have become closer. She's since often remarked that although she lost a husband, she regained a sister. It took me longer to agree, but that's another story.

Two planned dates for lunch with my parents got cancelled, on one of those dates Derrick had just been admitted into hospital after his stroke and on the other Dad was in hospital, another unplanned but short admission. Finally, we met up the day after Father's Day in June; it was a school closure day so Eva came with me. It is a treasured memory now because it was the last time that I saw Dad well, albeit frail. There was no grumpiness on either side that day. I was solicitous and patient with him and he was in a good mood, enjoying the company of his wife, two daughters and granddaughter, a glass (or two) of red wine with his lunch. The pub was in the village Asenby, where Dad's family had lived when he was a child, so we went past his childhood home and he reminisced about some of the mischief he and his six brothers had got up to as children.

If there was any recognition from his GP of Dad coming towards the end of life – in terms of defining it as the last year of life – I did not know about it. I didn't attend any GP appointments with Dad and it never came up at hospital appointments. In retrospect, I wonder if any GP appointments might have revealed more information but I don't know. Dad's transition between living and dying may also have been obscured by his determination to continue living, physical but not cognitive frailty, being proud of still 'working', joking about maybe retiring at 90, and so on. He and Mum lived in their own home without any input from any professionals. My parents both drove; Dad drove them home after our lunch at the pub in Asenby, despite me worrying about whether he should be driving after a couple of glasses of lunchtime wine. I have written a paper and a blog piece (Almack 2019, 2020) about how his situation reflects that of a wider population of older frail people who are still often invisible within the current paradigms of palliative and end-of-life care. That shift towards being in the last year of life for someone like my Dad can be so gradual it is only recognised with hindsight. I won't revisit all that detail in this chapter, however, when Dad was admitted to hospital as an emergency in July 2011, none of us (his family) thought he'd be in hospital more than a few days. Although my research related to end of life, death and dying, I didn't have a nursing or medical background. It highlights a clear disjuncture between knowing 'in theory' what end of life looks like and being able to recognise it as a daughter caring for a father. However, I was in a position to have discussions with colleagues with such backgrounds. I remember one such conversation after Dad had been in hospital perhaps a couple of weeks, when a colleague matter-of-factly advised I should organise a referral to the palliative care team. That came as quite a shock to me.

Those last seven weeks of his life were difficult, distressing and bewildering. The first time I saw Dad in hospital was the day after admission. The day of Jill's 50th birthday. A family gathering had been planned at her behest, to bury her husband's ashes. Her husband's three adult children were there, two with partners and children, and my mum, Andrew with his wife, Ann, and their two children, myself and Eva. Andrew lived a short drive from my parents' house, so Mum came over with him and his family and she then went home via the hospital with me and Eva. Dad was so pleased to see us, but almost immediately distressed by an urgent need for the commode next to his bed. He gestured for us to move away, although the curtain around his bed only provided visual privacy. At the end of visiting hours, Eva and I went back to my parents' house with Mum. 'Our' room in their house was small with twin beds and not a lot a space to move around. We spent so many nights in that room over the coming weeks. I've asked Eva what she remembers about that time, but she doesn't recall much other than she didn't mind sharing a bedroom with me and she liked the journeys in the car with me. She would have been 14 and I've since reflected on how well we got on, spending so much time in fairly fraught circumstances, being away from home and sharing a bedroom. We'd get home when we could, and every time we headed back to Nottingham I would be in tears, thinking I might not see Dad again. Eva would put her hand on my shoulder. She was a mature 14-year-old and a great comfort to me during those weeks. She and I had a holiday booked in Devon and I didn't want to go. Mum and Jill said we should go, and that if we abandoned our holiday, Dad might think he was dying. Silently I thought 'but I think he could be dying'. We did go to Devon; Eva sent a postcard to her granddad every day but on the third or fourth day we decided to travel back home to Nottingham and then up to Yorkshire the following day.

One of the few positives about those weeks was that Dad and I became much closer again. I have always loved my Dad and I was very close to him when I was growing up. I have memories of just the two of us doing stuff together, such as flying an acrobatic kite on the cricket field across from our house. We used to go horse-riding together, not a middle-class pursuit as such but a connection for my Dad to working with horses on his grandfather's farm. He had endless patience, teaching me how to ride my bike and years later, driving lessons. When I was little, I would watch for him coming home from work and run out to open the garage doors, hop in the car with him and we'd sing songs. Most of my childhood memories about him are about just the two of us. Andrew and Jill don't feature although I know they have their own special memories about him. We all recall his presence and his patience, suggesting he had time for each of us. But Dad and I grew more distant when I left home. Dad left school when he was 14, as he often mentioned and after leaving school, worked at Cundall Manor (since turned into a boarding school) as a footman. All the staff were signed up to the Territorial Army so at the start of the Second World War, he was among the first to be called up. He first went to Scotland for training, he had some fond memories of this time. Then from 1942 (aged 20) to 1945 he was in Burma (Myanmar), a period of time he rarely spoke about. When he came back, he trained to be a plumber and, during our childhood until he retired, he had his own plumbing and heating business. I left a rural working-class culture in Yorkshire for a very different life. I lived in London for two years, leaving home just before my 18th birthday and then moved to Nottingham to do my degree, a city I have lived in ever since. While I had lived within and understood the context of a rural working-class culture that the rest of my family of origin remained (and remains) rooted in, I think my life became increasingly unintelligible to my family. I was the first (only) sibling to go to university and then not only did a degree but a masters and a PhD. I gave up a full-time job in my mid-30s to do a PhD, a decision that my family found quite baffling. I felt caught between two worlds, with 'an increasing sense of distance from (my) familial habitus' (Almack and Churchill 2007: 48). My experience resonates with accounts I have read and discussions I have had with other working-class women transgressing the norms of class, gender and sexuality we grew up with, being rendered 'out of place' (Wilkens 2019: 121). I know Dad was proud of my achievements, but I don't think he ever quite understood what I did. Andrew's job working as a service engineer was more familiar to him, and for a while Andrew also worked for Dad in his plumbing business. Dad spent a lot of time working alongside Jill in her pub kitchen. By contrast, he found it difficult to relate to the areas I worked in. First, working in statutory and voluntary sectors in domestic violence and homelessness and then in academia, researching lesbian parenthood for my PhD and later all my work relating to death and dying. I also found it difficult to explain what I did, sometimes Dad would ask and I would say something along the lines of I read, write, think! My academic career has been a research-only career so I didn't even have teaching, which might have been more relatable to explain. I feel that all these factors combined created a distance between us not helped by limited visits 'home' and levels of grumpiness on both sides that somehow we couldn't bridge until he was dying.

After his death, I would find myself wondering where his thoughts went during those long last weeks in hospital, when he was often alone. Did he think back to his childhood on a farm, with nine siblings and his parents (he had a lot of funny stories about the escapades he and his six brothers got up to); or back to the war years that he could never talk about? Or to thinking about meeting Mum; family; holidays we'd enjoyed (caravan holidays and an annual holiday to Criccieth in North Wales); cricket (a sport he enjoyed playing and watching); his three grandchildren. I wished I had asked him. Increasingly since his death I find myself appreciating my childhood. I felt misunderstood as a teenager and was often labelled by my parents as 'different' (from my siblings) or perhaps 'difficult'. But I had a secure loving childhood.

Amid all the coming and going during Dad's last weeks in hospital and increasingly frequent visits to see Dad in hospital, he and I became closer again. One day I was sitting at his bedside and a nurse came to do a blood test. He took hold of my hand, which initially felt odd, uncomfortable. I don't think I had held his hand since childhood. But he held on after the nurse had left the room, and subsequently I always held his hand when sitting with him. Another time he was sitting in a chair having a blood transfusion. He'd been told to sit still and his shoulders were aching; I gave him a massage as I used to do many years ago when I lived at home and he would be aching after a day's manual work. A closer relationship blossomed between him and Eva too. I heard him murmur 'my lovely Eva' one time as we were leaving. She would also sit and hold his hand, a crossword book resting on her lap. She'd consult with her granddad and fill in the words with her other hand.

Dad died on a Sunday. It was only on the Friday – 9th September – that he seemed to acknowledge death was close when he said to Mum and Jill, who were with him that afternoon, 'I'm not going to make it out of here, am I?'. I have a clear recollection of Jill telling me about this and I have since wondered and wished I had been there to ask – did he have any fears or did he accept death was close and so on? Only recently I have asked Jill and Mum about this, to find out if it led to any conversation. Neither of them remembers Dad saying those words. In all the conversations I have had with Mum, Jill and Andrew in the course of writing about Dad's death, it has been fascinating to learn how different our recall of events and memories are, and the differences in how we communicate. I wonder if it is something about my family members having more of a tendency to take things 'at face value' whereas I have always wanted to know more, always asking questions, and possibly that's led me into research where it is my job to probe and find out more!

I had driven up on Wednesday 7th September, having dropped Eva off at school, planning to be back in the evening. While still on my way, Jill phoned to tell me to go straight to the hospital as Dad had taken a turn for the worse. I wanted Eva to be there too and arranged that a friend would drive her up to M1 to the Yorkshire Sculpture Park and I drove from the hospital to pick her up. She didn't have anything with her, other than the school uniform she was wearing. We all gathered around Dad's bed on the Thursday, he was mostly sleeping. Mum became uneasy and felt it was wrong that we were all sitting round 'waiting for him to die' and on her wishes, we all headed home. Eva and I for once travelling back to our home, not to my parents' home, mainly to pack some more clothes. We headed back within 24 hours and I spent a long time with him on the Saturday, although by then he was near death. I spoke with him, and so too did the nurses when they came through. He was the only man in the ward. By then he wasn't really conscious, but when I reminisced about running out to meet him when he came home from work, he opened his eyes and on other reminiscences, I think I caught a glimmer of a smile.

I had left Eva with Mum who had decided that she had said her 'goodbyes' to her husband. Then Andrew turned up at the hospital with Mum. He wanted to stay for a while but Mum wanted to go home. I didn't really feel I had any choice but to take her home. I was torn between wanting to be with Dad and feeling responsible for Eva and Mum. On the Sunday morning I was up early and went for a run. It had become part of a kind of self-care routine, getting a bit of time to myself. Only later I noted that my running routes followed the same paths as Dad's walking routes although I went further than he had been able to manage on his walks in his later years. On coming back, I helped Mum with a job in the garden, showered and planned to set off to the hospital. But I was just leaving the house when Andrew phoned with news that Dad had died. Mum broke down and I remember her saying 'What am I going to do without you, Doug?' Eva came down and we all sat in the kitchen. I was desperate to get to the hospital and devastated not to have been there with Dad when he died. The only scrap of consolation I subsequently found about not being with him was that I had delayed getting to the hospital that Sunday morning to do a job for Mum. During his weeks in hospital, Dad often said 'Look after Mum'. After the phone call, Andrew and family came over. His daughter was inconsolable. I wasn't sure how I could legitimately leave, who would stay with Mum? Somehow, we ended up with Andrew and Ann's children staying with Mum, he and Ann, Eva and I driving in our own cars to the hospital. Eva stayed in the car rather than enter the hospital.

We couldn't see Dad straight away – a local GP was certifying his death. We spoke to the two members of staff who had been with him when he died. They had been repositioning him and his death had, in the end, been too sudden to notify us to come in. They were tearful, which in an odd way was comforting, seeming to show they had really cared about him. I think Andrew must have spoken about funeral arrangements because one of them said she could play 'Amazing Grace' (a song my Dad requested be played at his funeral) on a recorder that she always brought in at the weekend. It was bizarre but strangely moving. I sat and held Dad's hand and sobbed uncontrollably. I felt his spirit was still with us and I just wanted to stay with him. But Andrew spoke of getting back to Mum and I was aware Eva was sat outside in our car. So, we left. Eva and I went into Skipton to get sandwiches for everyone from Marks & Spencer and we had this unreal picnic back at my mum's. I don't remember much about the next few days other than the funeral director visiting and being irritated by her reverent tone of voice. At one point she asked where we wanted the funeral procession to set off from – Mum and Andrew were thinking from the funeral home but I intercepted and asked if we could have him brought home first. It was just a gesture; he was dead after all. But he loved his home so much and the only time I saw him really upset during those long weeks in hospital was when he spoke of missing his lovely home.

After Dad's death, I was initially numb. Eva and I came home, and Eva started back at school. I had a new module to teach at the start of the semester to nursing students. It's all a blur now. I do remember Eva and I having a shopping trip out the Meadowhall near Sheffield, to find some clothes for Eva to wear at the funeral. I'm not sure why we choose to go there, we'd never been before or since. I gave my students some 'independent learning' for the week of Dad's funeral, telling them in advance why I wouldn't be there the following week. There was a stunned silence in the room that I couldn't make sense of, but of course, I was telling them that my Dad had just died, and it was so recent that we still had the funeral to attend to. I found it very hard to unpack the bag that I'd used as a suitcase all that summer; it had never been fully unpacked and now the finality of unpacking it properly was too hard to face for some time.

Dad's funeral was held on 20 September so we were soon back at my parents' house for a few days. Other family members had visited Dad at the funeral home and Eva and I decided we would go to see him. We didn't stay long; having felt Dad's spirit with me by his bedside after he had just died, his body in the coffin was nothing more than his body. On the day of the funeral, I got tasked with preparations for the funeral buffet. It kept me busy but I was then undone when Andrew turned up with a big board of photographs of Dad from over the years.

Andrew gave the eulogy at the funeral; Mum had asked him to do so, perceiving him now to be the (male) head of the family. I recall my feminist hackles rising but I didn't say anything. And I couldn't have done it. I was never prouder of Andrew who delivered a brilliant and loving tribute for Dad. So many condolence cards arrived for Mum and so many describing Dad as a true 'gentle man'; one of 'the last of his kind'. Many friends sent me cards too. I still have them, along with the crossword book we were working through with Dad in hospital. I loathed doing crosswords (still do) but acquired a new patience over those long weeks of hospital visits. A patience I try but often fail to extend to Mum who still does the crossword in her daily newspaper.

I didn't really want to see people, friends. There were many kind gestures. I would come home from work to find presents on my doorstep – including one from my lovely hairdresser who had left a bag with a bottle of wine, chocolate and a running magazine, which thoughtfully combined three things I enjoy. I went out with a friend for an early evening drink, but she asked me (meaning well) to tell her about my dad – I couldn't speak without crying and hurried home. I cried a lot. Mostly in the car. I would drive Eva to school and then go on to work, crying, then gather myself together to get into the office – which was based in a hospital. I didn't sleep well, replaying in my mind where did his thoughts go during those long weeks in hospital; why hadn't we tried harder to get him home or into a hospice. But most especially I was grief stricken that he had died alone – meaning without family around him.

I started having bad stomach pains, so bad that I would be doubled over with pain. I went to see my GP. I asked, could it be grief? She ordered a raft of tests and thought it might be gallstones. All the tests came back clear, but I still had the pains. Sometime later I attended a conference presentation when Jane Ribbens McCarthy was talking about *embodied grief* (McCarthy and Prokhovnik 2014). And it struck me, I had intuitively sensed it was embodied grief I had experienced. And more curiously, the diagnosis that Dad had been given on that last admission into hospital before he died was a suspected gallbladder infection or gallstones.

While I was struggling to face the final unpacking of the case that I had used all summer, Mum's way of coping was to get busy and start a clear-out of all Dad's things. He had a garage full of tools and I begged her not to start clearing the garage until I arrived. She went ahead and made a start, nevertheless. She is the opposite of being a hoarder. Dad's medals from the Second World War went to Andrew. I asked for a wooden box that I had always been fascinated by, that sat on his dresser. It came from India, where Dad had periods of leave during the war years. We never spoke about it, but I am curious that he hung on to it all those years, given his memories of the war years were too painful to revisit. I am quite certain it meant a lot to him. Quite certain too that if Mum had had her way, it might have been in a charity shop many years earlier. I also have his old wooden handled gardening tools; a long six foot ruler that he used when cutting glass – that would now be called vintage or antique; and his walking stick. I love having these things. The wooden box is on my dresser, the ruler is propped up in the kitchen. His walking stick rests in the hallway and sometime when passing I stop and hold the worn handle, thinking of Dad. I wish I had gone on more walks with him. I take meticulous care of his gardening tools, as he did. If I ever use them and put them back in the shed without first cleaning and oiling them, I feel guilty. Although I must confess, over the intervening years, my standards have slipped to below par.

A couple of years later, my old car broke down and was not worth repairing. At the same time, Mum had come to a decision to stop driving and so I 'inherited' my parents' car, mostly driven by my dad. I went up to Yorkshire to pick it up. As I set off home, I put the radio on and realised I hadn't properly worked out all the dashboard features. The radio was set to Radio Two, a station I never listen to, but I didn't know how to switch to another station. But then the song 'Amazing Grace' was played;

the song Dad requested was played at his funeral. It felt uncanny but deeply comforting. Another time, Eva and I were driving from friends in York to visit Mum and Jill in Dishforth. It was a perfect winter's day, blue skies and sunshine. Eva fell asleep and without her reading the map, I was unsure of the route. The route I navigated took me past Cundall Manor where Dad had worked in service as a young man – I had never seen the place before. Then through Topcliffe where he went to school and past Asenby where he was born. Again, it felt he was with me in an other-worldly way; it was a serene and beautiful experience.

Grief of course can catch one unawares, and I found this difficult to manage when it happened at work. I worked in a research centre studying the delivery and experience of palliative and end-of-life care. One day I was in Norfolk, meeting with and interviewing staff at a hospice. Towards the end of the day, we had a visit to a care home with specialist end-of-life care beds. The care home manager said we could look in one of the rooms as the gentleman who had taken up that bed had died the day before. I found tears welling up in my eyes and I had to excuse myself. I came to realise that when I was tired, my resilience would be low and grief could again feel raw. Another time, we were doing media training and I was observing a colleague talking about the Liverpool Care Pathway and how the body starts to shut down; again, I had to leave the room. I often found tears running down my cheeks during my weekly yoga class. Our teacher, Mike, commented to me at the end of one class that he hoped he would have someone who loved him as much after he died.

Some months after Dad's death, I began to feel stuck in my grief, the same thoughts going around and around in my head. In June 2012, I decided to seek out a bereavement counsellor. I can't recall much of the detail of those sessions, but it helped enormously. I have a quote I keep on the wall in my workroom at home from Kübler-Ross's book which says grief must be witnessed to be healed (Kübler-Ross and Kessler 2005). This resonates with my experience. The counsellor encouraged and supported me to contact the Community Hospital where Dad died, to seek out the two nurses who cared for Dad during his final hours. I wanted to ask if he had been in pain; had it been a peaceful end or was there any agitation; were they able to keep him company. I got through to the matron who told me the two staff have since left, one retired and one had moved to Australia. She gently advised I seek bereavement counselling to which I replied, 'I am having bereavement counselling'. Really, I wanted to yell 'IT'S BECAUSE I'M HAVING BEREAVEMENT COUNSELLING THAT I'VE FELT ABLE TO PHONE YOU'. I had to let the unresolved thoughts go in the end – and counselling helped me do so.

I have been puzzled by how haunted I was by not providing Dad with what are deemed aspects of a 'good death'. My work means I'm fully aware of the policy rhetoric relating to end-of-life care. In particular, notions about dying at home being a proxy measure for a 'good death'; also dying surrounded by loved ones in a familiar setting. I've written and read about problematising and critiquing these notions. And yet, it continued to trouble me in ways that seemed not to trouble other members of my family. Indeed, my immediate family members seemed to be coping better and this made me feel more isolated. I didn't feel able to speak with them about it in that first year of my grief and I certainly didn't disclose I was having bereavement counselling; at that time, I didn't reveal much about my life to my family of origin. During a particularly difficult period of my life, I was off work for some months and during this same period my family met at a funeral of my favourite uncle. I was terribly upset and my parents and siblings were at a loss to know how to comfort me; they had never have seen me so upset. Later that day, Jill asked when I was going back to work and when I said I wasn't sure, she rolled her eyes at me. Their approach was much more 'get a grip' and I felt unsupported. Later, a close friend helped me understand their responses better. When she observed me struggling, she said she was at a loss to know what to do and so often did nothing.[1] She also recalls that it scared her, because I was the strongest person she knew and if I wasn't coping well with life, then it could happen to anyone.

The actual process of writing papers and this chapter about Dad's dying and death has led to my initiation of conversations with Mum and siblings which I doubt would have otherwise taken place. It has been difficult talking to Mum about Dad's death; it is clearly painful for her. She talks about him in other ways, saying things like 'Oh, Doug would have liked this' or 'Doug wouldn't have enjoyed this'. They were together for nearly 60 years. She speaks of feeling relieved that Dad's suffering had ended but also of an almost bigger grief – the sudden death of her sister two years earlier. Mum's sister, Marjorie, lived just up the road from Mum and Dad and they saw each other most days. They were the youngest sisters in a family of seven children. During the war, Marjorie worked in the land army, but she would come home to Middlesbrough some weekends. Mum was the only child still at home with her parents and her Dad did long shifts on the railways. One weekend when Marjorie was visiting, she and Mum were having breakfast with their Mum, when she (their Mum) suddenly felt ill, collapsed and died of a brain aneurysm. I think that loss shaped Mum's life and brought her closer to Marjorie. Then Marjorie died very suddenly, in her garden one morning while hanging out washing. Fortunately, there were builders next door who rushed over, so we know it wasn't a lingering death. But the suddenness was devastating for Mum.

As part of that process of talking to my siblings I think we have grown to understand each other better. They have also both read this chapter and commented on it. Jill told me she thought it would be heavy going and depressing to read but instead she felt I had made talking about such a 'devastating' experience feel natural and okay. Through our conversations, I have also learnt more (and, just as importantly, shared more) about the different ways we have grieved. Jill talked to me about experiencing guilt, feeling that she never fully grieved for Dad. She was grieving for Derrick, her husband, who had died just six months earlier. On the day Derrick died, she had spent many hours at his bedside, along with his three adult children. On leaving, they had just reached the exit when a nurse caught them up to tell them Derrick had died. Jill believes he waited for them to leave before he died. My close colleague Glenys Caswell, who researched dying alone, suggests there is evidence that some people would prefer to be alone as they are coming to the end of their lives (Caswell 2019). Jill felt this was the case for Derrick and Dad. I recognise that dying alone isn't necessarily a 'bad' death but I am less convinced by the notion that patients might manage their own dying so that they could be alone at the moment of death. In Dad's case, he lived on through the Saturday night after we had all left and into Sunday morning.

In speaking to Andrew and having his comments on this chapter, it has helped ease my feelings of guilt about not being with Dad when he died. Andrew acknowledges my feelings of guilt but he feels very strongly that it felt wrong to sit around Dad's bedside waiting for him to die. He doesn't think keeping a vigil by the bedside of a dying loved one is something families should feel obliged or expected to do. He also spoke to me about his views that dying at home would be far more stressful and upsetting for a family to deal with and he wonders how people deal with any 'aura' left in a home after someone has died at home. Andrew's overwhelming memory of Dad's death is not so much about experiencing grief but rather being thankful that Dad had had a good long life, content at home with his wife, TV, books, garden and lovely walks from their doorstep. Andrew has just retired this year (2020) and he spoke to me about how it has made him think more about Dad and he hopes to enjoy a long and happy retirement just as Dad did.

The other major significance for me in asking my siblings to recall memories of Dad's dying and death are their recollections of my role. I have always felt I could have done more to get him moved off the surgical ward in the District General Hospital; pushed more for active treatment to be replaced or supplemented by supportive or palliative care. But my siblings were, and remain, grateful for what I did. I was surprised to learn that Jill feels Dad would not have been moved to the Community Hospital without my intervention. Andrew commented that, after our conversations during the writing of this chapter, he hopes I understand better that he and Jill feel I did more than enough. He said it was comforting when I was there; that I pushed for answers and information. Ann feels the same and said I fought hard for Dad and she especially liked that I would use my 'Doctor' title where it might help! They all felt my work meant I knew what questions to ask. It is immensely gratifying and comforting to know this, given that one of my enduring thoughts is that I wished I had done more.

These conversations with my siblings and their comments on this chapter have given me a different perspective on Dad's end of life and my subsequent grief. I have mentioned 'hindsight' several times, for example, the changing relationship of care with my Mum; recognising Dad's transition to end of life. It is also in hindsight that I understand ways in which working as an academic in the field of dying, death and bereavement may have 'complicated' rather than eased my grief. At the same time, drawing on this very personal experience (and finding out more from family members) as part of my work (this chapter and Almack 2019, forthcoming, 2022) has helped me make peace with it. I have felt compelled to write about Dad's dying and death even though I find it emotionally demanding. The first paper I had published took me about five years to write from starting it to feeling brave enough to send it out for review. In writing this chapter I have been trying to reflect why I feel the need to do this 'work'. Initially, I didn't find writing the academic papers cathartic, although people tend to assume it must be. But this chapter has felt cathartic, perhaps because it is a more personal account, which feels less distancing than an academic paper (albeit that my journal papers about Dad's death have been auto-ethnographical). I hope this work might contribute in some small way to changing practice or getting people to think and talk about death, dying and bereavement. But perhaps most importantly, it feels in some way to be an honouring of Dad's life and death and has been a way to continue my relationship with him. An unexpected corollary of this writing is, that is through the process of having more conversations with my siblings (and each of us being open with the other) we have become closer – and Dad would be very happy about that.

Acknowledgements Thanks to my daughter who has been a witness to this evolving relationship of bonds (and with whom I have the strongest bond); to my Mum, sister and brother for their patience with my questions and in memory of my lovely Dad, Leonard Douglas Almack (Doug to all who knew him).

Note

1. I do want to note that in more recent years, my siblings have grown to be more understanding of mental wellbeing being on par with physical wellbeing.

References

Almack, K. (2019). Uncertain trajectories in old age and implications for families and for palliative and end of life care policy and practice. *Death Studies*, https://doi.org/10.1080/07481187.2019.1671539.

Almack, K. (2020). Identifying end of life: The invisible transitions between living and dying amongst our oldest generations. Posted on March 30, 2020. https://eapcnet.wordpress.com/2020/03/30/identifying-end-of-life-the-invisible-transitions-between-living-and-dying-amongst-our-oldest-generations/. Accessed 1 October 2020.

Almack, K (forthcoming 2022). A death in the family: experiences of dying and death in which everyday family practices are embedded and enacted. Families, Relationships and Society, special issue.

Almack, K. & Churchill, H. (2007) Power and the PhD Journey: 'Getting in' and 'Getting on'. In Gilles, V. & Lucey, H. (eds.) *Power, Knowledge and the Academy: The Institutional is Political* (pp. 36–52). Basingstoke: Palgrave.

Caswell, G. (2019) 'A stark and lonely death': Representations of dying alone in popular culture. In Teodorescu, A and Jacobsen, M.H. (eds.) *Death in contemporary popular culture* (pp. 38–50). London: Routledge.

Kubler-Ross, E. & Kessler D. (2005). *On Grief and Grieving: Finding the Meaning of Grief Through the Five Stages of Loss*. New York: Scribner.

Ribbens McCarthy, J. & Prokhovnik, R. (2014). Embodied Relationality and Caring after Death. *Body & Society,* 20**,** 18–43.

Wilkens, J. (2019). All change please: education, mobility and habitus dislocation. In King, A., Almack, K. & Jone, R. L. (eds.) *Intersections of ageing, gender and sexuality: Multidisciplinary international perspectives* (pp 119–136). Bristol: Policy Press.

5

A Bittersweet Legacy

Gordon Riches

Looking Back (for the First Time, with a Purpose)

It is hard to disentangle my feelings about my parents' deaths from the changing phases of my own life. I was at a very different stage as a father and husband when my dad died compared with the death of my mum 18 years later. It's fair to say the impact of each loss *should* have been quite different. Until I wrote this, I would have happily pointed out how they were bound to be different, and how working with bereaved people helped me process my own grief when later my mum died. Now that I have been invited to describe their deaths in some detail, my responses to both seem embarrassingly similar and surprisingly uninformed by my research activity. What follows is a discovery of grief postponed, filtered through learned attitudes and contextual circumstances.

G. Riches (✉)
University of Derby, Derby, UK

My father died when I was 32. I had been in post as a lecturer in education for just four years. I dealt with my dad's death when I was the father of three relatively young sons and with little insight into the nature of loss and grief. I probably did so with an over-confidence in what snippets of psychology and sociology had landed me with what at the time seemed a dream job. By contrast, when Mum died, I was 50 and at a very different stage in my academic career. I was in the middle of an extended research project exploring the impact of a child's death on marital and family relationships. Nearly two decades later the 'dream job' had disappeared along with secondary teacher training; I had to adjust accordingly. Following a Masters in Sociology Research in Health Care my career was sustained initially by teaching behavioural sciences to midwifery, nursing and social work students, then to teaching sociology to undergraduates. There was also pressure to publish in journals that contributed to the University's research standing in national league tables. One of my mature students – Pam Dawson – invited me to a conference of The Compassionate Friends, a charity that supports bereaved parents and their families. At the same time Pam Abbott was appointed head of my faculty. Both colleagues were instrumental in much of my subsequent research career – Pam Dawson as a facilitator into the culture of bereavement support, and Pam Abbott as someone who both encouraged and helped fund a research project into child bereavement.

Therefore, when my mother died, with this new academic interest, I should have been better prepared to face her death with a clearer insight into my own manner of dealing with its impact. In addition, by the time my mother had the stroke that led to her death, my sons were in late adolescence/early adulthood. This had implications too in my own, my wife's – and their – reactions to my mum's death. There are further complications. Two years following my father's funeral my mum attempted suicide and burned down the family home. This resulted in a strange and strained dynamic in our respective relationships with each other – particularly with my wife, who is also called Pam.

Given this context, as far as my own grieving is concerned, I responded ineptly to my dad's death and 20 years later I should have been a little better prepared to manage the emotions that mum's death provoked. 'A little better' isn't just a turn of phrase. There is much I regret in the way I dealt with both deaths.

He Didn't Go Gently, Ever

As a child I was told that death was just a 'fact of life', a view common in the rural culture to which my family belonged. I remember eating pork from the family pig whose ears I'd scratched. I remember the excuse of being 'cruel to be kind' (when Dad drowned a litter of new-born kittens), and I remember the need for, and method of, 'culling' chickens that were too old to lay eggs. Stoicism and pragmatism in the face of death is a definite frame of mind I can trace back through to my earliest memories. The ability to shut down emotions in the face of practical necessity is, I know, typical of the way many men deal with loss and grief. This is particularly marked among farmers.

My dad was 70 when he had his third heart attack – the one that finally finished him off. It was brought on as he struggled to carry new window frames upstairs to replace the rotten ones he'd knocked out from the front bedroom windows. He'd already been diagnosed with heart disease which in those days had little effective treatment. For many years after he died, I used his refusal to take it easy and his lifelong heavy smoking as a reason to feel he had pretty much only himself to blame.

My relationship with him was typical of many kids of my generation. Ambivalence best describes it. Our father-son relationship was full of contradictions. Emotional distance in men was normal. He found it hard to show physical affection and almost impossible to play with me. Stoicism, frugality, the importance of hard work – all were bred through years of the Depression and two World Wars (he was born in 1910). I often felt I was a disappointment to him, being the object of a mother's overly protective love. I know now that this was the likely outcome of her losing her first baby. Where Dad was one of a family of ten boys, so poor they went to school without shoes, I was the spoiled only son who, to be frank, was pretty shiftless. He criticised my poor workmanship in those jobs I was required to complete. As we lived on a smallholding, there was plenty to do. On Sundays I would escape more chores by going to church with my mum. He was quick to anger and my parents' relationship with each other could be best described as volatile. Their relationship with my adopted elder sister (my cousin by birth) was worse. Six years older than me, she married and left for Australia when I was 15.

My father was 36 when I was born and from early middle age he suffered increasing pain from rheumatoid arthritis. As a child I had little sympathy for this condition and grew up with his physical flinching, temper and frequent complaining as normal, particularly as it was combined with remarkable physical strength and capacity to complete quite challenging projects: building a double garage and grain store out of telegraph poles; felling trees and splitting their trunks with steel wedges; using a cross-cut saw (with me on the other end) to produce logs for winter; laying hedges and digging out ditches. Consequently, I denied or ignored his ill-health, seeing only his extraordinary cussedness that manifested itself as strength, resilience and often anger. I was away at college when he arranged to go into hospital for a hip replacement. That seemed to help with the pain and afterwards he relied less on his walking sticks. Although my college vacations were spent back at home, I found temporary full-time work during the long summers and, in my head, I was away for good, already waking up to a world very different to that of my parents. Immersion in theories of education and how family life impacted views of the world prompted a lot of introspection. I had become physically as well as more emotionally distant – married and preoccupied with a young family – when it became clear that he had heart disease and had already experienced two 'attacks'. He was finally forced to go into hospital at the end of the summer of 1980. My wife and I had taken our three sons to the south of France in an old camper-van, our first time abroad. Mum said he refused to accept how ill he was until we were safely back. He was hospitalised early in September soon after we returned and was deteriorating rapidly.

My memory of the days leading up to his death is vivid. Hospital visiting was strictly regulated and Mum and I would attend both morning and evening. His breathing was awfully laboured, and he complained of disturbing dreams. Near the end he described in graphic detail how he had been forced to undergo an enema. Then he was as near to tears as I'd ever seen him. Why he had to undergo this indignity I still do not know, but at the time I hadn't the wit nor confidence to question it. During the time between morning and evening visiting on the day before Dad died,

I took my mother to the Malvern Hills. Not too far from our home in rural Warwickshire, the Malverns had been a place they'd loved. Set a few miles outside the County Town of Worcester, Mum had pipe-dreams of retiring there. It held a sense of peace for her. We reminisced about their lives together and walked to British Camp (an Iron Age hill fort). Returning in the late afternoon the nurse on duty said his end was near and suggested we stay. His breathing had become worse. He fought for each breath. He struggled in and out of consciousness. Oddly, very early the next morning, just before he died, we were ushered to a waiting room by the ward sister and called back only after the ward staff had laid him out, complete with a flower (a rose I think, but this could be a false memory) on his chest. So, after less than two weeks in hospital, just before his 70th birthday, at the end he died alone, or with strangers. Such were provincial hospitals in those days.

From this point on I was 'taken over' by a sense of responsibility to manage the consequences of his dying. Only later would I come across the concept of 'ghastly euphoria' to describe the adrenaline that drove my self-belief in being able to deal with this nightmare. At one point, my mum actually said, 'Do you have to sound quite so cheerful when you speak to people?' In researching background for our book on bereaved parents, 'An Intimate Loneliness', these initial emotions – at an academic level at least – made more sense. At the time, any personal feelings of loss were put firmly on hold. I stayed with Mum over the following week, sleeping on top of the double bed with her for the first three nights, answering the 'phone to speak to friends and relatives who wanted to offer condolences, talking with the funeral director and helping make arrangements for his funeral. The only sense of loss I remember was of a pair of Dad's leather gloves that I took to wearing and which I left in a shop when I paid the bill. My annoyance at this carelessness and the memory of it far outweighs its literal importance.

His funeral was a big event. While often irritable at home, in his work he was funny and charming, highly thought of by his customers and successful in promoting his company's agricultural products as well as giving advice on cattle feed and fertilisers. Hence, the church was packed and the procession to his grave seemed endless. As this is going back nearly 40 years, I have forgotten many details of that day, but one event still rankles. A farmer who came up to us, put his arm round my mum and looking at me said 'You're the man of the house now, you've got to look after her'. At the time this felt too much to ask. I had a family of my own, a full-time job and now additional responsibility for supporting my mother. Living over 50 miles away didn't make it any easier. I'm embarrassed that at this time my overwhelming feelings were of anger – anger at my father for doing such a physically impossible job that he brought on a final heart attack, and acute annoyance that neither he nor my mother had foreseen the problems she would face living by herself in an old house with large garden and ten acres of fields, chickens, hedges and ditches to maintain. The house was isolated from mains water, sewage and gas, with just electricity, a well for drinking water and rainwater tanks for all other washing and irrigation – and only an outdoor lavatory. Winter was always a challenge. Now without Dad, it would become doubly difficult for Mum alone. Alone that is, except for the chickens and the dog.

Returning home to my own family and work, I was preoccupied with how to manage my mother's practical problems, along with supporting her obvious deep distress at Dad's death. I did not experience any feelings of grief. I literally felt only anger, no real sense of personal sadness, just a feeling of resentment towards responsibilities I hadn't bargained for. Hence, I brushed off attempts at sympathy. Dad had lived a good life. Maybe he could have lived past 70 if he'd not smoked or put such a strain on his heart, but I avoided any exploration of what his loss actually meant to me. For two years, on and off, I kept sadness at bay by remembering the times he had been mean to me, even meaner to my older sister, and to my mum. No sense of loss or regret came near to the frustration I felt with my mother's increasing depression, with her refusal to consider selling up and moving closer. I rang often, fetched her over most weekends or drove over by myself to be with her, ending up doing the jobs that dad would have done. Two miserable winters passed and although I had taken Mum to see any number of houses both near to us and close to where she currently lived, she couldn't – or wouldn't – move. The whole problem boiled over when I had a phone call from my aunt – Mum's sister. There had been a fire. My aunt was on her way. I should go too. But mum was okay, so not to worry.

The house was gutted, Mum was in an ambulance on her way to hospital, two fire engines and a police car were in the drive. Three hours later, after police interrogations, my aunt and I were allowed to leave. It became clear that it had been no accident. Paraffin had been liberally tipped around the house, ignited and Mum had gone to bed. Further details about her survival and escape are still painful to recount. This event certainly eclipsed my father's death. Health services pronounced my mother mentally fit; depressed at worst. The psychiatrist who discharged her told me this wasn't unusual, though taking the house along with attempting to take one's life was relatively rare. My wife was incandescent. Never on the best of terms (typical mother/daughter-in-law tensions) this event brought their latent conflict into a blazing row in the hospital ward.

I shall be eternally grateful to my line-manager at university. I needed time off and went into some detail about why. His words are still clear in my memory: 'Don't feel guilty enough to bring your mother to live with you. It'll destroy your marriage and your family. Do whatever you can short of that'. I am in even more debt to my aunt and uncle. Mum and the dog went to live with them for the two years it took to sell the ruins of our home and the land that went with it, and to find a house in which she was prepared to live. I know this is a digression from my father's actual death but it helps justify why its consequences allowed me to avoid facing it squarely as his son. Instead, circumstances encouraged me to continue to prioritise my responsibility to my mum – seeing myself solely as Dad's widow's care worker, certainly not as his bereaved offspring. Underlying this too was a sense of exasperation with the loss of what had been my home for 18 years. I realise now that this was a defence – a denial that I was affected by the loss of my father. My aunt (my mum's younger sister) and uncle were the true support givers. I was far more surplus to requirements than I was prepared to admit.

In the end, it was the sausages and mash that got to me. One evening sometime after Mum went to live with her sister, the memory of me, a small boy, staying up long enough to see Dad come home from work and wait while he ate his dinner, overwhelmed me. My mother cooked delicious sausages and mash and he always left some on the side of his plate just so I could finish it off. For no apparent reason I could smell and taste that greasy mash and those crunchy sausages. These feelings of sadness were strongest when I was on my own, in the evenings, walking the dogs. It didn't happen all at once. But gradually, over the months that followed, more good memories forced themselves unannounced into my idle moments. I could produce a substantial list easily now. Then, each one came with a good deal of pain. It did not relieve the anger and in some ways it made it worse, shifting the target from my father to life in general, and to the lousy end we all face. I also felt anger with myself and guilt for not caring he'd died, or how he'd died, or how much he'd suffered beforehand, because it was becoming clearer, after all, that I did care. His manner of dying wasn't easy, and as far as I recall, the health service made it worse. He had to fight to die. He wasn't fighting to live. In the end his breathing was so difficult it was dreadful to hear. I was angry that he had to die like that.

The very late start to my grieving didn't relieve the frustration with my mother either. Compassion for her and the sadness that drove her came much later. At the time I carried on being a father, a husband and an employee. These routines and responsibilities kept me anchored and purposeful. Alone, I sometimes ruminated on the misery of it all. What had felt like a relatively stable, predictable life, bracketed by sons behind me and my father ahead of me had shifted with his death. I had become next in line and it was disturbing.

In many ways I was – and probably still am – a lot like my father. I handled his death in the same way that my mum described him handling the death of their first-born child. Her name was Dorothy and she lived for just four hours. This was two years before I was born, and I didn't hear the full story from my mother until nearly 18 years later. As a child though, she would hold me tight and tell me that I was her miracle; that I should have had a sister but she didn't live; that my father took her away and had her buried but she didn't know where; that he refused to talk about it and that he'd get angry and say she shouldn't talk about it either because it would only upset her. From what she said it seemed he was attempting to manage her grief, much like I was. Maybe it's just that they were both part of a generation recently surviving a war. Most of them wouldn't talk about any of it. Our similarities and my thoughts about how I wanted to be different have turned out to be a kind of legacy. He rarely drank alcohol. Neither do I. I often use the phrase 'As my old dad used to say....', because he had a repertoire of phrases, sayings, daft jokes and words of wisdom. I still wear the gold ring my mum bought him for their engagement. She gave it to me sometime after his death, explaining that he never wore it. For myself, the good outweighs the bad and I can remember him fondly. For my elder sister, I find it harder to understand what seemed to be their eternal, nagging and sometimes explosive conflict. He was good to her too, but also, more often, very short-tempered and even physically controlling. I wish I could have done more for her and that guilt lies unresolved, even though we talked about it on the occasions I visited her in Australia. Those were hard days for my parents' generation, harder than I appreciated at the time. They were the result of circumstances that mostly were concealed from me as a child.

My own fatherhood has been different. The product of a higher education, supervised in my last master's degree by a feminist academic, and well-versed in the sociology of oppression, I was – and still am – what some would call a 'member of the privileged liberal elite': a 'snowflake'. I had few inhibitions playing on the floor with my kids when they were little – and even less with my grand-kids now. We spent every long summer holiday camping or caravanning. I took my sons to football, helped cook their meals, listened to their stories, helped them through schools and universities. Though there's always some of the old masculine reserve, I tell them I love them and that I am proud of them, and I know they love me. They still hug me even though I barely come up to their shoulders. They still find uses for me – as chauffeur, 'babysitter' (though rarely on my own) and sounding board. I know how lucky I am. I wish I had hugged my father more. I only really appreciated what he and my mum did for me far too late to tell them.

Mother Love

Neither of my parents faded away quietly. Where my father finally died as a result of attempting major house improvements, my mother died from a massive stroke experienced while standing on the top of a stepladder, cleaning cob-webs off the top of the curtains. At least I assume that was what she was doing because that was how I found her, on the floor, unconscious, step-ladder intact and upright, feather duster abandoned. She had lain there for a good few hours. Her neighbour rang me to say the milk was still on the step. She always took the milk in early, so the neighbour guessed something was wrong. By lunchtime, as the milk still hadn't moved, she rang to say I ought to go over. The journey was always over an hour's drive, depending on the traffic, so it must have been around 2 pm when I got in. Phoning 999 the operator suggested I put her in the recovery position while I waited for the ambulance. It was obvious how bad she was as she was too stiff and fixed to move, and cold. I covered her with rugs and lay with her till the ambulance arrived. I followed it into hospital. The doctor who examined her confirmed what I had already suspected, she was unlikely to recover. We – I – agreed that other than making her comfortable (what a cruel euphemism) the medical staff would not attempt any treatment. She would have been 86 next birthday and had survived Dad by 18 years,

My mother was a proud, private and very independent person. It was she who badgered my father to be more ambitious, supporting him from being the milkman she married, through to a white-collar job as salaried sales representative. It was she, a farmer's daughter, who pushed for the small-holding they eventually bought. Hence, she would manage her home and present herself 'properly' before anyone was allowed in. She couldn't have born being seen as she was in hospital, or how she would have been had she lived. Although I don't think she would have lived, my acceptance of the doctor's prognosis felt like I had agreed to her dying. Then – and still now – I can live with that decision. If I feel any guilt, it is with the length of time I waited for the milk to disappear off the step.

The first day seemed endless. Mum was put on a saline drip in a single room and I stayed until it was late. The nurse who brought me tea said I should talk to her. She told me that although stroke victims couldn't move or speak and appeared comatose, they could probably hear. I retold as many of her favourite childhood memories as I could recall. There were lots. Since I was little, she had loved to tell me stories of when she was a girl, of growing up on a farm in Herefordshire, of her sisters and brother who had become a racing cyclist. She confided so much in me when I was young.

I retold her those familiar stories of her childhood and the more recent good memories of our own lives as a family. Over the next couple of weeks this became a routine. I'd get up, walk the dogs, help with the breakfast, then drive over to the hospital and spend the day just talking to her. She never recovered or responded. Over the weekends Pam came with me but during the week she was at work and I went alone. As with my father, I missed her actual dying but this time by a couple of hours. One morning I arrived at the hospital to be told she had 'passed' around 8 am and as they knew I was coming they didn't attempt to contact me. It had never occurred to me during these visits to say 'goodbye' and even if it had, it was now too late. My mother died in 1997. I was completing interviews and writing up the results of the research Pam Dawson and I had undertaken into the impact of children's deaths on family relationships. This was finally published in 2000, but up to when my Mum died, and for a couple of years previously, she and I had talked about death and how families coped with the loss of a son or daughter. This was not unfamiliar territory as part of my childhood routine was going with Mum to tend the family graves. These included my uncle's grave – Mum's younger brother, killed by a bull when he was 14. I was introduced to death early on and can remember being taken in to see my grandma (Dad's mother) soon after she had died, laid out in their front room. This was before I started primary school. My mum said she looked so peaceful it was good for me to see there was nothing to be afraid of with dying.

Death was never far away from Mum's narratives. The last few years before she died felt like the corresponding bookend to the relationship I'd had with her as a child. From as long as I can remember, and even during the holidays after I'd started school, she would take me shopping, take me to see her sister, take me to visit her friends. All of them were 'Aunties' even though no relation. I'd sit for what seemed like hours listening to their conversations. She also read stories to me. *The Famous Five* and *The Secret Garden* are still there in my mind. She'd tell me her own stories about how she'd gone to work in the Post Office rather than go into service or work on her father's farm and how she met my father and all the other men who courted her. I was not only her son; I was her confidant. Years later, at Teacher Training College, I ended up writing my final year's dissertation on D. H. Lawrence, feeling a certain resonance with his portrayal in *Sons and Lovers*. Maybe I owe my academic success to her ambitions for me. It is likely that I owe my interest in the social sciences to those hours I spent listening to women's conversations.

The closeness of our relationship when I was young perhaps explains the strength of my distancing from it when I left home. My mother was a staunch Conservative. She had a picture of Margaret Thatcher on her mantelpiece. She was an ardent churchgoer and managed to keep me in the faith until late adolescence. I was even confirmed. My wife was none of these things and by my early twenties, neither was I. Higher education was a revelation. However, in those last few years Mum had me to herself again. The lads were too old to visit their grandma but were often at home when I fetched her over. Pam accompanied me in the early days and was happy to go with us to the cinema or, once, to see Ken Dodd whom Mum loved. Mostly, I would drive over by myself, mow the lawns because the house she'd bought still had a huge garden, then sit on her favourite garden bench just talking into the late evening. We still have that bench in our garden; another legacy. They made things to last in those days.

Often these conversations would involve my bereavement research and she talked again about how awful it was not to know where her first baby was buried. However, for the first time she told me Dorothy had lived for four hours and that she had some form of birth defect. She said she felt guilt for this and, in my view completely misguidedly, linked it to struggling with an escaping calf while she was pregnant. She also confided more of the story of Uncle Eddie. It seems he and his brother were actually goading the bull when it attacked. She also told of the circumstances of my sister's adoption and of the pressure put on her by her own mother to take in a 'wild' two-year old who had been passed around the extended family after her mother had died in a subsequent childbirth. It had been my father who agreed to take her but only on condition that she was legally adopted, saying she had been messed around enough. I think in those last few years we were closer than for a long time. Her health remained pretty strong. She still drove her car to church and to the shops but close to the end her optician had told her that her eyesight was not good enough to drive. She also suffered from a sense of vertigo. It had not stopped her from climbing that stepladder to dust the curtain tops. She still read a good deal, kept a diary and tended the garden except for the mowing.

Driving over to the hospital I saw fields of rapeseed gradually change from green to yellow. Every year it reminds me of that April, of the morning she died, and of the ensuing catalogue of tasks that had to be completed. My sister was the other side of the world, so registering the death, arranging the funeral, putting a notice in the paper, contacting a solicitor all gave me things to put on a list – jobs to be ticked off that fully occupied my mind. My mum's Conservatism even extended to her choice of a true blue country solicitor to act as her executor, to draw up her will and lodge it, together with the house deeds, in a safety-deposit box in his 'country' practice. It was he who encouraged her to stay in the house she eventually demolished rather than supporting me in suggesting she move to somewhere more practical. By the time my mum died, his practice had been taken over by a larger company and he had disappeared. So too, unfortunately had my mum's will, the house deeds and any records relating to the service he had provided. This was sorted eventually by a very efficient solicitor in the practice that had absorbed his. She acted along with me as executor and clearly felt some responsibility for correcting his negligence but the procedure was messy and drawn out. Where my dad's death had allowed me to avoid my own feelings by focusing on managing my mum's grief, her death had left a barrage of practical and complicated legal tasks to complete, thereby providing plenty of excuses once again to avoid facing how I felt.

Although the funeral must have been among the first of these tasks, as with my dad's, I have little recollection of it. An abiding memory, crystallised through a photo, is of my three sons all dressed in suits and dark ties. It was the first time I'd seen them looking so smart and their support, along with my wife's, is something for which I remain very grateful. I felt far less alone this time, than I did at my dad's funeral. Putting Mum's house up for sale and disposing of its contents seemed daunting. Even though there was nothing left of 'our' previous home and contents, during the 15 or so years in her current house she had acquired a lot of stuff. She loved a bargain and to my embarrassment if I was with her she would attempt to haggle even in department stores. 'How much for cash?' was her usual gambit once she'd decided to buy something. Consequently, the house was full of furniture, nick-knacks, ornaments, books, saved letters, gardening equipment, receipts and records of Dad's work and her state pension. I encouraged my aunt and family to have first choice over the house contents. I was also able to pay my aunt back a little for the care she had shown my mother by staying with her the night my uncle died. I was, for the first time, present when someone took their final breath. It was far gentler than my father's and at home, rather than in hospital. Disposing of Mum's belongings was very bittersweet. In the end when the house was sold and a deadline loomed, the sheer amount of it meant many trips to the tip. Her pride and joy – a dark brown Ercol sideboard – we kept in our own home, eventually putting it on eBay and selling it to someone who was taking it abroad to his house in France. He said he was going to strip the varnish and paint it lots of different colours. Mum would have had a fit! My sister wasn't able to come from Australia for the funeral nor did I expect her to. She had visited three times, once when she had very young children and Dad was still alive, and twice when Mum was in her most recent home. Face to face, their relationship was rarely less than fractious, yet half a world away they got on fine through airmail letters. Mum had kept them all, along with diaries from the last ten years. I sent these to my sister. I hoped retaining the letters symbolised an affection they might have held for each other even though it was never expressed.

With Dad it was the sausages and mash that got me, a long time after his death. With Mum it was much sooner and less unexpected. By the side of her bed was a half-finished book. The thought that she'd never read to the end proclaimed the finality and pathos of her death. Her wallet, handbag, driving license, jewellery were all close personal possessions that were a part of her. Looking at them, wondering what to do with them, brought home how her life – all our lives – produce stuff that is only meaningful when they are being used, worn, or kept as evidence of who we are. I guess I was more intimately familiar with her life towards its end than with Dad's and having to dispose of things she valued, memories she kept, books she had read, was more difficult than I had anticipated. In the 12 months following her death I experienced very mixed emotions. On the one hand, I still felt guilt at not getting to her soon enough after her stroke. On the other, I felt grateful for her relatively uncomplicated and brief dying when compared with my dad. I also felt an enormous sense of release from responsibility and for a very limited time, a sense of our financial pressures easing. If I felt grief, it was wrapped up in my rationalisation that she had completed her life successfully and had lived it largely on her own terms. Soon after Mum's death, I attended an annual Bereavement Research Conference. A colleague with whom I have worked many times before was generous enough to listen to my account of the day my mother died. This retelling was very valuable and helped me clear some of the flashbacks of her lying on the floor while I waited for the ambulance that had, until then, occupied some of the nights when I couldn't sleep.

Mortality as a Fact of Life

Going to church as a child I was familiar with the parable of the wise and foolish virgins. Now it seems even more relevant as I grow older. I count myself lucky that I have outlived my dad by nearly two years at the time of writing this. He always said he wanted to live to be 90 and then get shot by a jealous husband. Mum died halfway through her 85th year, which feels like another landmark to aim for. My research has given me the privilege of listening to many parents sharing how their children died or were killed. Sitting with family members whose worlds were shattered through loss I have been unable to avoid the insight that life is horribly fragile. I think I've known this all my life and the fact that it is so close has familiarised me to its reality but hardened me to its consequences. From a research perspective, I have recorded in detail how each loss is catastrophic to those closest, and how the events, illnesses and accidents that lie behind them are often arbitrary, usually unpredictable and frighteningly common.

At an emotional level, I recognise how experience of past and current loss has contributed to both my relationship with death and my strategies for coping with grief. My research allowed me to discover the guilt Mum felt for losing her first baby. This, when I was nearly 50 and she was close to the end of her life. Being able to witness her sense of guilt and maybe offer a modicum of reassurance is itself a form of legacy. It has taken years for me to acknowledge how I feel about losing my parents. I deal with loss by attempting to belittle it, by believing it doesn't matter so much and that it is a natural and inevitable part of life. There were so many practical consequences to deal with after they died, occurring over such an extended period, that I was able to convince myself that I was over it when the last task was sorted. Before they died our lives had diverged, distance had separated us, and I cannot honestly say that the time I gave up to be with my mum during her later years was that generous. I failed to truly appreciate the start in life she and my Dad gave me but I have come to realise that my experience as a child of listening to my mother's stories and to those long conversations with her women friends laid the groundwork for feeling at home doing ethnographic research. Also, in a modest way, their academic ambitions for me were finally realised. Reading this through, it's clear I still see death with a mixture of anger, humour and denial. I also accept grief as an inevitable consequence of loss, but a consequence that I still work quite hard to avoid.

At an objective level, researching death and grief has reinforced my awareness of how provisional all our lives are. I know the knock on the door can come at any time. If it's for me, not so bad. I have few regrets and know I have lived a privileged and charmed life compared to many, lucky to be still here. I am a strong advocate of euthanasia – another legacy of my father's death, or at least his manner of dying. If the knock is for anyone in my close family, I know that the rest of us will survive, but we will be changed, and our relationships will be challenged and may not pass the tests that grief demands. In practical terms, I have learned much from the consequences of my parents' deaths. We have downsized twice. Much of the accumulated detritus we collected over the years has gone to charity shops or the recycling centre. The garden is small and easily maintained. The costs of running the house are manageable by whichever of the two of us survive the other. We live on a bus route if we can no longer drive. There is a convenience store within walking (or mobility scooter) distance. We have made a will. We have stipulated no funeral – straight to environmentally friendly shallow unmarked woodland graves with the cost-saving to be used for a family party at a later date. I have stayed as close to my own sons as is possible given their own busy lives and family commitments. We have tried to be useful grandparents and have shared in the care of our grandchildren. We hope to be around long enough for them to have grown into busy lives where they are not too upset at losing us.

In conclusion, I recognise that my personal account mirrors the data we collected when exploring the question of why so many bereaved parents experienced marital conflict following a child's death. Previous research, as well as our own, described how men often grieve differently to women. When it comes to loss, men seem less capable of processing their emotions. They appear to be more inclined to use anger, denial, projection, practical projects and rationalisation to avoid the pain of exploring how they feel. Looking back, as this exercise has encouraged me to do, I know that my parents did their best under circumstances too difficult for me to ever truly comprehend. At many points since their deaths I have felt resentment at the things I felt they did wrong and used it as an excuse to avoid thinking about the many more things I know they did right. I have used the fact that they both completed their 'natural lifespans' to avoid truly examining how bad I felt when they were no longer there, preferring to deal with their deaths as a life-stage to be completed with as little emotional fuss as possible. Most of all, I avoided counting up the things I missed, the absences in my life when they were gone, the lives we shared and the legacy of good memories with which they left me.

I continue to discover them.

6

Two Traumatic Bereavements

Colin Murray Parkes

I

It was during the late summer of 1969 when I returned home by car from a visit to St Christopher's Hospice. As I drew up at my house in Chorleywood I was surprised to see my wife, Patricia, standing at the front door. She came up to the car and got in beside me. The following dialogue is an approximation to what I now recall:

> 'It's your Dad' she said, 'Your Mum's at home, you need to get over there, she's on her own. They say he's dead.'
> 'Dead?' Patricia nodded, 'The doctor phoned – a stroke, it was very sudden, – she's on her own'. I sat at the wheel trying to get my head round the news.
> 'Dead?', my father had been in bed during the week with the flu but nothing serious. I couldn't believe it. I sat there, stunned.
> 'Your mother needs you.'

C. M. Parkes (✉)
St Christopher's Hospice, London, UK

'I know, I know, but give me a minute.'
'Oh, Colin, I'm sorry, I can't come with you, it's the children, there's nobody else to look after them.'
'That's OK, I'm all right.' I was back in control.

My parent's house, old stables converted into a bungalow, with fine views across the Hertfordshire countryside to Shenley, half an hour by car from Chorleywood. I drove there in a bewildered state of mind. I was trying to make sense of the news. Dad, aged 68, was a semi-retired lawyer. He had been working, visiting his office in New Barnet, three days a week. A large and formerly athletic man, he had suffered from osteoarthritis and it had been hard and painful for him to carry so heavy a body on his ageing, arthritic hips. In addition, he had had a cancer of the bowel which, though successfully removed along with his rectum, had left him with a colostomy, an opening in his abdominal wall, through which the contents of his colon passed into a plastic bag. His body had become a burden to himself and to my mother. This said, there was no reason for him to die. He took capsules for blood pressure, but nobody had suggested that his life might be at risk. It didn't make sense.

When I arrived, it was to find a group of neighbours standing in the driveway. The doctor had been and gone, and mother had shut herself in the house and would not open the door. I rang, knocked, and called out,

'It's Colin, Mum.' The door opened, my mother looked out, shrunken and grey.
'I'm sorry you've come. (Pause) You'll take me away from him.'
'No I won't.' I said, 'I want to be with him too'.

My father lay on his side, on the floor by the bed; a very solid presence, in his pyjamas and dressing gown. There was a cut on his brow where he had fallen, but it was not bleeding. I reached out and touched his brow, remembering how often he had proudly carried me on those shoulders and I had clutched him round the head, equally proud. My tears came as I knelt, then lay, on the floor and held him. I felt my mother's arm on mine. She was lying, on his other side, on the floor, the three of us, together, for the last time, ever.

After a long time, there was a ring at the door. The GP had returned with the death certificate. Mother sighed, 'I suppose we must leave him now'. She went to make a cup of tea while the GP and I hauled him into bed and washed traces of blood from his face. By the time we had finished, his body looked clean and tidy, but something had gone, he was not there anymore. Neither I nor my mother needed to spend more time with him. It seemed that the time we had spent on the floor had made it easier for both of us to let go of him. *This was lesson number one.*

We sat on the sofa in the living room, with the GP, all three of us weeping quietly together. Dad and the GP had been friends for many years and I felt warmed by this evidence of the doctor's genuine affection. He had seen my father during the preceding week and told him that his blood pressure was much too high. It seemed that this hypertension had caused a massive stroke, some blood vessel in his brain had burst and disrupted that delicate structure. Dad must have tried to get out of bed before he fell forward and struck his head. The fact that there was little blood indicated that his heart had stopped, he had died very rapidly.

My experience of hospice had taught me not to be afraid to cry but any embarrassment I might have felt was dispelled by this GP's sharing of his own grief.

I was dreading having to break the news to the extended family and friends. I found it difficult to organise my thoughts. Images of Dad lying inert on the floor, and the sight of his pallid face, swam in my memory and interrupted my ability to think clearly. The first person I phoned was my brother Roger, he answered at once but I found myself unable to find words, 'What is it, Col?' he asked, alarmed. At last I stammered out some kind of explanation and soon both of us were crying together.

The second call, to Patricia, was slightly easier, I began to get the words in order and the sound of her gentle voice comforted me. After that I phoned the children, then started on Dad's friends, family and others. Before long I had the story pat and had calmed down enough to comfort them. By the tenth call I realised that I had stopped feeling. From then on, although I continued to miss my Dad, I was able to acknowledge the full reality of his death.

Sudden, unexpected deaths are a common cause of PTSD (Post-Traumatic Stress Disorder) which can now be treated by EMDR (Eye

Movement Desensitisation and Reprogramming). This is a complex method that focuses attention on the most painful traumatic memory that is repeated again and again until it gradually diminishes. It seems that my ten telephone calls may have had the same influence. Even the most horrific memories get organised, they may even get boring if repeated again and again. *That was lesson number two.*

It seems ungrateful to say so, but the sympathy I received from my colleagues and friends over the next few weeks was hard to accept. I was repeatedly reminded that I had changed from the consultant and expert on bereavement, to the recipient of care and concern, the grief doctor had become a grief patient. I was touched by their kindness but unsettled by it. Did I need a shoulder to cry on? No, I already had that, and had made good use of it. Did I need someone to talk to? I did not think so although, with hindsight, it has taken writing an auto-biography to help me to review the importance of my father in my life. My discomfort arose from a vague feeling that I had lost status. At the same time the place I was in felt unfamiliar. I became aware that grief is a foreign country.

I began to understand one of the reasons that my father, and other people, distrust psychiatrists; by making people an object of study and care we subtlety downgrade them in status from person to object, and from equals to subordinates. I was now in a different world and wondering if I could get back to the old one. I do think that we need to recognise and respect the gap that exists between our patients and ourselves and be careful not to misuse our status. *This was lesson number three.*

I cannot pretend that the experience of my father's death subsequently haunted me or profoundly changed my psychological adjustment or the direction of my researches. Any such influences had taken place much earlier in my life and by the time he died I had become autonomous. Neither did the timely death of my mother in old age although the way she died has lingered and influenced both my care of patients undergoing palliative care in old age and the anticipation of my own death in old age.

II

My mother had many friends several of them very close. With their support and that of my brother and myself she mastered her grief, carried on and outlived my father by over 30 years. She needed little help from me and, perhaps because of bad experiences with her own mother-in-law, was determined not to become a 'burden' to her children and grandchildren. Instead she took pains to make all of us welcome to her house. She turned down several proposals of marriage on the grounds that she did not want to spend the rest of her life 'looking after another sick old man'. I began to realise how stressful it had been to her to nurse that weak but heavy old man who was so far removed from the romantic and athletic lover who had married his 'little woman'.

Gwen continued to live in the house in Shenley and divided it in two, letting out a flat to bring in income. She soon became a friend of her tenants. In later years, she was able to provide free accommodation, through the Home Share scheme, to couples in the flat, in return for a little help in the house and garden. She took great pleasure in entertaining her growing family and her circle of friends. At age 96 she was still up for a game of football with her great grandchildren.

I was able to visit her weekly and we both enjoyed our teas together. In due course she developed macular degeneration, a form of blindness, but tackled this in the same positive way in which she tackled all her problems. Together we visited a shop for the disabled in London and returned home laden with devices for the blind.

In her late 90s she retained sufficient vision to get about the house and look after herself. And when, in due course, her hearing became impaired, she proudly announced that she had an expensive 'computer' in each ear. In the end it was the loss of her teeth that proved her main source of annoyance. Meanwhile her friends were dying, one by one.

Dying, in great old age, is not necessarily traumatic for the family or for the patient but, sadly, in my mother's case it was very painful. The notes that follow are taken from my diary:

22.07.03

Ruth (my mother's carer) phoned at breakfast time to say that my mother has fallen while attempting to reach her commode during the night. I drove at once to Shenley where I was told that she has eaten and drunk nothing for three days, she is now dehydrated and very weak. She has been cared for over the weekend by my brother and daughter-in-law, Roger and Tessa. Dr H, her GP, who visited yesterday, thinks she has cystitis and ordered a blood test.

Mother appears somewhat breathless with rapid pulse and respiration. The poor old lady's cheeks are fallen in and she is clearly suffering but pathetically grateful for any comfort given. She is conscious and coherent and has a three inch cut on her elbow. Dr H visited again at mid-day and confirmed my suspicion that she has broncho-pneumonia. She declined his offer of hospital admission. He prescribed amoxycillin.

I decided to stay with her and drove home to fetch clothes, computer etc. The District Nurse came late to dress her wound but refused to take blood for two more days. I nagged Mother to drink during the day and this improved her hydration. She is clearly tired and unable to concentrate on conversation for long. At her request I deflected numerous requests from the family to visit her.

23.07.03

Mother slept well and her respiratory rate had dropped by the morning. GP called and found her temperature normal. But Mother says she feels much less well. Any attempt to take more than a few sips of water makes her feel sick and all movement is painful. I coaxed her into a chair for a few hours but her breathing got worse during the day and, in the late afternoon I was shocked to find her coughing frothy sputum. A phone call to the GP confirmed my fear that she has pulmonary oedema, heart failure. The outlook is very bad and I phoned the family to warn them.

Tonight it is clear that heart failure is causing her chest to fill up with froth. The old lady is unable to cough it up and is breathing, with difficulty, through the bubbles. From time to time I sit her up to help her cough and lift her up the bed. She strokes my face and says, 'My dear darling'.

24.07.03

About 1 am her breathing improved and she went to sleep. This morning she is still very ill but is no longer coughing up frothy sputum. I conclude that the amoxycillin is taking effect.

During the day she managed to take a few sips of water but anything more substantial nauseates her. I only managed to get her out of bed for an hour.

Because she seemed better I left her with my brother's wife, Tessa, who is staying the weekend, while I went to Newbury to lecture on 'Traumatic Bereavement and Disasters' to Cruse Bereavement Care. The meeting went well.

25.07.03

No change in Mother's condition. The blood test shows that she is uraemic with high creatinine levels. This may be attributable to dehydration. Dr H advises that she go into hospital for a drip and Mother agrees. If he is right she may feel much better when rehydrated but I have misgivings about prolonging active treatment. Tessa accompanied her to the Medical Observation Unit... and she was soon on a drip.

26.07.03

Mother has lost heart. The technician hurt her when taking X-rays of her chest and every movement seems painful. Fortunately, she is semi-comatose much of the time. My second daughter, Jennifer; her husband, John; and their two boys are on holiday in Italy. I told Mum that I had spoken to Jennifer and heard the boys swimming and shouting in the pool. Jenny had sent her love and asked if she should hurry back. Mum said, 'Oh don't let them give up their holiday, I would hate that'.

28.07.03 (SUN)

The last two days have been hellish for the old lady. I have been at her side most of the time with grand-daughters, Caz and Liz, with Tessa, sharing the care. She has been unconscious much of the time but, when awake, her malaise has been awful and all movement painful...

Today Mum suffered 'total pain', could not even bear us to hold her hand. She was asking for euthanasia. A new team of doctors have taken over and wanted to change her anti-biotic because a blood culture has shown that she has a coliform septicaemia.

She asked Liz to let her die. Liz was in tears. I approached the doctors and suggested that active treatment be terminated and a syringe driver be set up to relieve her pain. They agreed and a Palliative Care Nurse arrived later to supervise this. When Liz and Caz returned from their lunch together I asked Liz if she could see anything different, the look of relief on her face when she realised that the drip had been taken down was good to see. At last we are getting something right.

29.07.03

Her consultant visited and wanted to carry out further investigations with a view to further therapy. I argued that she has multi organ failure, is suffering and, at 98, is ready to die. I told him that the family had backed my recommendation to stop active treatment and give palliative care.

Mother's pain is less and she was unconscious during much of the day. She was able to say 'Goodbye' to my brother's son, Brandon, and express her love to Liz and all of us. She can now hold hands without pain and seems more peaceful. I left to give Roger time with her alone.

30.07.03

I phoned the ward this morning to ask about Mother's condition. A nurse told me that there was 'No Change' but five minutes later the ward sister phoned to say that she was much worse. When Patricia and I arrived on the ward an hour later there was no nurse in her room. She lay on her back with her mouth open, looking just as she had for days, but quite dead and cold. She had obviously been dead for many hours.

Thank goodness her sufferings are over. The hospital staff moved swiftly to obtain the death certificate and we were able to certify the death and arrange the funeral without further delay.

With hindsight I regret the decision to transfer her to a Medical Observation Unit, focused on investigation and treatment, rather than to a Palliative Care Unit. At aged 98 she was clearly dying but I had remembered her wish to live to see Caz (Caroline), her third grand-daughter, married in August, and this blinded me to the growing evidence that she was not going to make it.

It is now clear that my mother had died of sepsis caused by a fatal strain of *E. coli*. *Escherichia coli* is very common in the bowel, however, in very young and very old people, with impaired immune responses, it can cause sepsis and be rapidly fatal.

The internet contains many essays on the treatment of sepsis but the only plan is for cure, no attention is given to palliative care or hospice even when the patient is, like my mother, in extreme old age. The fact that sepsis can sometimes be cured seems to blind the medical staff to the fact that, in old age, life is a fatal disease; her time had come. The diagnosis was unimportant. I regret that I did not act sooner to persuade the medical team to introduce palliative care.

In this case the palliative care nurse had come as soon as she was called and set up a continuous syringe driver strapped to Mother's arm to deliver an opioid drug in sufficient dosage to relieve pain without knocking her out. Mum knew that she was dying and was able to say 'Goodbye' to her close family in the best possible way. I regret that I did not stay over the last night of her life but, knowing Mum, she may have waited to let go of life until the visitors were all gone and the room quiet. I hope so.

Her funeral followed the same pattern as that of Eric, her husband:

7.08.03

On a glorious summer day the chapel at Garston Crematorium was packed with people of all ages who had come to say 'Goodbye' to Mother. Roger and myself, with Tessa and Patricia, followed the coffin as an organist played extracts from Verdi and other operatic composers whom Mother had heard in her visits to Covent Garden Opera House. The service was taken by a lay preacher who knew her through the Radlett Music Club. Keelin Watson sang 'Pie Jesu' from Fauré's Requiem and Roger, at mother's own request, read the piece in Ecclesiastes about life's harvest.

> For everything there is a season, a time for every activity under heaven.
> A time to be born and a time to die.
> A time to plant and a time to harvest...
> (NCT Ecclesiastes 3.v.1–2.)

The three generations, children, grandchildren and great grandchildren were represented by myself, Brandon and Alex to read eulogies. As the preacher spoke the words 'Lord, now lettest thou thy servant depart in peace' a curtain closed and she was gone.

Fifty or so people returned to mother's house for the wake which had been prepared with loving care by her carer Ruth and several neighbours. We stood, talked and reminisced while John Hughes took pictures. This was the last of many parties that Mother had hosted at Long Meadow and it seemed strange that she was not there to greet the guests. The only survivor of her closest friends, Daphie Horden, was in tears much of the time and Wanda, the grand-daughter who had lived with her for a while, also shared the tears, but the rest of us felt little need to mourn. In fact, the party was generally cheerful as seems fitting in the wake of a long life well lived.

My most vivid recollection is of her great grandson, Alex, standing proudly between Brandon and myself and nodding his head and laughing as Brandon described his own memories of his grandmother. I have been inundated with cards and letters of sympathy but have been too busy to grieve.

III

Although my attachment to my mother had always been stronger than that to my father, his untimely death had given rise to much greater grief than that of my mother. Her death had put an end to her suffering and given rise to a feeling of relief. But I deeply regret my failure to resist the doctor's attempts to prolong her life, to give her the opportunity to die at home and to provide pain relief when and where it was most needed.

As I, in my turn, pass my 92nd year and face the prospect of my own death, my mother's experience is a harsh reminder that doctors are not necessarily the best people to prepare people for death. True palliative care can control most of the physical symptoms but more is needed. I once upset Cicely Saunders by reminding her, unfairly, of the words of Tom Lehrer's song.

> He's a cure for all your sorrows,
> He's' a cure for your distress,
> It's the old dope pedlar,
> With his powdered happiness.

So, in all humility, I expect no funeral better than the traditional, ramshackle vestige of Christian liturgy interspersed with eulogies from those who love me and a glimpse of the glorious Missa Brevis, written for Patricia, conducted by its composer, Michael Cayton, and sung by members of the Chiltern Choir. I hope that the congregation will find in my death a good ending.

7

Death, Dislocation and Discovery over Five (or Should that Be Six or Even Seven?) Decades

Rosaline S. Barbour

Introduction

As Woodthorpe points out: '(e)veryone is an "insider" when it comes to death, due to its universal reach' (2011, p. 100). This is one of the premises of this volume, the editors having invited contributors, as fellow academics, to write about the deaths of their parents. Death always seems to catch us on the hop, with a mix of burning hurt and bewilderment – even for those who are well-versed in the sociology of death and dying. Here, I reflect on my experiences in the wake of my father's death 52 years ago in the late 1960s, and my mother's more recent death 15 years ago (in the middle of the first decade of the twenty-first century). Over the five decades that span my experiences of the death of my two parents, social mores have certainly undergone significant changes and this sets the scene for a re-examination of my own experiences. The comment in parentheses in the title of this chapter acknowledges that reflection and

R. S. Barbour (✉)
The Open University, Milton Keynes, UK
e-mail: rose.barbour@open.ac.uk

engagement continue well beyond the actual death and immediate period of bereavement.

The burgeoning field of death studies notwithstanding, and the many parallels identified, the experience remains for each of us, at least in some respects, unique. However, bereavement and our responses are mediated by a host of other factors, which merit unpicking in order to gain some analytical – indeed, sociological – insights into what would otherwise remain an isolated personal experience.

Writing this piece has involved reliving and sometimes dramatically re-interpreting long-past events. As Letherby attests: '… the 'I' who writes is not singular but plural, enmeshed in a web of relational interdependencies' (Brennan and Letherby 2017, p. 164) – for me this has most notably meant interacting with my former self/selves. It has involved remembering, re-casting, re-constructing and layering of meaning.

Of course, memory is a somewhat unreliable and potentially mischievous thing. As the journalist Deborah Orr observes in her posthumously published memoir of a Scottish childhood (in many respects reminiscent of my own): 'Yet old memories shape you, whether they're real, imagined, a dream, a photograph you've seen or someone else's memory, passed on through your own perfidious filter.' (2020, p. 19)

Further, Brennan and Letherby argue that auto/biography is rigorous precisely because it highlights explicitly the social location of the researcher and makes clear their 'role in the process of *constructing* rather than discovering the story/the knowledge' (2017, p. 157). This I have tried to do, being careful not to take advantage of my narrative privilege (Adams 2008) in order to impute, without good reason, thoughts and insights to my former self/selves.

For Brose, '(T)he (professional) biography mediates between subjective and social time structures, whose synchronization remains constantly "precarious"' (1982, p. 387, paraphrased/translated by Bergmann 1992). As such, it occupies what Rose would call a 'psy-shaped space' – an 'internal zone' 'with its own characteristics' that lies within each human being. Rose justifies invoking psychology in this description, even though its (i.e. psy-shaped space's) 'relation to the complex and contradictory domain of authorized psychological knowledge is one of bricolage, translation and hybridization' (Rose 1999, afterword, p. 265). It is this subjectified environment that provides the ethical repertoires for those who are only 'professionals' of themselves – 'experts of their own existence.' (1999, p. 265). Within a 'psy-shaped space' '… a plurality of forms of selfhood are represented as solutions to the dilemmas of existence, shaped by age, gender, class, race and much more' (Rose 1999, p. 265). My account, accordingly, invokes social and cultural time, biographical time, age, gender, social class, and locality, straying even into religious beliefs and political affiliations – an illustration, perhaps, of the uncertainty, plurality and fluidity that characterise the 'liquid modernity' articulated by Bauman (2000).

A sociologist is never really 'off duty' and sociology can prove to be a valuable resource in difficult times. As Letherby cogently puts it: 'sociology, in turn, affects the way that I do grief' (Brennan and Letherby 2017, p. 163). Grief – or at least, re-visiting of the experience of the death of both of my parents – for me has led to a re-examination and re-evaluation of relevant sociological theories, all concerned with elaborating the relationship between self and society in its many forms.

My First Encounter with 'Doing Death'

My father died in 1968, two days after my 16th birthday. This followed a lengthy period of hospitalisation, following a heart attack. My mother visited him every day, courtesy of a more affluent friend who elected to drive her the 26 miles between our home in Forres (in Morayshire, Scotland) and the hospital in Inverness, while I visited at weekends. Over the first few weeks he spent in hospital I studied for and sat my 'O' level exams, before catching chickenpox, which – due to my father's immunosuppressed status – prevented me for six weeks from visiting the hospital (a difficult situation currently mirrored by the situation of many during the COVID-19 pandemic). This was rendered especially challenging, since the further complication of a blood clot necessitated having his leg amputated, but only after an agonising wait until he was deemed strong enough to withstand this operation. Unable to visit him over this period, I was prevented from seeing him in person prior to this operation, when his chances of survival were 'touch-and-go'. I took to writing him daily letters to be delivered by my mother, who reported that he was delighted at such unexpected evidence of how much I cared about him. Miraculously he survived the operation and eventually we had an emotive reunion on the hospital ward, with all three of us (my father, mother and myself) shedding tears of joy. My father told me he had never realised how much I loved him until receiving my regular letters.

By this time, I had a summer job at a local hotel, making beds, washing dishes, and cleaning, but visited whenever my schedule allowed. My (successful) 'O' level results arrived on my 16th birthday, just after my father had suffered a relapse, having, it was thought, caught a chill while being fitted for an artificial leg. He was told of my results by my mother and had professed himself 'very proud'. Since I was an only child this was, possibly, all the more meaningful for him. Two days later he died, having, it was thought, suffered a further heart attack. The run-up to his death was, thus, both agonisingly protracted and sudden. My mother had kept me fully informed of my father's progress and setbacks and I had also heard her telling the story to various acquaintances who asked how he was getting on. However, perhaps we had 'let our guard down' a bit, having rejoiced at his achieving the milestone of getting fitted for his artificial leg, and were, consequently, less prepared – if, indeed, one can ever be prepared – for his death.

In the run-up to the funeral I was informed by my mother and maternal grandmother (with whom we lived) that women did not attend the cemetery for the interment. Like the conforming (working class) women (and girl) that we were, we were left, instead, to adjust to a suddenly empty house and to prepare yet more tea for the returning male mourners. This involved considerable work, as 'tea' was not a term to be taken lightly, involving the preparation of copious amounts of sandwiches, cakes and biscuits (some of which had been provided by female friends and neighbours, a couple of whom stayed out of sight in the kitchen to bustle about and help). The energy that went into this left no doubt that it was considered important to 'put on a good spread'.

However, events nevertheless conspired to allocate me a central role. Although I had not previously realised, we were observing a specifically Scottish tradition, whereby male relatives each take a cord and lower the coffin into the grave. Either the undertakers – or, in the case of our family's variant, the most 'senior' male relative – is charged with furnishing each identified mourner with the appropriate small printed card, with a diagram of the coffin and location of each numbered cord.

My father's (identical twin) brother, whose role this supposedly was, was too overcome with grief (and, possibly, intimations of his own mortality) to talk sensibly and kept shaking his head when anyone looked expectantly in his direction or motioned to him that it was time to give out the cards. (This was prior to the cortege leaving our house, where the eulogy and funeral tea had been hosted.) Less than a week after my sixteenth birthday, then, I found myself having to assume responsibility for allocating coffin cords to male relatives and friends. I reasoned that someone had to carry out this task and no-one appeared to take offence at my stepping in. I had already gone to register the death, as my mother was too upset to venture out of the house. We didn't have a telephone, so this had necessitated a visit to the municipal offices. I realised, and quietly accepted, at the time, that these adults – my mother and uncle – both of whom I had somehow expected to manage the situation, were unable to fulfil my expectations. However, these expectations were, in equal part, vague, but unquestioned. It now occurs, with the benefit, or over-layering, of experience, that my stepping into these unanticipated roles marked a progression from being a child to assuming responsibility as an emergent young adult. Given that attendance at the graveside and the taking of coffin cords were privileges/responsibilities reserved for men I had also crossed the boundary conferred by gender.

Aftermath

The only person with whom I discussed my father's death was my mother. My friends did not mention it at all, but I noted that they took pains to be especially kind towards me, while appearing relieved that I had not lost my sense of humour and capacity for enjoying myself.

My grandmother, with whom we had lived since my grandfather's death (when I was three years old) died within a year of my father. Possibly because I was still grieving for my father (alongside my mother), this death does not particularly stand out in my memory. In some ways it was a relief, as my grandmother had been suffering from Alzheimer's for several years. As a family, prior to my father's death, we had felt we were almost at breaking point in terms of coping with her behaviour and associated wandering, with the added concern regarding her frailty – the enduring consequences of the onset of polio as a young wife and mother. Uncannily, from the time of my father's hospital admission until her own death, my grandmother's behaviour, although challenging, reverted to a level at which my mother and I could just about cope.

After my grandmother's death, my mother courageously set about re-making her life, obtaining a housekeeper's job at a private boarding house, where she gradually increased her hours and responsibilities. Also, with encouragement from a friend, she started evening classes in woodwork (one of my father's many skills). Meantime, I had been offered a place at university. Although I had unconditional acceptance from all universities to which I had applied, I opted for Aberdeen, which was the one closest to home. Around this time my mother was being pressured to consider moving to a smaller council house, since the assumption appeared to be that I would be moving out permanently. I don't recall there ever having been a discussion, but it was decided that my mother would move with me to the city. Although I did not realise it at the time, this played an important role in shaping – and significantly curtailing – my experience as a student, living, initially in a residential caravan on the outskirts of the city. My comings and goings were compromised by my mother's steadfast refusal to have a telephone installed. (This followed the pattern in our previous home, news of my father's death having had to be relayed by a neighbour who lived three doors down from us.)

Perhaps still grieving and attempting to start afresh, my mother, for the first two years following her relocation to Aberdeen, assiduously avoided all ties with our former lives. She did forge a new life for herself, going to work, first in a department store and later – having (with my encouragement and support) attended evening classes at college and obtained some 'O' levels – at the 'Council Offices'. She even (after persistent suggestions and help from my erstwhile – middle class – boyfriend and his older solicitor brother) managed to buy a small flat in a residential area much closer to the city centre. She lived to enjoy nearly 20 years of retirement on a reasonable work pension, which provided for her modest lifestyle.

In the course of our third year in our new city I met Mike, who was to become my husband. We had a lot in common, as he had also come from a working-class family and had given up his work as a time-served and approved electrician to pursue further education. Mike had already suggested to me that the reason for my mother's rift from friends and family in my 'home town' was, in all likelihood, due to her having refused to listen to concerned 'others', who had probably advised her against moving with me when I left for university. I then encouraged my mother to contact a couple of her friends and wrote to her cousin, who still lived in the village where they had both grown up. This had the desired result and my mother resumed contact with these significant others, taking holidays with these three individuals and, even, returning to Forres. She did not, however, reinitiate contact with my father's family, which in retrospect seems odd, although only now I can begin to work out possible reasons for her reluctance.

I had taken Mike to visit friends in Forres not long after meeting him and enjoyed showing him around all my old haunts, including the shop that sold my favourite ice-cream. The owner, who had been a close friend of my uncle's (my father's twin brother), remembered me and greeted me enthusiastically. Shortly afterwards, while walking down the road, we were hailed by a man running after us, who turned out to be my uncle Jimmy (who must have received a phone call from his friend). He appeared to be delighted to see me and shook hands enthusiastically with Mike. For some reason, it did not seem to occur to either of us to exchange contact details, since I assumed that my uncle had my mother's address. I later explained to Mike that this could perhaps stand in for meeting my deceased father, given their striking resemblance.

As a child, however, I hadn't really processed this uncanny duplication of features – perhaps since their gestures and facial expressions when interacting with me were markedly different. However, I recall my incredulity when one of my acquaintances asked, shortly after my father's death, 'Don't you find it really hard to still see your uncle?' Somewhat taken aback, I replied, 'No – why would I?' She elaborated: 'Well, they look so alike', to which I retorted, 'Well, not to me, they don't', leaving her looking puzzled. Perhaps, then, with the benefit of hindsight, this was why my mother studiously avoided making contact with my uncle. To grow up from birth with identical twin brothers as a backdrop is probably very different to meeting and marrying one of these men (when my mother was in her late 20s and my father in his mid-40s).

Following completion of my PhD, Mike and I made the first of what were to be many geographical moves in order to pursue our careers, characterised, for me, by a succession of short-term contracts over the next 20 years (including one post back in Aberdeen where my mother still lived). Mike's trajectory proved to be even more perilous, as there were very few jobs in his specialist area, resulting in very lengthy periods of unemployment. While back working on a research project in Aberdeen I tended to arrange to meet my mother for lunch, often driving her to a country pub or restaurant. On reflection, I'm not sure whether this was spurred by the desire to provide a treat for her or by a preference for meeting on 'neutral ground'.

Inevitably, perhaps, given the distance – both geographical and in terms of lifestyle –my mother and I grew apart over time and successive career moves, although we stayed in regular contact. She took a great deal of pleasure in the time she spent with our son, Alasdair (born 14 years after we married and a welcome surprise for a 'grandmother-in-waiting'). As a young child, Alasdair occasionally had sleepovers with her and she delighted in fussing over the preparations for these visits.

My mother's health was marred by a succession of illnesses, including hyperthyroidism, arteriosclerosis, and an emergency hospital admission for a perforated ulcer. It proved to be challenging and frustrating to glean information about her condition, due to geographical distance and the need to rely on somewhat garbled accounts from my mother – and, on the occasion of the emergency hospital admission, the friend who had posed as 'next of kin'. This was entirely in keeping with my mother's characteristic diffidence combined with her pride in not bothering or making demands of anyone. She was far from alone in this, as such behaviour is relatively common amongst Scots from the Moray coast, and, indeed, the whole of the north east of the country.

Encouraged by the success of an 80th birthday lunch (with her cousin and my father's cousin) that I had organised for my mother, I planned a weekend stay further from home to mark her 82nd birthday. It was when, on waking up one morning in our twin bedroom and seeing my mother mistakenly trying to don my cardigan, that I was forced to acknowledge how serious her own Alzheimer's had become. This observation was particularly striking, since the cardigan in question was a vivid shade of green – a colour that my mother had always studiously avoided, insisting it was unlucky. My mother's attachment to what was, in effect, a medieval superstition – deriving from the colour of the Islamic flag of the Moorish slavers (Dearden 1976) – was as inexplicable and incongruous as it was firm and unwavering. Clearly the time had come, however, to accept that my mother could not continue to live independently and required residential care. We managed to find a care home that suited her needs and she lived there for the next 18 months or so before she died.

Re-engaging with Death

This time around, I was the executor and (as only child) the person responsible for making all the decisions in the 'uncertain world' that the bereaved face (Hockey et al. 2001). Exley, in a review article, paraphrases their conclusions: 'The world of the bereaved is …one of few 'rules', in which, in late modernity the person is left to draw on traditional practices of grieving and memorial combined with more idiosyncratic choices, to try to do the "right thing"' (2004, p. 11).

The first 'uncertainty' that I faced related to the timing of the funeral and what I – mistakenly, as it turned out – had assumed was a short turn-around time. From somewhere –probably discussions surrounding my father's funeral – I had formed the 'certainty' that burial needed to take place after an interval of no longer than three days following the death. In telephone conversations with the funeral director I had invoked this idea and the person on the other end of the line did not refute this assumption. It was only during the third telephone call with this 'firm' that it was revealed that 'the body' could be 'kept' for later burial. This was a revelation to me and meant that I need not, as I had planned, make a hurried return from our holiday home in France, having arrived there, alone, on the day of my mother's death and intending to spend ten days or so before flying back to Scotland. Presumably 'the body' was going to be refrigerated, but I seethed at the withholding of this crucial information, raging, in phone calls to my husband in our home in Scotland, about 'the ridiculous attachment to needless euphemism in the face of the reality of death'. Indeed, for some considerable time afterwards I took it upon myself to impart to anyone who might be interested, this hard-won piece of 'essential information'.

At my father's funeral service, the minister, whom I'd known via Sunday School and Bible Class delivered what, on reflection, was really an 'off the peg' oration, my father having, under duress, been a regular, but somewhat disengaged church-goer. This time around, when making arrangements for my mother's funeral, the current incumbent at the same church, in 2005, had liaised with me (at the time in France) by phone and email and I'd furnished quite a bit of information about my mother's life and interests. I wished to avoid the somewhat impersonal renditions at both my father's and my grandmother's funerals and had, undoubtedly, also been influenced by the changes in funeral practice that had evolved over the intervening years. These shifts were characterised by the growing prevalence of secular alternatives (which would have certainly been my own preferred route) and natural burials, complete with idiosyncratic touches and a broadening of ideas as to what was 'acceptable'.

My mother and, to an extent, my grandmother (although, by this stage partly diminished by Alzheimer's) had been on hand to oversee my choice of clothes for my father's funeral, slightly surprising me by ruling that my new mini skirt would be acceptable attire. This time around I was left to my own devices and elected to wear my 'go to' brown trouser suit – veteran of many academic meetings – suitably modest, but not 'showy'.

At the graveside the minister asked whether I was intending to take a cord – something I hadn't considered as a possibility (especially given my former experience). In retrospect, I'm surprised at the extent to which I had, apparently, internalised gendered – and, it would appear, outdated – expectations about how I should behave at this funeral. All these years later, it seemed I still entertained the worry about what others might think – the pursuit of 'respectability' – that 'most ubiquitous signifier of class' (Skeggs 1997, p. 1).

When I hesitated about taking a cord, the minister reminded me that I had just one chance to do this and added that lots of women now did this. I was surprised at how challenging this was – perhaps due to the somewhat overzealous efforts of our strong 17-year-old son. The minister had said that he'd hold my handbag and, at the end of the oration, he handed it back, saying 'You'd better take this – it's really not my colour'. This made me laugh and seemed light years away from the pomp and unnecessary coldness of the approach taken at my father's funeral. I was also very impressed at his apparent ability to 'read' me and to know that this comment would not cause me offence or be deemed inappropriate.

My mother had long expressed the desire to be buried alongside my father, which inevitably brought back memories of visiting my father's grave for the first time. The gravestone which my mother and I had chosen was suitably modest – medium sized, black granite with a thistle engraved at the top. While the 'old cemetery' in another part of the town featured many elaborate Victorian headstones, those in the 'new cemetery' were generally of the same order as ours – apart from those of local families of Italian origin, which frequently boasted a photograph of the deceased. Frith observes that the cemetery can be 'a space where families communicate their wealth, social status and aesthetic taste' (2005, p. xix). The converse can also apply – our choice reflected not just our taste, but our desire not to stand out from the crowd – in short to 'know our place'.

The inscription on the gravestone – chiselled after the stipulated interval following my father's funeral – was in simple gold lettering, giving my father's name, dates and stating that he was the 'beloved husband of Susanna MacLeod Souter.' While I had never questioned it at the time, it came to me, reading this inscription as we assembled around my father's (and about to be mother's) grave, that I was completely written out of this earlier process, not even having merited a mention on the gravestone (although I remain unsure as to the extent to which this is, or was then, common practice). Looking at the inscription, the minister provided – as an apparently casual observation – the comment that proved to be perhaps the most comforting of all, remarking, 'Thirty-seven years – it's a long time to be a widow.' My mother had grieved deeply and protractedly and it was certainly possible to view her life after my father's death as manifestly diminished.

While not subscribing to the notion that she was at long last re-joining my father, I felt glad that her suffering was, at least, at an end. One unlooked-for benefit of Alzheimer's which assailed her in her final years – the 'disadvantaged dying' of which Exley (2004) speaks – was that she did not appear to remember my father, although she would, occasionally, when I visited her at her care home, ask where her own parents were. As she was insistent in her quest for answers to this question, I felt compelled to gently remind her that they were dead. When she would burst into tears, I found that the best way to calm her down was to mention that the person in question would have been 116 years old or so. (Writing this on 18th May, I realise that this would have been my father's 114th birthday.)

Continuity, Distance and Dislocation

Such chronological musings as those above relating to the age my father would have attained, do also, of course, presage one's own decline and death. While this is inevitable it is not necessarily readily internalised:

> as Updike (in *Toward the End of Time*) illustrates, we aren't all screaming (about the proximity of death) partly because we are never fully convinced by the age we are, the age that others, including one's own mirror, together conspire to bestow upon us. (Segal 2013, p. 158)

This rang true for me, and on further reflection, part of the reason for this was also, perhaps, the realisation that I had, in effect, been the 'adult' in our relationship for some time, starting with the responsibilities I had assumed when my father died, and further compounded by the assault of Alzheimer's on my mother's capacity to make decisions for herself.

Returning to the town where I was born and had spent the first 18 years of my life transported me back in time and, coupled with my recent bereavement, had the effect of threatening my somewhat unsteady confidence; partly due to my lack of familiarity with the conventions and rituals surrounding burial ceremonies, and partly due to my hazy recollections of this small town (since my mother had also relocated to the city where

I studied as an undergraduate and post graduate). Not only had I returned infrequently to Forres, I had subsequently moved many times (in addition to three moves within the city where I was studying). I had experienced considerable disruption, having moved (not once – but twice) from one end of the UK to the other and to various points in between, to take up various short-term research contracts.

Given the precarious nature of such employment, we compromised by electing to live between two places (purchasing four additional properties and renting a further two different properties in order to accommodate five fixed-term posts and one permanent post). During this period, we also moved our family home three times by choice (only once for work). Thus, profound dislocation – frequently accompanied by financial losses – was a permanent feature not just of my professional life, but also of my family life. Enumerating these many moves today graphically highlights for me the extent of the dislocation and expense (both of energy and money) involved – particularly as all of these moves involved us in renovating run-down (and, consequently, affordable) properties. These upheavals have all conspired to make for an exceedingly tenuous 'sense of belonging'. My life has been markedly different from that of my parents, my mother having been born and raised only nine miles from Forres, while my father lived there throughout his 62 years. Even my mother's subsequent move to Aberdeen at the age of 49 involved a relatively short distance of 78 miles – still within the embrace of the somewhat distinctive culture of the north east of Scotland.

As there had been some delay between my mother's death and the funeral, I had the opportunity to publicise the graveside service and long-lost relatives and even a school friend turned up. It was surprisingly enjoyable to reconnect with these individuals, including an elderly white-haired man, who, of course, had to introduce himself, given my lengthy absence from the town. This individual, James (now apparently called 'Jim' by everyone else), had been my favourite cousin as a child some 13 years younger than him (and was the son of my uncle Jimmy, my father's twin).

All of the individuals attending the service had continued to live locally, while I had left, first of all to attend university in Aberdeen (accompanied by my mother, who seems, looking back from today's vantage point, to have cut virtually all ties). Nearly three years previously, in order to celebrate my mother's 80th birthday, I had organised a surprise stay in a nice hotel, with a lunch along with my mother's cousin and my father's cousin – neither of whom my mother had seen for some time. My father's cousin, Les, was present at the graveside and took a cord, while my mother's cousin was, by this stage, living in a care home, and judged by the staff there to be too confused to attend. The cemetery is adjacent to the field where Les ran a pony trekking business and I had regularly, as an 8–14-year-old, chatted amicably with John the gravedigger while he went about his business, revived by frequent cups of tea and home baking provided by his wife (always referred to by us as Mrs Donaldson), who often also welcomed us children to the table. When visiting my father's grave to look at the wreaths the day after the funeral I had speculated as to why John (whom I had spotted working in the graveyard), hadn't come to greet us. My mother explained that he was being respectful and giving us a bit of space. The Donaldson family, by the time of my mother's death, were, of course, long-gone, but I felt strangely soothed by my easy familiarity with the place, although, of course, the cemetery had expanded greatly.

The whole experience was characterised – apart from the inevitable grief – by a mixture of nostalgia, and regret. Incredibly, given that I hadn't seen my favourite cousin since my father's funeral 37 years previously – and had not made the efforts to stay in touch described by Hanley (2017), except in my imagination – James still sensed when it was best to put a consoling arm around my shoulders and when to leave me alone. None of the other people present at the graveside had known me as a very young child and refrained from making similar overtures. Looking back on the day it occurs to me that I felt more comfortable with the minister (whom I had met for the first time the previous evening) than I did with the 'supporting cast' who were simultaneously 'known' and yet 'unknown'.

Our nuclear family home at the time of my mother's death was some 140 miles from my childhood home, where the funeral was to take place and the cemetery was located some distance from Aberdeen, where my mother had lived for the past 35 years. This narrowed down options and my husband, son and myself had decided to stay for two nights in the hotel closest to the graveyard (which also happened to be the one where

I had taken my mother to celebrate her 80th birthday). This, then, was the obvious choice for the post-funeral gathering – a soup and sandwich lunch, which was the most appropriate given the late morning timing of the funeral. I was not entirely sure why – given that Mike and I were regular and enthusiastic hosts of parties and various gatherings – but I felt considerable, if slightly guilty, relief that the funeral lunch was to be held in a neutral space rather than our home. It was a relatively enjoyable and uplifting event, allowing me to have an informal chat with everyone present.

Social Class

My experiences and reactions were, of course, mitigated by the passage of time – although relatively few intervening funerals. The change of which I was most acutely aware, however, was that of having drifted – or, perhaps, on further reflection, having persevered and struggled – into another social class, by virtue of my education and employment as an academic. My more distressing feelings throughout the day of my mother's funeral were coupled with a not totally unpleasant sense of having stepped outside the confines of my previous life. Lindsay Hanley, in her book *Respectable*, captures very well the conflicting emotions involved in the sense of dislocation which I experienced:

> Changing class is like emigrating from one side of the world to the other, where you have to rescind your old passport, learn a new language and make gargantuan efforts if you are not to lose touch completely with the people and habits of your old life, even if they are among the relationships and things that are dearest to your heart. (Hanley 2017, p.x)

In terms of my extended family I was – and remain – the first and only person (with the exception of our son) to have attended university. My mother had been Dux (the top pupil) of her village school and proudly displayed the commemorating photograph, which had appeared in the local paper (the only photograph of her as a child that I recall having seen). She explained that the family could not afford to keep more than one child at school beyond the age of 14 (when she had left) and that her younger brother was accorded this privilege.

During my time as an undergraduate in the early 1970s it became suddenly, and inexplicably, fashionable to claim working class origins and connections – however erroneously. I could, of course, win hands down at this 'game', being able to cite – in my case truthfully – my father's role (amongst other duties at the Royal Air Force base where he had been employed) as bin man. As a youngster I had eagerly celebrated those rare occasions when he and his colleagues would park the truck outside our council house and come indoors for afternoon tea and cakes, providing me with a rare and much-prized opportunity to socialise in male company. Otherwise I resigned myself to distantly observing, in the passing, my father standing on the street corner with his friends, talking and smoking. The rubbish truck made quite an impression on me (possibly because we didn't own a car) and I felt incredibly proud when it parked outside – always a surprise for me, although not for my mother and grandmother, who had prepared the tea, cakes and biscuits. I was puzzled and upset when my attempted rendition of 'My old man's a dustman' (a popular refrain at the time) – and intended kindly/proudly – invoked extreme displeasure from my father. He certainly had a temper and, it was alleged, I had inherited this trait from him. Indeed, when he succumbed to the heart attack that would protractedly lead to his death (some months later) we were having one of our many altercations – probably about something incredibly trivial, as I cannot recall the source of our disagreement.

Since I felt largely culpable for my father's heart attack – despite the doctor's assessment that my father's smoking had greatly impaired his health – I had found particularly challenging my enforced absence from his hospital bedside. Friends were supportive – although employing very few words to convey this. There had been no special dispensation at school, however. My English teacher, who had always manifested a visceral dislike of me, chose to demand (without the week's warning unfailingly accorded us prior to my chickenpox-induced absence) that I present my essay to the class. This teacher suspected that I was somehow cheating and regularly sought to humiliate me. Looking back with what I hope is the greater tolerance accorded by the passage of time and sociological insight, I realise that he was equally a prisoner of expectations shaped by his social class position and that, for him, my high marks were somehow an aberration requiring explanation.

I started university two years after my father's death. The disingenuous embracing, by my fellow undergraduate students, of working class credentials possibly blunted my sense of dislocation and certainly did not prepare me for what was to come as I pursued an academic career (largely through default rather than closely articulated design). In retrospect I have come to recognise just how challenging I had found – and continued to find – the world of academia. A seam of class privilege runs through the entire venture, causing insecurity and multiple hurts for those of us with humble origins: from the casually disdainful ex-public schoolboy who conducted my (unsuccessful) postdoctoral job interview, dressed in T-shirt and jeans and with his long legs crossed and resting on the table; to many comments from (mostly – but not exclusively – male) colleagues over the ensuing years, along the lines of 'I never had you down as someone who … likes opera/attends gallery openings'.

My mother's fervent – although unspoken – wish was that I might, just might, become a teacher. She was perplexed when I continued my studies to complete a doctorate, despite having married (at the age of 20) while still an undergraduate, since settling for a first degree and going to teacher training college, would, in her eyes, have afforded the perfect opportunity to combine a 'career' and motherhood. Looking back from today's vantage point, 20 seems a very young age for committing to marriage, although, in working class circles at this time, one was deemed to be virtually 'past it' at this age. Throughout my writing of this piece, I've discussed most of my observations with Mike – in contrast to the odd mention of an idea arising during the preparation of many articles and several books. When I reflected that I had been exceedingly lucky, as the desire to escape my mother's meticulous oversight could easily have led me into a disastrous marriage, my husband of 47 years replied in his self-deprecating way, 'Well, maybe you did!'. He too grew up in the north east of Scotland and is undoubtedly still marked by this working-class upbringing and unsentimental – at times even taciturn – approach to life. There is, of course, a grain of truth in his facetious comment, as our lives were undoubtedly rendered more difficult – although, simultaneously comforting – by the shared dislocation (in terms of class and place) we have experienced.

At university I had encountered feminism and, thereafter for some considerable time, continued to view everything through the prism of gender rather than social class – which, in the context of my own life, is probably even more significant. Adhering to the dictum 'the personal is political', I was resolute in my ambitions and, perhaps, dismissed rather harshly my mother's musings about my future. My mother certainly made up for such slights (real or imagined on her part) when I proudly – but mistakenly – shared with her my delight at having been cited for the very first time. She perused the proffered article and remarked, scathingly, 'Well, he certainly doesn't think much of you – he calls you 'Barbour!' This hurt and amused me in equal measure.

This incident calls to mind the many insights of the novelist, poet, and playwright Jessie Kesson (an astute commentator on north east of Scotland mores) who spent her early childhood only a few miles from where my mother was born and grew up. Kesson, who died in 1993, and whose work is celebrated in an anthology, has one of her characters in a (previously unpublished) short story describe her mother as someone 'who loved me in her own bitter way' (Kesson 2000).

Gaining Analytical Purchase

In life – and, I was finding, in the face of death too – this social class dislocation has caused me to step back and sometimes to look on or look back in some amusement, verging, at times, on disbelief. In between the poignant moments at both funerals, there were moments of amusement and, even, genuine hilarity.

At my father's funeral, when family and friends were having tea and sandwiches prior to the arrival of the minister, I overheard my cousin (he of the later snowy white hair) recounting that the absence of my father's brother-in-law was due to his advanced illness (cancer – my mother later clarified to me in a whisper – although the word itself was never mentioned). My cousin somewhat gleefully explained that the last time this man had been seen – by somebody else – he had 'a head the size of a sugar bowl'. The other surreal moment at my father's funeral was provided by my reliably eccentric aunt Dais(y) (Margueritte) who was my father's younger sister. As the hearse drove away, she tripped across the small lawn, moving surprisingly gracefully despite her considerable bulk, sweeping her hand over her brow in the manner of Saturday matinee actresses and crying, 'Don, Don…' (my father's name). My mother even ventured a faintly amused lift of her eyebrow as this occurred.

The 'head the size of a sugar bowl' comment had struck me as being memorable and out-of-sync, although I was too distressed to think more about this at the time. However, I certainly stored this comment away and have revisited it from time to time (uncannily presaging my career as a qualitative researcher, being exactly, I realise, what one does with field-notes). It struck a chord with me in precisely the way that the comedy series 'Shameless' unfailingly does. Despite having experienced a social class reallocation similar to my own, Mike still cannot bear to watch this television programme, saying that it is simply too painfully close to his own life experience. This reaction is certainly not due to a lack of humour, as, having been the only other person to have overheard the minister's somewhat camp aside at my mother's graveside, he also laughed spontaneously and still fondly recalls his amusement.

My mother's funeral was, by contrast to my father's, shorter and less eventful. Thinking back to this event, and fondly remembering two of my attending cousins who have since died, I have found reassurance in Walter's (1999) assertion, paraphrased by Exley, that wishing to maintain 'meaningful bonds (and relationships) with those who have died should not be seen as 'pathological' grief, but rather as part of the reflexive construction of self-identity and relationships engaged with on a daily basis' (2004).

I was surprised that the son of my mother's closest school friend turned up at my mother's graveside. Although I had only once met him very briefly, our mothers had regularly gone on holiday together (some 10–15 years earlier), generally accompanied by this son, who lived at home and worked, I now recalled, as I took in his eminently suitable attire, at a funeral parlour. He clearly expected to be given a cord, but, with the number of male relatives attending and with my taking a cord myself, there were not enough to allocate him one. He was obviously displeased and left rather pointedly immediately after the graveside service, despite me taking pains to personally invite him to come to the lunch being provided at the nearby hotel. I found myself thinking back to my mother's comments about being on holiday with her friend, Hilda, and this son. Apparently, Hilda used to reassure my mother that there was no need to be modest when dressing and undressing, as 'Finlay's seen it all, with his job'.

Talking about being emotionally affected during fieldwork, Wilkins suggests: 'An analytic exploration is achieved through grasping the behaviour emotionally and then working with and beyond that to sociological insight' (1993, p. 97). In a similar vein, amusement and humour may also hold a key to better understanding the impact and meaning of situations and experiences.

Conclusion

I hope these observations serve to illustrate the complex interweaving of various influences and also underline the uniqueness and rawness of the bereavement experience, despite increasing maturity and analytic – even sociological – insights.

There are two significant gaps in sociological theorising, both of which are relevant in seeking to understand my bereavement experiences through a sociological lens. While the discipline of sociology has traditionally favoured the public realm, there is a growing acknowledgement of the need to engage more with various forms of subjectivity, as documented by commentators, such as Bailey (2000).

The relative neglect of social class in research into death and dying is noted by Howarth (2007), who calls for research into working-class experiences. However, this focuses on working-class cultures, reflecting sociology's fascination with the collective, leading to the 'working classes' being 'massified', as Skeggs (1997, p. 3) puts it. Social class also operates at the individual, and perhaps equally invidious, level – possibly all the more poignant for the lack of recognition given to this aspect. 'Class is something beneath your clothes, under your skin, in your reflexes, in your psyche, at the very core of your being' (Kuhn 1995, p. 98). What, then, of differences between individuals occupying this class position or, indeed, what of situations where there is a clash of cultures or class?

Skeggs (1997) usefully highlights the possibility of using concepts such as 'respectability' as analytical tools. For the upwardly socially mobile individual (or, in our case, couple) the other side of the coin relates to concerns to avoid being seen as 'pretentious'. While my upper middle-class colleagues sometimes questioned my access to various signifiers of cultural capital, these same habits and possessions were likely to elicit a charge (unspoken, of course – but nonetheless disturbing) of 'pretention' from family members and friends occupying a lower social class position. It wasn't until I read Friedman's publication that I came to realise the 'profound psychological imprint of social mobility' (2016, p. 145), which goes some way towards explaining why I would have felt very uneasy about hosting my mother's funeral tea in our home, where our paintings and antiquarian books could have graphically highlighted our social mobility and 'taste' now sharply differentiated from those characterising my 'primary habitus': 'those childhood dispositions that will always act as the 'scaffolding' of habitus' (Wacquant 2014, p. 6 – paraphrased by Friedman 2016, p. 45).

The term 'habitus' was coined by the much-revered French sociologist Bourdieu and speaks to the same theoretical concerns as does Rose's (1999) notion of 'psy-shaped spaces'. Bourdieu talked of the 'contradictions of succession', 'where the upwardly socially mobile experience "success" as "failure", as a betrayal of those who have nurtured and created them'. (Friedman 2016, p. 141). This appears to be an example of an aspect of 'the fractured habitus', reflecting 'the complex relationalities of the contemporary individual – often engaged in unconnected relational matrices' (Silva 2016, pp. 86–87, paraphrasing Bourdieu 2002, p. 510). Silva points out that Bourdieu's views 'shifted over time from a unitary to a more fluid and changing perspective on the "habitus"' (2016, p. 86). For example: the assertion that the habitus is 'an open system of dispositions that is constantly subjected to experiences, and therefore constantly affected by them in a way that reinforces or modifies its structures' (Bourdieu and Wacquant 1992). 'Thus the habitus can be creative and initiate changes in dispositions' (Cockerham 2005).

Silva (2016) argues that Bourdieu's 'consecrated position in the academic field gives him the strength – guts – to transgress and incorporate psychoanalytic thinking together with sociological reflexivity', although he did not further develop the potential of these 'constant negotiations'. Interestingly, it appears that Bourdieu, himself, experienced a dramatic shift in terms of his social class position, having been born into humble circumstances (Friedman 2016). I suspect, that, in the academic milieu which he came to inhabit, such personal revelations – not to mention forays into autobiography – might well have damaged his reputation. This may partly explain why he chose not to extrapolate further on his concept of the 'fractured habitus'.

Aarseth, Layton and Nielsen (2016) point out that 'rapid social transformations or social mobility may entail conditions that are markedly different from those in which the habitus was produced.' They suggest that: 'What appears to be lacking in Bourdieu's theory is a concept of how objective contradictions entwine with relationally produced emotional tension, and how these emotional conflicts are then handled by the subject'. They continue: 'we argue that considering conflicts in the *habitus* provides a potentially productive meeting place between a Bourdieusian and a psychoanalytic relational concept of socialized subjectivity' (2016, p. 150).

Again, this meeting of sociology and psychology might afford the key to better understanding the tensions that can arise for the individual seeking to negotiate those incommensurate 'unconnected relational matrices' (Silva 2016) – affording conflicting sets of expectations and explanations that frequently conspire to deny a sense of wholeness.

From the outset I recognised that writing this chapter, reflecting on the deaths of both of my parents, was going to be an emotional journey. I experienced feelings ranging from mild sadness through all-pervasive discomfort/unease, to real anguish/lament, and I shed quite a few tears. However, what occasioned these emotions – certainly those at the extreme end of the spectrum – were not the memories of my parents' deaths, but the visceral realisation both of the multiple ways and extent to which my life has been beset, shaped, and constrained by the painful ramifications of what Friedman (2016) would term long-range social mobility and the many dislocations involved. As Friedman puts it: 'mobility influences social, familial and intimate relationships, as well as the ontological coherence of the self' (2016, p. 129). I was forced to concede that my hitherto largely unquestioned and casually invoked life narrative – one of happy self-advancement – was inadequate and sometimes misleading, even for myself.

To my surprise, in writing this chapter, I found that critically examining my emotional responses has led me to revisit some strands of sociological theory, to interrogate these and, ultimately, to go some way towards reconciling some conceptual tensions that I have experienced. These tensions have been a feature throughout my engagement with sociology, colouring and troubling my interactions with those parts of sociological theory that have particularly intrigued me. They concern the elusive but nevertheless compelling strand of resonance or dissonance with my own experiences and perceptions. Perhaps sociologists of a qualitative bent inevitably engage in reflexivity, but there are, nevertheless, limits to this – as evidenced by the relative lack of personal revelations in the writing that is eventually submitted for publication. I wonder whether – despite their restraint in terms of academic writing – others privately relate to theory in this way – or is it just me?? (Or is even posing this question merely another vivid manifestation of my 'habitus clivé' and its related self-doubt?)

References

Aarseth, H., Layton, L. and Nielsen, H.B. (2016). "Conflicts in the habitus: The emotional work of becoming modern." *The Sociological Review*, 64(1), 148–165.

Adams, T. E. (2008). A Review of Narrative Ethics. *Qualitative Inquiry*, 14(2), 175–194.

Bailey, J. (2000). Some meanings of 'the private' in sociological thought. *Sociology*, 34(3), 381–401.

Bauman, Z. (2000). *Liquid Modernity*, New Jersey: Wiley.

Bergmann, W. (1992). The problem of time in sociology: An overview of the literature on the state of theory and research on the sociology of time 1900–82. *Time and Society*, 1, 81–134.

Bourdieu, P. (2002). *The Bachelors' Ball*. Cambridge: Polity.
Bourdieu, P. and Wacquant, L. (1992). *An Invitation to a Reflexive Sociology*. Chicago: University of Chicago Press.
Brennan, M. and Letherby, G. (2017). Auto/biographical approaches to researching death and bereavement: Connections, continuing contrasts. *Mortality*, 22(2), 155–169.
Brose, H-G. (1982). Die Vermittlung von sozialen and biographischen Zeitstrukturen. In *Kölner Zeitschrift für Soziologie und Sozialpsychologie*, Sonderheft 24, 385–407.
Cockerham, W. (2005). Health lifestyle theory and the convergence of agency and structure. *Journal of Health and Social Behavior*, 46(1), 51–67.
Dearden, S. (1976). *A Nest of Corsairs: The Fighting Karamanlis of the Barbary Coast*. London: John Murray.
Exley, C. (2004). Review article: The sociology of dying, death and bereavement. *Sociology of Health and Illness*, 26(1), 110–122.
Friedman, S. (2016). Habitus clivé and the emotional work of becoming modern. *The Sociological Review*, 64(1), 129–147.
Frith, R. (2005). Foreword: The body in the sacred garden. In D. Francis, L. Kellaher and G. Neophytou (Eds.) *The Secret Cemetery* (pp.xv-xxii). Oxford: Berg Publishers.
Hanley, L. (2017). *Respectable: Crossing the Class Divide*. London: Penguin.
Hockey, J., Katz, J. and Small, N. (Eds.) (2001). *Grief, Mourning and Death Ritual*. Buckingham: Open University Press.
Howarth, G. (2007). Whatever happened to the working class; An examination of working-class cultures in the sociology of death. *Health Sociology Review*, 16, 425–435.
Kesson, J. (2000). Railway journey. In *Somewhere Beyond: A Jessie Kesson Companion* (pp. 3–9). I. Murray (ed.), Edinburgh: B&W Publishing.
Kuhn, A. (1995). *Family Secrets: Acts of Memory and Imagination*. London: Verso.
Orr, D. (2020). *Motherwell: A Girlhood*, London: Weidenfeld & Nicolson.
Rose, N. (1999). *Governing the Soul: The Shaping of the Private Self*. London: Routledge.
Segal, L. (2013). *Out of Time: The Pleasures and the Perils of Ageing*, London: Verso.
Skeggs, B. (1997). *Formations of Class and Gender*. London: Sage.
Silva, E.B. (2016). Habitus: Beyond sociology. *The Sociological Review*, 64(1), 73–92.

Wacquant, L. (2014). Homines in extremis: What fighting scholars teach us about habitus. *Body and Society*, 20(2), 3–17.

Walter, T. (1999). *The Revival of Death*, London: Routledge.

Wilkins, R. (1993). 'Taking it personally': A note on emotion and autobiography. *Sociology*, 27(1), 93–100.

Woodthorpe, K. (2011). Researching death: Methodological reflections on the management of critical distance. *International Journal of Social Research Methodology*, 14, 99–109.

8

Bereavement, Sacred-Secrecy and Dreams

Douglas Davies

Rationale

This retrospective consideration of my parents' deaths circles around the three ideas of sacred-secrecy, opacity, and personhood. These will need some detailed explanation because they are far from common currency within death studies and because they will help explain why I was, initially, rather hesitant in accepting the invitation to contribute to this volume. However, having accepted, the chapter seemed to generate its own rationale through the interplay of personal reflection and these theoretical perspectives and will, I hope, complement other narratives in this book while also contributing to bereavement and memory theories within death studies.

D. Davies (✉)
University of Durham, Durham, UK
e-mail: Douglas.davies@durham.ac.uk

Accepting Invitations

As for my original hesitation, it lasted some months, and when I did accept the invitation I had no real sense of what I wanted to write, except that the phrase 'sacred secrecy', kept coming to mind. I will explain later not only why it was there in the first place but also why I came to see it as germane in terms of grief, and how two additional notions – 'opacity' and 'personhood'- joined it as complements in a chapter that then assumed a life of its own. Even so, this account remains a 'work in progress', with decades of emotions behind it and, doubtless, further possibilities ahead. Still, leaving the future to its own devices for the moment, what of that invitation and its certain pressure 'to write' on one's parents' deaths? This I found intrinsically problematic, not because of any writers' block, something I have been fortunate enough not to encounter in my publishing career, but because of a degree of personal reticence about being 'public' on what I have, hitherto, deemed 'private' matters. The issue was just what to say and not to say, or more particularly, what to write and not to write. While still pondering that challenging question, nevertheless, I decided to accept the invitation, mindful of the fact that here, as with some but not all other 'invitations', I was party to that complex process of personal and professional networks deeply embedded in reciprocity theory (Mauss 1954; Kujala and Danielsbacka 2019). Academic life, as with much in life at large, frequently depends upon such personal relationships as well as drawing upon professional obligations. This is far from an irrelevant observation because British and many other universities, academies, and organisations depend for their integrity and claims to scholarly standards not only upon mutual professional obligation but also upon levels of trust that emerge across the years. And this is certainly true for death studies, and the various disciplinary bases from which it derives its methods and practices. While this volume reflects such friendship and collegiality perhaps it also achieves something more when those who share a focused interest express aspects of their life and thought that go beyond, or beneath, their usual published work.

Writing Not Speaking

Such personal factors are obviously significant even when someone may not be given to following conventions of social media to express social-selves and inner identity to 'friends' and 'followers'. This is not to deny the value some gain from telling their own stories of loss, and marking memories through online media. Indeed, this chapter may also provide a similar personal benefit even though my own preference is not entirely with 'social media'. Here much depends on the marriage of genre and topic, not least because 'writing' can be quite unlike 'talking', whether engaging with a single friend, a small group of the like-minded, or a larger conference involving diverse attitudes. With writing, nuance is much more difficult because of the vital silences … unfinished … sentences…. in spoken forms, and because of the tone underlying all verbal exchanges, especially intimate and deeply personal ones. Writing remains curious, however, precisely in that sense of running lines and paragraphs, one before another, leaving open the question of priority amid many equally vital elements. Moreover, that linear mode does not seem to me to be the way my mind works in its myriad creative flitting of emotion, mood and memory that must somehow be manipulated into a sensible script and accompanying narrative if one is to avoid anything like free-flowing consciousness. It is now a long time since the French anthropologist Claude Lévi-Strauss (1962) reminded us that the narratives that constitute myths seem to think themselves in us, with much the same occurring when writing shifts into its own zone of flow. Many will also recognise that additionally strange process of reading but not recognising what one wrote some years before, making even our own text as strange a country as any foreign destination. But write I must since I did accept the invitation to share in this collection.

Parental Cameos

Despite these introductory paragraphs, I have a sense that by now you ask, 'Why doesn't he get to the point and tell us what happened?' One answer, echoing my initial uncertainty over this venture, brings me to my first substantial issue enshrined in the notion of 'sacred secrecy'. However, while still maintaining the theoretical tension, let me begin to 'get to the point' by sharing a cameo of my parents, my mother, who died on 22 April 1991, aged 74, and my father on 14 January 1994, aged 81. Already this means a retrospective view across more than 25 years from the time when I was already in my mid-40s to my present seventh decade. This duration covers shifts of image and memory, for the experience of the death of a parent, as with most personal bereavements, is not just the experience of a day or two, or even months or a few years. Indeed, that is a key feature of this particular account. My entire prior life-experience frames it, and the many ensuing years transform it, a point that will recur when I discuss my parents' appearance in my dreams.

While many images, from the photos taken in my old Box-Brownie to more sophisticated cameras, fill a family album that I look at perhaps every couple of years, only one stands framed in my home. In describing this, let me say that I seem to be 'thinking aloud' about some of these things for the first time. This photograph shows the sun-tanned, smiling, faces of a white haired mother and greying-white haired father, both looking out from behind dense foliage of a weeping-willow. One of Father's hands, holds back some leafy branch as both look with the same focus and intent to some near distance. The context was the garden of the house they often visited from Wales when I lived in Nottingham; two significant locations underlying this story. As with all accounts, each moment is a confluence of many others, with this photograph distilling and intensifying many in the album that holds images of our family life including their marriage in St. Cadoc's Church Bedlinog, the Valleys' village of my mother's family, where my father, originally from nearby Gelligaer, came to live. Other photos cover holidays, visits, celebrations, with a few extending to previous and, to me at least, unknown relatives. They include houses, gardens, and dogs. In these my father, Llewellyn James, was always slightly shy and not really wanting to be caught on camera while my mother, Gwladys Evelyn, was ever-ready for the portrait. Indeed, I smile to myself while writing and recalling those dispositions, thinking of just how many tales could be told of them at different times and places.

As for the willow-tree moment, it captures a relaxed, happy, 'natural', and couple-companionate pair. That, perhaps, is why this particular photograph holds pride of place, something I do not think I have consciously or explicitly considered before writing this. Married as very young adults, they were together for more than 50 years before my mother died first and my father just a couple of years later. As with all spouses, they had their joys and sorrows, not least some critical mid-life years when cancer demanded major operations for my mother, with recovery hosting many unexpected years of ongoing companionship. Their one child – myself – arrived after they had already been married a decade, something that involves a distinctive episode of its own, meriting praise for a legendary local General Practitioner, Dr F.H. D'Souza, a splendid Indian Catholic, and surgeon whose repute is easily discoverable online, and to whom my parents, and later myself, owed debts of clinical gratitude – indeed, for being here at all. His very large family included several sons with whom I was at school. He died aged 53, and his grave is near that of my parents in Bedlinog's Graigfargoed Cemetery where, in due course, I anticipate my remains will also lie.

My parents' wider families were important for them as for me. My mother's three sisters and one brother, now all dead, were strongly networked; their parents lived into old age and saw them into adulthood, while my maternal cousins remain important to me. My father had one younger sister, now deceased, but whose five daughters, their children and grand-children, also still live in South Wales. My father's mother died while he was still a child. His father's post-war self was, as far as I can make out, deeply problematic, leaving them to live with an aunt in poor circumstances. Despite gaining a scholarship to one of the most prestigious grammar schools in Wales, he had to leave primary school and work, partly to support his younger sister. As a 14-year-old small boy he started in the mines, continuing there largely until retirement. So much could be said about that, as about my mother as a miner's wife. Let me simply say that, as I write in June 2020, issues of slavery, ethnicities, and Black identity are much in the press – rightly so. Yet my reading of British culture history also notes the enormous blank on the 'slavery' map of constrained lives intensified during the Industrial Revolution whose own 'imperialism' and 'colonialisation' included the intra-UK domination of girls and boys, let alone of men and women, working in factories and mines at an age when, today, many parents curate their offspring's lives to extreme limits. Britain had its own work-slaves, a negativity that remains even as one can deeply appreciate the 'community' and male comradeship of workers and intuitive alliance of their wives. My mother's father had even started in the pits aged 12. The fact that both he, and my father, survived their working lives was remarkable, a credit to their physical strength and mental alertness: all apart from pneumoconiosis or 'the dust', a distinctive health issue for my father, albeit accepted without complaint. As for my mother, she never 'worked' after marrying, but kept the home, my father and myself, and played her part in her family's network. These details are, as it seems to me, integral to my parents' deaths, as to their lives, and help fill my emotional-intellectual canvass of those events.

Absent Details

Also, these details move us closer towards the 'sacred secrecy' motif framing the absence of more intimate, personal and private, details in this chapter. I imagine that for some readers this will be a disappointment since there is a certain 'something', a curiosity and even vicarious pleasure, in glimpsing such moments in other people's lives. I know that, because I also like them in biographies, and I half criticise my own partiality and obscurity over that silent core of this account. Yet, I cannot apologise, and pursue this line because I dislike the prevailing cultural propensity to photograph, record, and reveal 'all' in our days. Even though that 'all' is, inevitably, a highly selective, cosmeticised, curated 'all'. Some may well share this view, others not. Still, we all live as different folk; contexts form us, times bind us, as do the emotional dynamics of our psychological constitutions. And it is with just such dynamics in mind that, shortly, I will consider sacred secrecy, a concept that makes personal sense, and might make sense to you, only in the light of episodes of my own academic trajectory, itself an important aspect of this book, part of whose goal is to speak of our parents' death in the light of our knowledge of 'mortality' and what in more recent years we designate as death studies. Certainly, all knowledge is one, and the confluence of past thoughts and experiences, make us who we are. For me, this has involved a complex interplay of family, core and peripheral friends, colleagues, and networked acquaintances within university and church in the UK and beyond. Factually, none of my family was 'university'; religion-wise my mother's family was Church in Wales, hence my provenance on that score; my father was a very occasional, though happy, attender.

Personal Cameo

What, then, of this author and writer of lines? One academically launched by The Lewis School Pengam, the selective Grammar School of East Glamorgan Valleys and parts of Monmouthshire, for which my father had a 'passed the scholarship' but could not join. In fact, it is only now, in writing, that I realise he had never spoken of that 'scholarship' opportunity. Others told me of it. He was, however, so pleased that I was there and it was excellent when he and my mother would come to events in its old chapel. Moreover, I had, never until now, considered the thoughts such realities might have prompted. This, itself, is a reminder of that whole domain of existence where we do not, when younger, pursue or ask after our parents' life-experiences, being perhaps too preoccupied with our own lives. The present often exerts a pressure that somehow seems to render redundant a questioning of the past, except for those moments when something prompts a personal episode. What I do recall my father rather rhetorically asking me to promise was that I would never go down a mine – itself a cultural motif and personal idiom known by not a few working-class boys of that era in Wales, and for whose fathers 'education' was of the essence. In making that point, and adding that I have never so 'descended', I am almost – but not quite – breaking my approach to 'sacred secrecy', but I do so in respect of those men and women's hard-earned support of their children's education. Such 'education' and its germinating concepts take a lifetime to develop and flourish. In my case involving a two-fold adventure, one engaging social anthropology and sociology, especially focused on religion, notably Mormonism, and death studies, another engaging theology. Between 1966 and 1974 I was inducted to these social scientific and arts-humanities disciplines at Durham and Oxford, classic times and places for those fields. Decades of ensuing interdisciplinary promiscuity, research and teaching, interbred these domains and with some additional interests in psychology and biology generated a body of eclectic work. Prompted by the invitation to write for this book that pool of potential theoretical orientations has yielded the triad of sacred-secrecy, opacity, and personhood as an analytical base for a personal pondering of parental death.

Opacity

While yet again delaying my account of the sacred-secrecy motif, and to prepare for it, I need to insert my theoretical perspective on opacity. This notion struck me decades ago at Nottingham University's Theology Department when teaching a Pastoral Theology course. Coming from a psychological direction it reminded me then, and still does, of the depths of our personhood that are not immediately – nor perhaps ever – accessible to us. This is something that more recent cognitive studies of complex mental operations have made all the clearer, reinforcing the awareness that I do not 'understand' myself in any full sense. Taking the general lead from the 'theory of mind', which prompts us to accept others as 'like' myself in mental capacities and therefore apt for mutual engagement, we might also speak of a 'theory of opacity', involving its own 'unknowns'. If I have some idea of the opacity of myself to myself, then I can be similarly aware of the opaque limitations of others to themselves. So, too, with my parents as partly opaque to me, to themselves, and I think to each other. Moreover, sickness, terminal illness, dying, death, grief, and memory, all carry opacities of their own.

Such thoughts remind me of the theological argument of St Paul in his near ecstatic yet utterly realistic chapter on love – once the stable of church wedding ceremonies – where he speaks of our present human knowledge of things as resembling an image in a not so clear mirror, an image observed – 'through a glass, darkly' (KJV) or 'in a mirror dimly' (RSV). Charles Wesley, in a commentary from an almost former era, neatly catches the 'puzzle' or enigma element of the Greek text on how we see, when saying 'our thoughts … are puzzling, intricate, and everything is a kind of riddle to us', a description that will resonate with many today as they ponder themselves, let alone others (Wesley 1831. Entry on 1. Corinthians 13:12). For Paul, in post-mortal resurrection existence such puzzles would be transformed into clarity. Meanwhile, for all of us I suspect, there remains, as it were, the enigmatic variations of identity, not least when being with a parent while dying and dead, at their funerals, and over the many subsequent years of active and passive memory.

As for those dying-dead circumstances, it is relatively easy to speak of things we can label and socially share: empathy with suffering, the waiting, the minute by minute passing of time, anxiety, fear, breathing, anticipation, expectation, calm, tears, peace, naturalness, stillness, sadness, dismay alongside the poignant reality of events (Mannix 2017). But it is practically impossible 'to describe' now, in retrospect, what was, at the time felt, experienced, encountered, thought, and appropriated into our very embodiment. Feeling is one thing, description after the event is another. Yet it is that second-order activity that easily prevails in the retrospective narrative. It is precisely in the death-bed context that one opacity meets another, whether in eye-to-eye, or hand-to-hand, meeting and touch. And this is positive not negative. To know that many of us carry such past moments with us is an important reality of its own, even if, and perhaps especially if, every detail is kept private. For such episodes of embodiment are, existentially, profound in and of themselves, while much else can be a story told, a narrative constructed and shared after the event.

Moreover, being together during serious illness, terminal diagnosis, and in moving to the end of life is not, in some respects totally unlike healthy-togetherness in terms of sustaining opacities. This is, itself, a reminder that things not shared when healthy and together are hardly going to be easier to share when the end comes. Likewise, it is, perhaps, a lesson to regard the ordinariness of 'normal' life as its own potent time of shared significance, thoughts, and words. Though, as a caveat, there are, doubtless, opaque domains of life and death that are far from 'ordinary', even pathological, and can benefit from various kinds of professional counselling. Still, many 'ordinary' band-widths of opacity are utterly as they should be, and help sustain individual creativity. If I did detail what passed between all involved when my parents died, the ensuing narratives – though very 'ordinary' in their way – would achieve a story whose opaque subtexts would lie unseen. Though providing some readers with their own emotional parallels and, in that, affording some degree of comfort or shared empathy, something quite considerable would be lost in the process, at least as far as I am concerned, and to that I now – finally – turn, in the notion of sacred-secrecy.

Sacred-Secrecy

Only now, having sketched the notion of opacity, can this theme of sacred-secrecy be broached. Its odd designation originated within my academic study of Mormonism that began in 1969 and led, albeit as a non-Mormon, to decades engaging with members of The Church of Jesus Christ of Latter-day Saints (LDS), largely through 'participant observation', that well-known though problematic notion that often includes long-term friendship and personal shifts in understanding of 'others'. One dimension of devout Mormon religious and cultural life involves participation in rites, not only at the many local meeting houses but also, most importantly, at regional Temples, there being but two in the UK and around 150 across the world. While these temple-ritual events have often been designated in defamatory fashion as 'secret', implying some negativity, my own monographs on the Saints have, of course, accounted for their existence and significance but have never detailed wording or performance, nor sought to defame them. This was not because of lack of information, some Saints have certainly alluded to them, and ex-members talked about them with me, while their form and content are readily available in published and, even, online visual formats, 'disclosed' by some who may feel alienated from or by Temples. I have, rather, not depicted them precisely because they are very special for the devout whose own custom is not to speak publicly about them. It was with that preserved piety in mind that I preferred to account for these rites in terms of 'sacred-secrecy' (Davies 2000; Davies 2014). Others have taken different positions, with one non-Mormon taking issues of authority over the use or non-use of materials as a basis for her descriptive accounts (McDannell 1997), and one Mormon specifically developing my notion of sacred-secrecy to analyse the management of self-identity by one well-known Mormon Apostle (Olaiz 2010).

It was, then, this LDS contextual background of 'sacred-secrecy' that came to mind when explicitly invited to write on my parents' death. Its 'capturing' of personal experience could, of course, also apply to many intimate aspects of human relationships, making the point that certain moments in life, especially between those 'close to' each other, are distinctively special. As such they capture an emotional significance whose force lies precisely in being kept between them, each to himself or herself. The secret is a treasure. This is true for many a Latter-day Saint within their religious culture and, I think, is also true for people who have found something 'precious' pervading the life and the dying of those they love. Though it lies beyond the scope of this chapter, it is also the case that if, for whatever reason, that relationship is ruptured the 'treasure' may invert to appear as radical loss. Pleasure becomes pain: love becomes hate. And this can happen with religious devotees as well as lovers, and I dare say for some parent-child relationships too.

Treasured Features

But here I remain with positive phenomena and speak of 'treasure' and something 'precious' within profoundly personal relationships and events that might, as we will see, be designated as 'sacred'. In this context, the sacred touches on what strengthens, brings unexpected emotion, blesses, or prompts wonder in special and perhaps entirely unexpected things. And above all, helps seal one's sense of identity.

In the history of religion, for example, Rudolph Otto famously spoke of the numinous' as a religious experience of the divine that, for him, involved a kind of great mystery that attracted, fascinated, and entailed its own thrill (Otto 1924; Davies 1984). I mention this in passing simply to highlight the potential effect of being with one's dying and dead. Within religious vocabulary numinous phenomena attract the description of 'ineffability', of things that cannot be put into words, and where so to do might be to lose what is precious. For it is precisely because emotions are sometimes inappropriately shoehorned into ill-fitting words that poetry often serves the deep things of life better than prose. Music is similar, and so is silence. For there is, in these phenomena an intensification of identity where we find ourselves in the land of fullness, excess, and the superfluity of meaning. This is what makes some 'religious' experiences remarkable. It is also what makes some relationships remarkable, not least at their physical ending where, in some contexts, death can also invite ineffability. And not least when a person encounters death for the first time, or in a particular kind of way.

This may help explain why some bereaved persons say that 'no one understands' their loss. For in some sense we do not 'understand' our own loss. Its comprehension takes time. If someone does say 'I understand' when they have little or no similar experience it easily sounds hollow. Though, in the UK, 'not speaking about death' or 'crossing the road' to avoid a bereaved person are idioms taken as expressions of avoidance of death, this may not tell the whole story, and may prompt too easy a criticism of people. For another side of bereavement and grief, one that touches on sacred secrecy, means that to try and spell out what happened is to lose the force of what did happen. This does not mean that 'keeping it to yourself' is somehow pathological, and that one should 'let it all out', as expressed in popular phrases allied with notions of grief.

There are, doubtless, contexts where those notions are applicable, where some 'secrets' can be 'told', but there are contexts where they are inapplicable. In cultural contexts where expression is not simply valued but expected, if not demanded, sacred secrecy is in potential peril of being denatured. Much could be said here, as when many a development of Freud's talking cure, albeit pre-occupied with the poignancy of symbols, asks too much of language. Others, following Jung, are happier to be symbol-accentuating analysts without verbally exhausting 'interpretations'. Everything cannot be 'said', as is evident in artistic representations of grief, whether in roadside, online, or headstone memorials.

Indeed, secrets and secrecy occupy a more significant place in personal, family, and social life than is often given satisfactory credit. One considerable exception lies in Georg Simmel's magisterial early twentieth century study of the sociology of secrecy which embraces the positive as well as potentially negative aspects of secrecy whether within marriage relationships or secret societies. Pursuing that dialectic with delicate nuance brings him to seeing that 'secrecy … is one of the greatest accomplishments of humanity' (Simmel 1906, p. 462). For him, secrets, and knowledge at large, are framed by language of reciprocity, with his 'reciprocal apprehension' and 'reciprocal knowledge' predating the rise of reciprocity theory in anthropology (Simmel 1906, pp. 442, 444). A generation later Sissela Bok's pursuit of secrecy across a swathe of social situations is more all-embracing, especially in terms of identity. She grasps the interplay of 'intimacy and privacy', and explores 'privacy as the condition of being protected from unwanted access by others', something that confers the 'protection of secrecy' with the aim of being 'less vulnerable, and more in control': while she does allude to the 'sacred' her concern lies with Durkheim's emphasis on formal religious ritual (Bok 1982, 6, pp. 10–11). However, she alludes to 'the sacredness of the self' when accentuating the 'unique' and 'unfathomable' nature of people, and when acknowledging that, 'they can never be entirely understood' her thought aligns with what has already been said above concerning opacity (Bok 1982, p21). She sees that 'human beings would lose their sense of identity and every shred of autonomy' if they had 'no capacity for keeping secrets and for choosing when to reveal them' (Bok 1982, p282). Even so, I think Bok's timely analysis dwells more on the potential for loss, whereas my preferred emphasis affirms the positivity of non-disclosed experience. Simmel, too, tends to dwell more on the negative rather than the positive dynamics of secrecy. In a moment we will move more clearly towards the positivity of secrecy when drawing on the existentially rich sociological work of Hans Mol as we apply it to contexts of bereavement.

Identities Sacralised

But, before invoking Mol's theory, it is worth calling to mind those many aspects of our deep emotional lives that make us who we are and continue to influence us over a lifetime. They enter into our sense of identity and change us, and this applies to experiences of loss with its feeling of being bereft, alone, and abandoned, just as to experiences of comfort, enhancement, and even of blessing. It is all too obvious, as already intimated, that these relationships experienced in ordinary life also affect times of illness, dying, death, and memory. This is why the actual period of 'death' involves what went before and influences what happens afterwards (Cleiren 1991). This is no 'stage theory' of grief but an acknowledgement both that elements of relationships, potentially, are intensified around the death-bed and that identities transform over time. Perhaps this very process is what that phrase – 'time heals' – both beloved and detested in some grief biographies is feeling towards. It is also why this chapter has included cameo accounts of my parents and of myself.

In all of this it is important to acknowledge the fact that people often differ markedly in quality of relationships, in the circumstances of terminal illness, pain, palliative contexts, and in being with the dying. There will be some, perhaps many, who sense a considerable need, and want to 'say what happened' as their mother or father died and as they responded afterwards. They will, in all probability, speak of it in changing ways as subsequent days, months, and years move on. Reiterating something already alluded to above, they may tell of anxiety, fear, pain, palliative care, relief, anguished breathing, moments that seemed like an age; of the passing of day and night, wishing that it would all come to an end, as well as of relief, calm and quiet and perhaps of enormous relief when 'it is over' (Mannix 2017). Or, perhaps, of how their sense of things seemed out of kilter with how the world at large simply seemed to continue as normal.

They want to speak of what happened, perhaps especially when several family members are involved, making that death a shared event. Such a family moment possesses a particular capacity to grow as the diverse perspectives of a surviving spouse and of elder and younger siblings contribute to the tale that is told. Things are unlikely to be perceived in the same way by any two individuals being with the third at his or her death. And it may be quite different again for the single 'child' being with the one dying parent, and then with the other. In glossing this variety, it is worth considering the truth of the vernacular expression 'you had to be there' in order to 'get' what happened. Though that phrase is often used in humour – you won't really 'get' the joke, because 'you had to be there' to 'get it' – I am sure that something similar surrounds experiences of the dying of those we love. The ineffability of it involves the embodied

8 Bereavement, Sacred-Secrecy and Dreams

emotion of it, and in our society just now we have a limited vocabulary for bodily felt states, something that is replicated in social science and its limited terminology and analyses of mood, tone, and ethos. In some ways we might say that this is why sacred-secrecy frames a kind of blessing, or for some, albeit a relative minority, a curse.

Just what we make of relationships is entirely the point as far as dying, death, and memory are concerned. The intensity of bonding between some is only as remarkable as is its lack between others. Here the contemporary 'continuing bonds' discussion of bereavement offers a fruitful backcloth for a point that I do not think has, as yet, been made (Klass and Steffen 2018). It is one that bears an affinity with the sacred-secrecy motif and can be derived from sociologist Hans Mol's highly creative theory of the sacralisation of identity (1976). He argued that entities helping forge a person's or a group's sense of identity, and which aid both their integration and survival are, in turn, accorded positive priority. The many expressions of priority include notions of care, concern, and respect, as well as that identity-source being placed beyond question or contradiction. Hence the high cultural value placed upon the mother, family, clan, political institutions, and religious groups, and within the latter upon key religious figures who are regarded with awe and worship. To own a profound source of one's identity is to revere, protect, and defend it. For it assures one's own 'being'. This we may say is evident in attitudes of devotees towards such figures as Jesus in Christianity, the Prophet Mohammed in Islam, and the figure of Gautama and his ensuing Sangha community in Buddhism. In the mutual interplay of key figure and believers lies the identity that accounts for their piety on the one hand and, sometimes, vehemence towards blasphemers on the other. The greater an identity found through attachment to such a figure, the greater is the respect, awe, indeed, even worship, accorded to that figure.

But, what of death, bereavement, and identity in terms of that interplay of the dead and their surviving kin? Here there is considerable scope for analysis, especially in terms of our sacred-secrecy motif and of personhood and dividuality to which we pass in a moment. Here the key hypothesis is that parents who have radically influenced their offspring's sense of identity will be accorded a high status of appreciation. In Mol's terminology, parents will be sacralised as profound meaning-makers of their children's sense of identity – notably in 'western' societies with their strong parent-focused form of socialisation, something that is not always the case in other societies (Davies 2020a). It is just here that I see an intersection between Mol on the sacralisation of identity and my view of sacred-secrecy. Though I cannot pursue this fully here, enough has been said to signpost how the notions of sacred-secrecy and the sacralisation of identity engage both with the bereaved person's sense of identity, and the status accorded to the deceased parents.

Personhood, Dividuality over Individuality

It is precisely here, then, that I bring into consideration the notion of personhood to partner both sacred secrecy and opacity. Just how we think of our personhood is an astonishingly complex issue. It varies from culture to culture, social class to social class, gender, and even between family and family-like groups. As a simple basis for discussion let me take the common western idea of 'the individual' and its 'individualism' as a fairly conventionally accepted perspective on the self-contained and relatively insular 'self'. But even to speak of this as 'common' is to give far too much credit to a form of intellectual and, in British terms, of a middle-class model of intellectual life. In saying this I must concede that, in some ways, my preceding account of both opacity and sacred secrecy reflects this individual-individualist model of personhood. That I accept, indeed, if one aligns all three one is already developing a picture of an intellectual and theoretically motivated perception of the world. I acknowledge that and see its near inevitability for someone whose lifetime has been rooted in analytical reflection on practice. But, there is more to be said than that. For the matrix of a significant dynamic of my personal identity lies in the working class, mining village context with extended kinship and other relationships that endure, and that despite a near entire adulthood of English, middle-class, academic and clerical contexts. A considerable element of adult identity depends upon dynamics of will, affection, and affinity. So much so that I sometimes think discussions of social mobility, including 'class values', accent-change or retention, ignore those and other motivating factors in human lives.

Moreover, there are aspects of life experience for millions of people for whom the 'individualist' model of personhood is inadequate, despite being preferred in many academic circles. But, among other available conceptual options, is that of dividual, complex, or partible personhood. I have already alluded to this above, and pursued this notion elsewhere as far as death studies and, indeed, palliative care, and pet-death are concerned and will not repeat its theoretical aetiology here (Davies 2017, 2020a, b). In essence this view identifies personhood as a composite of various elements, aspects, and characteristics of other people who have contributed to and entered into the making of this one 'self'. 'I' am, essentially, 'many', though just how 'others' make 'me' is an astonishingly complex issue, but vital none the less. This view is somewhat difficult to grasp in psychological terms even though we are now more accustomed than ever to understand how our parents' DNA does influence us to a remarkable extent.

To bring this notion of complex, dividual, or partible, personhood to the death of a parent is to accept a new kaleidoscopic view of emotions, reflections, and perceptive awareness that is available solely in terms of 'the individual' model of personhood. Cole Porter's 1940s lyrics, 'Every time we say goodbye I die a little', is not only a jazz favourite, but with its many French parallels based on *partir c'est mourir un peu*, gives as good a popular basis to partible personhood as might any more theoretical account. Correspondingly, grief, in its many manifestations, can be as creatively approached by the dividual as by the individual model when considering the inner transformations of personal identity that the physical death of a parent brings about. Just which 'part' of my partible or dividual 'self' died when my mother died is one thing, so too when my father died. More than that, given their inextricable 'partnership', that which 'died' in my father when my mother died itself belongs to both that opacity and sacred secrecy we have already pondered in theoretical terms. Whatever it was, and I intuit it was considerable over his three years as a widower, it was also a factor in my awareness of those years, his being unwell, then with a terminal diagnosis, our final Christmas Day together, just the two of us at home in Wales, his rapid hospitalisation on Boxing Day, and death by 14th January. Being with him, when dead, inevitably resonated with being with my mother when dead, and with being with him and my deceased mother – his wife. Each of those contexts could fill a paper of descriptive phenomenology of bereavement. Other, larger families, and their networked presences would doubtless extend this exponentially.

Dreamtime Selves

Speaking personally, years have now passed and while that cameo photograph of my parents and the weeping willow still sits framed in my house, what of their images in my mind? Even more so, what of their co-constituting presence in my embodied self-awareness, attitudes, and emotions? What of the occasional postures, the shadow thrown by the sun on summer days that is my father's, the thumb-nail that so easily splits that is my mother's? All echoes of Katherine Young's insightful paper on embodied memory (Young 2000). And then what of the invisible, imaginative, and dynamic memories, not least those dreams in which they 'come to me'? (Davies 2017, pp.187–205). For me, these dreams are telling and constitute their own validation of the hypothetical notion of dividual personhood. They reveal just how these key 'other' persons are integral aspects of my 'self', of my personhood, or even more specifically of my composite, dividual, personhood. And in their own way such dreams develop, enhance, transform or even transcend the image of the 'dead' parent. Have they been 'desacralised' in Mol's terminology, or has our sacred-secrecy flourished further? Such issues are not entirely dissimilar from Allan Kellehear's recent published research on appearances of 'dead' kin attending and surrounding the time of some people's death (Kellehear 2020).

As, perhaps, you will already see, I find dreams significant, despite their uncertain status in what some might see as mainstream contemporary British society, though I am very alert to their significance in some communities' cultural heritage and praxis as, for example, in Islam (Edgar 2011). Personally speaking, I began keeping a kind of dream diary since 1979, triggered by one of my post-graduates then working on 'dreams'. My accounts record many a reflection on 'life, reality, and everything!', but often with a considerable emphasis on dreams and the intuitive awareness of the moods they carry. Mood, along with notions of social-cultural tone, being the largely untapped domain of social scientific scholarly analysis, albeit with a potentially stimulating substrate in Max Weber's sociology of religion, though that is issue for another day.

As for my dream-diary, while I but seldom read it for the 'past' I thought I would look at entries surrounding my parents' deaths and funerals for this chapter. However, still following the sacred-secrecy motif I will not repeat any personal detail recorded there as to what we did together, what one or other of them 'said', or how they looked. What I have found interesting is what was and was not written in terms of what remains in my memory today. For example, while I recorded the benefit of the funeral services held at St. Cadoc's Parish Church with many local folk and family present, I did not describe the nuanced, comforting, fact that the Vicar spoke so well of my mother's love of things natural, nor that when we arrived at Graigfargoed, one of the most isolated, mountainside, and picturesque of cemeteries, the local grave digger had lined her grave with ferns. This serendipitous synchronicity could not have been better. As for my father's funeral, I did find the briefest of references to the fact that the hearse got stuck as we turned into that same cemetery, and that a group of men, many who had known my father from their working days, got out of their cars and we pushed it fully on to the recently refurbished 'road'. This was no 'catastrophe' or hindrance to the solemnity of the event, no ritual gone wrong, nothing to complain about, but rather added a degree of reality to things as a manual, shared, act: its own form of community blessing.

But these are not the events or moments arising in my dreams. My dead are often very 'present' and sustaining. While sometimes depicting an aspect of our past relationships, drawing them out, as it were, the dream events somehow speak the truth, sometimes gritty and not always fuzzily pleasant but not, as yet at least, unpleasant or negative. For writing this, I looked back for the last dream-event. It was on 21st March (2020) just when the UK COVID-19 shut-down started. On this occasion I fell asleep in a chair, a late afternoon practice I often enjoy, and I met them, they were together. Again I will not depict the substance of that occasion, but it left me entirely positive and heartened. Its visual acuity was considerable; I think it was in colour. In analytical terms, my partible personhood was dynamically at its survival-flourishing best, not least, and probably precisely because of, the emergent cultural lock-down.

Concluding with Life

In moving to a conclusion, let me turn from dreams to the 'real life' influence of my parents, their death, and embodied 'memory'. I must be brief, partial, and highly selective in what I say. Speaking loosely and in a poignantly inadequate binary sense, there was my father's more rational and mother's more emotional intelligences, their mutual work ethic, endurance, and appreciation of beauty in 'nature'. Would I have loved gardening had I not kept an allotment with my father and grown vegetables for local horticultural shows? Would I have pursued anthropology if I had not inherited something of my mother's sense of being able to 'read them like a book'? Who knows? But, now, a quarter of a century after their deaths I have no real sense of being bereaved. Perhaps this reflects something of those professional males whose lives were, at the time of immediate bereavement, and still are embedded in interesting and engaging work and relationships. But it is also because, in some part of my dividual personhood I have never entirely 'lost' them. Today's favouring of versions of 'continuing bonds' theories over the attachment and loss models of grief offers its own partial explanation of this as would a great deal of the insight of people like Colin Murray Parkes (2006) and others on patterns of attachment, relationships, and identity. So, too, with Hans Mol's notion of 'commitment' in his theory of the sacralisation of identity that has, yet, still to be developed for death studies (Mol 1976). And, certainly, not least in terms of love, that aspect of life that could, itself, have been the basic topic for this extended reflection. It is the long-term duration of bereavement that allows for so many of these issues to develop, many of them in creative and life-sustaining ways. Here, of course, I would not wish to overlook or negate those for whom parental death has struck cords of fragmentation and deeply troubling memories that perhaps even grow with time. That just happens not to have been my experience, and I am grateful for that. Indeed, the entire theme of gratitude could also have been given high profile in this chapter. While alluding to gifts given and received at funerals Kompter once reminded us of Georg Simmel's 'beautiful essay "Faithfulness and Gratitude"', in which he spoke of 'the moral memory of mankind' (Kompter 2004, p. 203). This kind of memory offers one distinctive way of appreciating dreams as interpersonal phenomena. For, from the perspective of biology and social status persons are certainly 'dead', from the dynamic reality of personal awareness they may still play a vital role for the living. I am not the first to acknowledge parental attitude and those of their offspring when it comes to living and dying. Indeed, what Erikson said of life also applies to death. 'Healthy children will not fear life if their elders have enough integrity not to fear death' (Erikson 1965, p. 261). If that happens to be our lot we can consider ourselves fortunate, which in this case I am, and it is with that in mind that I am now glad that I did accept the invitation to engage with this mini parent-offspring in memoriam.

References

Bok, S. (1982). *Secrets: On the ethics of concealment and revelation.* New York: Pantheon Books.
Cleiren, M. P. H. D. (1991). *Adaptation after Bereavement.* Leiden: University Press.
Davies, D. J. (1984). *Meaning and Salvation in Religious Studies.* Leiden: Brill.
Davies, D. J. (2000). *The Mormon Culture of Salvation.* Aldershot: Ashgate.
Davies, D. J. (2014). 'Sacred-secrecy and the Latter-day Saints'. *International Journal of Mormon Studies.* January, 2014. https://www.ijmsonline.org/archives/3289.
Davies, D. J. (2017). *Death, Ritual, and Belief: The Rhetoric of Funerary Rites.* Third Edition. London: Bloomsbury.
Davies, D. J. (2020a). 'Dividual identity in grief theories, palliative and bereavement care.' *Palliative Care and Social Practice.* 14, 1–12.
Davies, D. J. (2020b). Grief in human and companion-animal loss, bonding, and dividual pet-personhood. In Michael Hviid Jacobsen and Anders Petersen (Eds.) *Exploring Grief, Towards and Sociology of Sorrow.* London: Routledge, pp. 153–168.
Edgar, I. R. (2011). *The Dream in Islam. From Qur'anic Tradition to Jihadist Inspiration.* New York, Oxford: Berghahn.
Erikson, E. (1965 [1950]). *Childhood and Society.* Harmondsworth: Penguin Books.

Kellehear, A. (2020). *Visitors at the End of Life*. New York: Columbia University Press.
Klass, D. and Steffen, E. M. (2018). *Continuing Bonds in Bereavement, New Directions for Research and Practice*. London: Routledge.
Kompter, A. E. (2004). 'Gratitude and Gift Exchange'. In Emmons, R. A. and McCullough M. E. (Eds.) *The Psychology of Gratitude*. Oxford: Oxford University Press, pp. 195–212.
Kujala, A. and Danielsbacka, M. (2019). *Reciprocity in Human Societies from Ancient Times to the Modern Welfare State*. London: Palgrave Macmillan.
Lévi-Strauss, C. (1962). *Totemism*. London: Merlin Press.
Mannix, K. (2017). *With the end in Mind: How to Live and Die Well*. London: Collins.
Mauss, M. (1954). *The Gift: Forms and Functions of Exchange in Archaic Society*. (Trans. Cunnison, I.) Glencoe: The Free Press.
McDannell, C. (1997). 'Sacred, Secret, and the Non-Mormon'. *Sunstone*, April, pp. 41–45.
Mol, H. (1976). *Identity and the Sacred*. Oxford: Blackwell.
Olaiz, H. (2010). SL10212: *Sacred Secrecy in the Teachings of President Boyd K. Packer*. Sunstone. January 1st 2010, https://www.sunstonemagazine.com/tag/sacred-secrecy/
Otto, R. ([1917] 1924). *The Idea of the Holy*. Oxford: Oxford University Press.
Parkes, C. M. (2006). *Love and Loss. The Roots of Grief and its Complications*. London: Routledge.
Simmel, G. (1906). The Sociology of Secrecy and of Secret Societies. *American Journal of Sociology.* 11(1906), 441–98.
Wesley, J. (1831. New Edition). *Explanatory Notes upon the New Testament*. London: John Mason.
Young, K. (2000). The Memory of the Flesh. *Body and Society,* 8(3), 25–48.

9

Conclusion: Recovering Ghosts

Caroline Pearce

As I write this, I have lived most of my life without parents. My perspective on the death of my parents is one of distance, of viewing the detail of dying and death not from a vantage point but from a stage removed. The immediacy, vividness is no longer there. I experience memories as faded, or at least somewhat static. I can retrieve only those from the collection of memories that have become 'set' in my mind, that have imprinted on my consciousness and been carefully constructed over time.

For this book we invited death, dying and bereavement scholars to narrate their own personal stories of parental death and bereavement – assuming such experiences can be narrated. Collected here are accounts, interpretations and memories told and retold through emotional and analytical lenses, with diverse perspectives, and capturing the passage of time.

Following my mother's death, I felt compelled to write my narrative and make sense of what had happened to me. My sociology

C. Pearce (✉)
University of Cambridge, Cambridge, UK
e-mail: cmp89@medschl.cam.ac.uk

undergraduate and master's dissertations were both concerned with my mother's illness and death. My first academic papers were autoethnographic accounts of the death of my mother (Pearce 2008, 2010). Throughout my early 20s I was, in the words of bereavement theory, 'preoccupied' with my loss.

Studying sociology, I was excited for the first time by academic study. Sociological theories and concepts transformed my perception of the world and myself. Applying those concepts to my own life felt liberating, as though I could manage and control my own narrative. Inspired by auto-ethnography and narrative theory, I believed that telling my story would allow me to become free of it. Certainly, telling my story did change the course of my life. It contributed to academic achievements that in turn enabled opportunities that would otherwise have been closed off to me.

My experience of parental death was prior to any professional and academic understanding of death and dying, in contrast to most of the accounts in this book. Yet, as the authors describe, such professional knowledge can still leave one unprepared for personal experiences. Ultimately for me, and in common with the other authors, understanding the relationship between my personal experiences and professional knowledge and theories was and remains an iterative process.

However, writing about such personal experiences, particularly in academic work, also brought with it a sense of shame. While I felt compelled to write my narrative, it also left me feeling exposed. Though I believed in the importance of what I wrote, afterward I often wished I could edit myself out. The insecurity of being an early academic was heightened by the fact that my first claims to academic credibility were tied to my personal story. My fear was that I wasn't really a good academic merely someone with a good sob story.

Perhaps it was because of this that initially I felt a resistance to reflecting on my own experience, something that felt unavoidable in editing this book. As Douglas Davies explained in Chap. 8, I too felt a hesitancy toward writing publicly about emotions deemed private. Yet in my case I had already written at length about my history with bereavement in various forums: academic papers, dissertations, blog posts. It was not then that I did not see the value in narrating personal experiences of death and dying but rather I felt I had exhausted the topic, and – to borrow a crude phrase – maybe it was time I got over it.

Though as I began to read the draft chapters here, I felt encouraged by their openness in sharing such personal accounts. It helped to remove the shame of self-exposure as I understood how meaningful it can be to share and understand another's experience. It is from this perspective that in this concluding chapter I reflect on the meaning and content of the these accounts, referring to my own experience to elucidate some of the salient aspects of parental death, dying and bereavement.

Stories and Silences

One of initial impulses to write about my experiences was a frustration and feeling of anger at research on bereaved children and adolescents and the various negative 'risks' to which early parental death exposed them. I felt a strong desire to resist this doomed narrative, and also felt completely disconnected from the identity of orphan. What happened to me was tragic, but I did not want to be treated as tragic. Narratives of post-traumatic growth I found equally restrictive. I did not want to be extraordinary, I wanted to be ordinary, to be normal.

Narratives can make us comprehensible to others, and to ourselves. Since childhood I had been given a story – a sad and tragic tale I describe in this chapter – and it was perhaps my discomfort, my wrestling with this story that made me perceptive to the role of stories and narratives. During my PhD field work on recovery following bereavement, I became aware of the powerful discourse in the literature that claimed telling one's story could assist in recovery from grief. Indeed, it was claimed to be healing and restorative. Yet I began to feel fatigued over what felt like a proliferation of stories, and specifically the use of stories as a means of liberation. Instead, I started to wonder whether it might be better to say nothing at all.

The flipside of the liberatory potential of telling one's story is what Douglas Davies described in Chap. 8. Drawing on the concept of 'sacred-secrecy' Douglas suggests that the emotional significance of an experience or relationship lies precisely in it being kept to oneself or between those involved. The process of describing an event or experience can cause it to lose its force, or sacredness. Like certain religious rituals, sacredness is fostered by the details of acts remaining secret only to those who participated and experienced it.

In Chap. 1, we discussed the notion of experiential knowledge – a concept that highlights the importance of experience to understanding or knowing a phenomenon. As editors we have sought to draw attention to the space in between an experience and the knowledge of it, and the limitations of portraying autobiographical events. Yet we also sought to argue that all knowledge is experiential knowledge, to the extent that all knowledge production processes are undertaken by experiencing embodied subjects. This process of knowledge production is something with which the authors of this book are acutely aware due to the depth of their experience in qualitative and ethnographic research. As researchers we rely on interviews and observations to help us understand the 'truth' of a phenomenon – asking those that have experienced something to relay it to us. Through this process both researcher and participant are constructing and re-constructing a narrative around what happened.

In my experience of interviewing people about bereavement, I have been struck by how people rarely express things in concrete terms. Transcribing interviews brought to my attention how often people use words such as 'like', 'sort of', 'kind of', 'thing'. It was as though words and language failed the narrator and their desire to communicate an experience. Or perhaps it was that the narrator feared that the act of capturing and describing – as Douglas described – may enact violence to the 'thing' (experiential, sensory realm) itself. Yet people continue to understand each other, make sense of each other, through these mumbles, utterances, metaphors, and gestures. Often, I walked away from an interview encounter carrying one impression but in the process of typing speech into words on a blank page it would impress upon me in a totally different way. A story articulated through language has already transformed the sensory experience being told. It is then transformed again once the story is listened to and read. It may be that at each stage something is lost – perhaps a sacredness?

As interviewers and ethnographers, we are constantly working the divide between what was experienced, encountered, observed, and our description, accounting, narrative of it. As such we recognise the importance of silences – what is not said – in how someone narrates themselves. This is what Douglas Davies in Chap. 8 described as the 'silent core' that remains in any account or act of disclosure; the things that are not or cannot be expressed. The interview lends itself to describing events, things that are tangible. Restricted by a dominant narrative form that encourages beginnings, middles and endings it may be that narrating experiences always transforms them into this conventional storyline. Yet of course silences give definition to these very events and narratives, playing an important role in shaping identities, and family histories. Silences however remain ambiguous and difficult to interpret (Baddeley and Singer 2010). Silences do not have to imply an active covering over or oppression of truths, but, as some authors have testified here, after a death many silences may be left behind without the chance of resolution.

The Limits of Shared Experience

In preparation for writing this chapter I revisited my master's degree dissertation, written in 2008. The dissertation was a qualitative study of women's experience of losing their mother during adolescence. Re-reading the dissertation, I noted my scepticism toward the idea that experiences can be shared. I was clearly resistant to the idea that all those who had lost a parent were somehow the same. Yet undeniably my interview data, along with my extensive reading of the literature, suggested that there were shared learning experiences.

In his 'Mourning Diary', written following the death of his mother, Roland Barthes (2011[1987]) describes sharing his feelings of grief to an acquaintance. Barthes expressed how he felt his enduring grief appeared to resist psychoanalytic notions of adaptation, to which his acquaintance responded: 'That's what mourning is'. This response bothered Barthes, who wrote: 'I can't endure seeing my suffering being reduced – being generalised … it's as if it were being stolen from me' (2011, p. 71). On becoming a bereaved person, one's subjective experience that feels so individual and unique, is opened up to the generalising effects of bereavement theories and concepts that explain grief as a linear, staged process.

In bereavement, it seems that one becomes another 'case': typical and normal or complicated and abnormal. In Chap. 6, Colin Murray Parkes momentarily questions his profession of psychiatry following his father's death: 'I began to understand one of the reasons that my father, and other people, distrust psychiatrists; by making people an object of study and care we subtlety downgrade them in status from person to object, and from equals to subordinates'. Becoming generalised, an object rather than a person can feel belittling as Colin identifies, contemplating that as one of the bereaved he now inhabited a 'different world'. Experiencing this gap however allowed him to recognise that psychiatrists and other professionals should not misuse their power with patients.

The resistance I felt to acknowledging the shared experiences between myself and other parentally bereaved young people, was in part a resistance to my grief becoming 'generalised': where my behaviour could be described as 'typical' or not and where I was another one of 'The Bereaved' – as Jenny Hockey noted in Chap. 3. Yet my discomfort also resulted from the disappointing realisation that shared experiences do not necessarily lead to healing. For some time after my mother's death I was looking to others to make sense of my loss, and I was frustrated to discover the meanings and narratives of others could not simply be supplanted into my own life. It was a feeling of loss to realise that just because something happened to me it did not mean I could also understand others who had undergone the same experience. In other words, I was acknowledging the gulf between my own and others perception and experience of the world.

I had not quite grasped then that the death of parent might indeed lead to shared experiences, but not necessarily because the event of parental death impacted everyone in the same way. I was viewing these shared reactions and emotions as a direct result of the death of a parent rather than reflective of the cultural assumptions around bereavement and death that existed in the western society in which I lived. The main lesson of this was recognising the significance of my positioning towards my research topic and to my own narrative, a lesson informed by my sociological education. As discussed above, and in Chap. 1, how experiences of death and bereavement are narrated is shaped by language and cultural discourses. Understanding the constructed nature of experiences, enabled me to perceive that instead of one single story of parental death or one set of learning experiences, the truth of any experience, event, person was multiple. Acknowledging that 'truth' didn't lie in any one story was for me a revelation that felt liberating.

In this anthology each author has presented how they confronted and managed death, specifically the death of one or both parents in their own lives, reflecting on how the experience of bereavement is interweaved with the different 'selves' they occupy. There is the professional, academic self, but also the self as daughter or son, the self that occupies a certain social class, ethnicity and gender. In Chap. 7, Rose Barbour writes how re-visiting the death of her parents 'led to a re-examination and re-evaluation of relevant sociological theories, all concerned with elaborating the relationship between self and society in its many forms'. This emphasises how, in documenting death and dying we are documenting not simply individual experiences but social experiences. As Arnason (2007) would argue, drawing on Bloch and Parry (1982), death provides an opportunity for societal norms and authority to be created, reborn or reaffirmed; in other words, society is constituted through death.

In attempting to discern the 'truth' of parental death, the culmination of my reflections resulted in a modest realisation: events happened to me and I observed and experienced them. But as individuals, the stories we tell are always in flux. From my own experience of narrating parental death, I realised I could tell multiple different stories, each one true in its own way. But it did not mean that if I told a story it held the 'truth' of me, or of my experience. Now I feel I can easily and healthily dissociate 'me' and 'my story' from my research. My interest in bereavement and end-of-life care is no longer a means of making sense of my past. Yet the connection to my narrative of bereavement was and remains largely an ambivalent one, an emotional state that very much characterised my feelings towards my parents before and after their deaths.

Dys-appearing

One of the themes of this book is to explore how it feels to lose the sense of buffer between life and death that a parent can provide. But for me, the death of my parents didn't make the prospect of my own death feel closer; death was always close. By the time I was 15, both my parents had died. In my youth death through old age felt like a distant prospect, yet the presence of death still loomed large in my daily life.

My father was not an active presence in my life and following my parent's separation, he moved back to his home country of Australia. I grew up with my sister under my mother's care in Derby, UK. His death when I was aged 11 therefore impacted me little at the time, his absence was unaltered by his death. However, it did make the impact of my mother's death four years later more profound as I had lost not only a mother but I was now an orphan, bereft of all parental support.

Throughout the whole of my childhood my mother's health was deteriorating. As I was growing and developing, she was dying. In my memory, my mother was always in decline. Before receiving the diagnosis of Multiple Sclerosis my mother suffered continual falls and imbalance. I have only faint memories of her walking with the support of walking sticks and I remember her mostly as a wheelchair user. For a disease that for some people can be manageable despite periods of relapse, my mother's trajectory was a dramatic and severe decline over a period of around ten years. Yet from my perspective living daily with my mother's ill body, the changes in her health were imperceptible. I experienced those years as a child and my memories appear to me as stuck in the seemingly endless present of my child mind.

For almost as long as I was a daughter, I was a carer. Because caring and illness were so entwined with my childhood it is not possible for me to identify when the dying period began. For my sister and I, it involved an increasingly arduous effort to limit the ill effects of my mother's unbounded body by acting as an extension to her body. In Chap. 3, Jenny Hockey described the dirty aspects of dying and her description of the smells of her father's illness resonated with me and reminded me how these sensory aspects of dying and death can fade over time.

It was not only that my mother had acquired a new identity but that – like Jenny's father – her identity had become 'spoiled' (Goffman 1968). In an article, I wrote about this process of identity 'transgression', drawing on Goffman's concept, describing it as: 'the name given to the process when an individual conducts some error; they lapse or fault in their performance. In effect to transgress is to be accorded a spoiled identity' (Pearce 2008). As a family, managing the 'impressions' we gave to the outside world was important as we feared being 'discredited' by the significant others around us (Goffman 1968). Yet my mother's body became increasingly difficult to maintain; she was in a continual process of unravelling. Her body began to 'dys-appear' (Leder 1990) to the point where only the 'dys', ill or bad, features were prominent. An illness like MS acts upon the body in a gradual fashion, destroying the body's capacities and abilities, and in Leder's terms brings to conscious awareness the many bodily functions that previously remained automatic, and outside of conscious reflection. It is not only one's body that changes but one's relationship to their environment, which brings to the fore the 'dys'-functioning aspects of the ill body. This process was especially marked for my mother, who seemed to experience an accelerated decline – as though decades of aging were compressed into one.

Returning to Jenny Hockey's account in Chap. 3, she presented a contrast between the continual smells of sickness and illness with a desire for cleanliness. Dressing up in nice clothes is a reprieve from the exhausting act of caring but also acts as a symbolic barrier against death and dying. By this I mean, that though our mother's health deteriorated, my sister and I remember her as elegant and beautiful. From her vast collection of different jewellery every day she would personally select earrings and a necklace to co-ordinate with the clothes she also carefully selected. I admire my mother's resolve to maintain her appearance, which went beyond vanity; it was a committed maintenance of self. It feels heartbreaking to try and fathom the despair she felt on rare days when she could not face getting out of bed, and to contemplate the monotony of her daily life in those few final years.

Performing Death

My mother was admitted to hospital in November 2000. She had felt unable to get out of bed and the General Practitioner (GP) came to visit. Her bowels had become obstructed. This wasn't unusual, my mother had been diagnosed with Crohn's disease in her late teens and so had spent a life with intestinal difficulties. Years seated in a wheelchair had further damaged her digestive process and going to the toilet had become quite an anxiety-ridden event. Lying there in bed with a distended abdomen the GP swiftly recommended for her to be transferred to hospital.

My sister and I were both familiar with the hospital having visited many times before for appointments and previous hospital stays. The journey to the ward, the beige corridors, were well known territory. For the next month we visited every day. She was nil by mouth, I assumed due to her obstructed bowel, but we would sometimes bring forbidden drinks and treats. She was placed on a ward, surrounded by five or maybe seven other beds, mostly elderly patients. My mother had recently turned 44; I felt very aware of our youthfulness.

She seemed to deteriorate quite rapidly while in hospital. At some point she developed pneumonia, though this only became apparent to me later when I read the death certificate. Sometimes when I visited, I couldn't tell whether my mother was aware that I was there or not. When she was alert her speech would be so mumbled it was even hard for my sister and I to understand. Because conversation was a strain, I used to read a book to her. It was a Maeve Binchy book that I had found in a pile of books and magazines on the ward. It was an author my mum liked, and she had many of her books. My mother read widely and had trained as a librarian. I assumed Binchy with its floral adorned covers was for her an easy comfort read, a sort of middle-aged chick lit. I would read it even if I didn't know she was listening.

As my usual caring duties were passed to someone else, there were fewer demands on our time together and I had the opportunity to simply spend time with my mother as a daughter, and not just someone to address her needs. We were close when I was a child, but our relationship suffered during my teenage years and I felt my mother did not have much interest in me. In Chaps. 3 and 4 Jenny Hockey and Kathryn Almack describe feeling their fathers had become more 'accessible' to them during illness, which is something I also experienced in the final weeks before my mother's death. One conversation during this time became particularly precious to me. I had mentioned I was reading one of her books from the bookshelf at home – *The Color Purple*. She seemed surprised. The conversation drifted to what I wanted to do with my life. 'I want to be a writer' I replied. I remember her nodding slightly – an error in my memory no doubt as she could no longer move her head by herself. It was the first time we had had a conversation about anything regarding my future or my interests for as long as I could remember, so overwhelmed our lives had become with simply managing illness.

Memories of this month-long hospital stay are some of those that later 'haunted' me the most, but I wonder whether it is only because I recall them more distinctly. One haunting memory involved a visit from the vicar of the church we attended. He was trying to comfort my mother and said a prayer. Then he added, 'We know Brenda's not going to be with us for much longer'. My mother started to cry saying, 'I don't want to die'. The Vicar looked at me confused, not able to understand what she's saying. 'What is she saying?' He asked me. I was forced to repeat those words spoken in horror: 'She said she doesn't want to die'.

At the time this horrified me on multiple levels: first the fact that my mother was going to die soon was news to me. It was approaching mid-December and we were planning for our mother to be home by Christmas. Though her condition had deteriorated considerably, my mother – as I mentioned above – to me was always in decline. I was so accustomed to decline I couldn't detect the point where decline became dying.

It was much later when I realised how completely my sister and I had been kept out of any discussions and decision-making over our mother's care and subsequent death. At the time, and in this particular hospital ward, our age had meant the staff had decided we were not suitably equipped to participate in decisions about our mother's care, despite being her primary carers for most of our lives. Neither were we able to disclose and discuss with our mother what care she wanted. Her reaction to the vicar's comment led me to believe she was also equally unaware that she was at the very end of life.

My second level of horror and disbelief was then to learn that my mother was still afraid of death. It was hard to comprehend my mother could want to persist living in her bodily state. Not only her physical capacity but our social existence had become so fragile that I think all three of us felt as though we were barely alive. I was horrified to learn that one may never come to terms with one's death, even when so close to the end.

Hauntings and Becomings

When a parent dies, one is faced with trying to understand the role that parent played in constructing one's own sense of personhood. As Douglas Davies detailed in Chap. 8, parents have an especially significant role in constructing their children's identities. And in Chap. 5, Gordon Riches delved deeply into questioning what he inherited from his parents managing to appreciate and critically acknowledge the various aspects of his emotional inheritance. Through this process of understanding one's inheritance, authors of this anthology have also sought to make sense of who their parents were. As children we embody our parents through physical resemblances, along with other cultural and social characteristics gained as part of our socialisation or cultural 'habitus', the concept developed by Pierre Bourdieu which Rose Barbour detailed in Chap. 7. Though as Douglas Davies suggests, our parents tend to remain opaque to us; aspects of their personhood remain inaccessible. This feeling of inaccessibility may result from a difficulty in viewing our parents objectively rather than through the perspective of a child, a lens that brings with it certain expectations and obligations. With any relationship however, identifying the extent to which others compose our sense of self, is as Sigmund Freud (1917) famously described, a complicated and potentially impossible task. As bereavement theory has moved away from descriptions of 'detaching' from the deceased person to 'recover' one's self, towards concepts of continued bonds and theories that foreground relational understandings of identity – as Kathryn Almack detailed in Chap. 4 – this has illustrated the ways in which our attachments to others – alive or deceased – influence and shape our subjectivity and sense of meaning (Pearce and Komaromy 2020).

Here the authors have written of their feelings of gratitude towards parents, while recognising both the positive and ambivalent legacies of parental death. The subtitle of this anthology – a kind of haunting – points precisely to these mixed legacies and the different ways parents might feature in our lives after death. However, the notion of 'haunting' might seem at odds with the examples of modern dying displayed here. Certainly, within the narratives religious rites are mentioned and notions of the afterlife alluded to, but these are deaths framed by medicine, health care systems and western conventions around disposal. While, at the same time, the authors have spent careers investigating and disrupting the boundary between life and death, carrying out research that has explored how people experience the ongoing presence of the deceased person and continue relationships after death.

The notion of haunting felt especially close to me as I did feel haunted by my mother for many years. Looking back at previous writing I noticed how the theme of haunting reoccurred. This was literal in the sense that I had recurring dreams about my mother. A powerful recurring image was my childhood home. Two years after my mother died, my sister and I sold our family home. Yet it seemed no matter what distances I travelled, in my dreams I continually walked down the same street, through the same door, into the empty, silent house. When I carried out research on the experience of losing a parent, bereaved children would describe feeling that they had lost the sense of a safety net (Pearce 2011). I felt that acutely. The idea of home no longer existed for me. Innocuous questions regarding where my 'home' is would fill me with despair. Despite the efforts of my dream self I could never 'go home' again.

This experience I later described as the liminality of grief (Pearce 2019). In this 'liminal space' one's identity is ambiguous to oneself as well as to others. Here one enters a new but formless sense of identity as bereaved person, and in the case of parental death, as orphan. For Colin Murray Parkes, in Chap. 6, sympathy from colleagues reminded him that his external identity had changed from 'the consultant and expert on bereavement to the grief doctor who had become a grief patient'. Such transitions can feel uncomfortable, and Colin described a vague feeling of losing status. In comparison, I had very little status to lose – indeed a teenage orphan seemed to grant me a new status, that could be both stigmatising and elevating. This feeling is captured in Dave Eggers' fictional memoir about the death of his parents in his late teens: 'We are unusual and tragic and alive. ...We are orphans. As orphans we are celebrities. We are foreign exchange people, from a place where there are still orphans. ...We are oddities, sideshows, talk show subjects. ...We are new and everyone else is old' (2000, p. 96).

Entering the 'foreign country' of grief could bring freedoms from longstanding responsibilities, even if one's new identity, is not yet clear. Following his mother's death Gordon Riches in Chap. 5 described feeling 'an enormous sense of release from responsibility'. The theme of responsibility and the mixture of emotions it brings permeates the accounts in this book, as the authors had to negotiate both the societal obligations around caring for one's parent and family responsibilities, and the individual characteristics of their relationships with their parents. In Chap. 3, Jenny Hockey writes of feeling threatened by her father's illness, what it might require from her and what it might take away. This feeling of being out of control and burdened contrasts with Carol Komaromy's experience in Chap. 2 of looking after her father Jim, where she recalled feelings of joy at his signs of improvement as it meant she might have more time to spend with and care for her father. For the authors here such responsibilities were often interlinked with social and cultural expectations around family roles. Indeed, such assumptions over caring responsibilities can have gendered implications. In Chap. 7, Rose Barbour described how following her father's death, she was informed by her mother and grandmother that women did not attend the cemetery for the interment, and that her role was to instead help prepare tea for the returning male mourners. Yet Rose found herself taking charge of what was then traditionally a male responsibility of allocating 'coffin cords'. In transgressing these gendered norms, Rose reflected that aged 16, the adults whom she expected to manage the situation of her father's funeral, 'were unable to fulfil my expectations', an experience that also served to demarcate her progression into adulthood.

When losing a parent in the transitional phase of adolescence one's progression into adulthood can be especially marked by a parent's death.

9 Conclusion: Recovering Ghosts

This contrasts with Colin's Murray Parke's experience of his father's death who notes that 'by the time he died I had become autonomous'. Becoming autonomous and one's own person, is an experience – or rite of passage – that can be stimulated by the death of a parent or becoming an orphan. Though of course, one's living relationships with their parents are often characterised by a desire to shape one's own sense of identity, separate from parental ties. The theme of geographical and emotional distance is apparent as the authors described experiences of growing beyond the world of their parents. The trajectories of Gordon Riches, Kathryn Almack and Rose Barbour are very much influenced by their access to higher education that demarcated a difference from their parents' generation. For example, when at college Gordon Riches described feeling he was 'already waking up to a world very different to that of my parents'. Further, as Rose Barbour described, the middle-class environs of working in higher education can increase awareness of one's class origins. Recognising one's possibilities are different from one's parents, and other family members can be both freeing and unsettling, fostering a feeling of being 'out of place'.

For Kathryn Almack, Gordon Riches and Rose Barbour, parental illness and death served to confront them with the scale of these distances as they navigated between two notions of 'home'. Written from the perspective of those emerging into adulthood in the post-war period, the narratives capture shifts in social mobility experienced by this generation, and the self-reflexivity of late 'liquid' modernity (Bauman 2000). Connecting these broader societal shifts with changes to individual sense of self-identity, lies the feeling of belonging (May 2011). On returning to one's hometown, a feeling of not belonging illustrates the distance one has travelled – emotionally and geographically – away from the place of childhood. This may invite positive emotions as well as uncomfortable feelings of exclusion – a feeling of not really belonging anywhere. It is a feeling of distance not only from place, but cultural habitus, and perhaps by extension a distance from one's parents. After a parent dies, the need to cling to origins may be felt more acutely in a desire to retain a sense of past and history. Yet the feeling of homelessness that both class transition and parental death can trigger demonstrates how belonging is not a permanent state, but something which is actively sustained (May 2011). The death of a parent brings to the fore an understanding that as we change, as others around us change, and as society changes, so does our sense of belonging, including where our home lies, and what the act of returning means.

Recovering Ghosts

In closing, I share an experience of returning home, an experience that helps to tie together these strands of inheritances, identity, hauntings and becomings, and that concludes my own narrative of parental death and bereavement. The act of returning home can confront us with the past, and with it cause us to re-encounter our former selves. Returning to her childhood home for her mother's funeral, Rose Barbour described the feeling of once again being in contact with people she had not seen since childhood, writing that it felt like being 'transported back in time'. From my own perspective, I have less and less need to return to my hometown. Yet when I have returned, it has felt as though I am revisiting the multiple ghosts of my past. I wonder how such a small space can contain so many versions of myself.

In late 2011, my maternal grandmother died. I was in India at the time, and she was in Australia where she had lived since she emigrated with her family decades earlier. My mother arrived in Australia as a teenager, completing school and further studies, and then at 23 she married my father there. For reasons I do not know, my mother was always keen to return to England and did so shortly with my father after getting married, leaving her parents and younger brother behind.

Grandma visited us occasionally throughout mine and my sister's childhood and we corresponded regularly, a practice that continued up until her death. I remember being very fond of Grandma as a child but also recall the arguments she and my mother had – in-person on her occasional visits or over the telephone. The complexities of their relationship were far beyond my comprehension as a child, and to this day I understand little of the nature of their relationship. My uncle had stayed in Australia and maintained a close relationship with his mother. After Grandma's death he had responsibility for disposing of her ashes and decided that they would be scattered on my mum's grave. It was several years later in 2016 when my uncle and Grandma made the journey from Australia to England. My sister and I travelled from different parts of the country to meet them – our modest family all descending into the middle of a small island.

It was implausibly hot August day as we met outside Derby train station before journeying to the village where my mother was buried in a small, quiet graveyard. We had brought flowers and cleaning equipment and when we arrived my sister and I busied ourselves by making the headstone look presentable. As none of us were sure whether the scattering of ashes in the cemetery was permitted, my uncle scattered them over the grass with little fanfare. We stood by the grave to say a few words and take photos to remember. I looked at the photo later in the day, seeing the ash resting on the grass, wondering whether it would be blown away or absorbed into the ground.

Our mother's early death caused a rupture in the generational order; her own mother dying 11 years after her. As Grandma's ashes were laid on top on my mother's grave, we literally layered one generation over the other. It was an odd sensation, a sense that we were trying to rectify the unsettling of time and temporality caused by my mother's death.

For our sparsely populated family tree it was an attempt at creating some family history. I felt ambivalent not knowing whether these two women would have wanted to be reunited in death or whether it was a fitting resolution to their relationship. As an adult, my mother had spent her life at a distance from her own parents and now this distance was collapsed, past and present folded in on one another. Despite my ambivalence, at least now, I thought, my mother was not alone.

References

Arnason, A. (2007). "Fall apart and put yourself together again": the anthropology of death and bereavement counselling in Britain. *Mortality*, 12 (1), 48–65.
Baddeley, J. and Singer, J. A. (2010). A loss in the family: silence, memory, and narrative identity after bereavement. *Memory*, 18(2), 198–207.
Barthes, R. (2011[1987]). *Mourning diary*. London: Notting Hill Editions.

Bauman, Z. (2000). *Liquid Modernity*. New Jersey: Wiley.

Bloch, M. and Parry, J. (1982). 'Introduction: Death and the regeneration of life' in Death and the regeneration of life (pp. 1–44). Cambridge: Cambridge University Press.

Eggers, D. (2000). *A heartbreaking work of staggering genius*. New York: Simon & Schuster.

Freud, S. (1917). Mourning and melancholia. In Philips, A (Ed.) (2006) *The Penguin Freud reader* (pp. 310–326). London: Penguin.

Goffman, E. (1968). *Asylums: Essays on the Social Situation of Mental Patients and Other Inmates*. Harmondsworth: Penguin.

Leder, D. (1990). *The absent body*. Chicago: University of Chicago Press.

May, V. (2011). Self, belonging and social change. *Sociology*, 45(3), 363–378.

Pearce, C. (2008). World Interrupted: An autoethnographic exploration into the rupture of self and family narratives following the onset of chronic illness and the death of a mother. *Qualitative Sociology Review*, 4(1), 131–149.

Pearce, C. (2010). The crises and freedoms of researching your own life. *Journal of Research Practice*, 6(1), M2.

Pearce, C. (2011). Girl, Interrupted: An exploration into the experience of grief following the death of a mother in young women's narratives. *Mortality*, 16(1), 35–53.

Pearce, C. (2019). *The public and private management of grief: recovering normal*. London: Palgrave.

Pearce, C. and Komaromy, C. (2020). Recovering the body in grief: physical absence and embodied presence. *Health*, https://doi.org/10.1177/1363459320931914.

Index[1]

A
Ariès, Philippe, 7
Attachments, 128, 137, 138, 188
Autobiography, 21–24, 150

B
Bauman, Zygmunt, 131, 191
Belonging, 75, 77, 114, 141, 191, 192
Bereavement, v, vii, 1–8, 12–20, 23, 24, 27, 53, 79, 94, 95, 98, 102, 112, 119–128, 130, 140, 148, 155–175, 177–183, 188, 189, 192
Bok, Sissela, 67
Bourdieu, Pierre, 149, 150, 188
Breaking bad news, 34
Brose, H-G., 130

C
Caring, 2, 6, 14, 79, 83, 86, 108, 184–186, 190
Childhood, 15, 16, 27, 35, 49, 63, 85, 87–89, 110, 111, 130, 142, 146, 149, 179, 184, 189, 191, 192
Class
  middle-class, 134, 149, 191
  working-class, 84, 87, 88, 132, 135, 144, 145, 148, 161

D
De Beauvoir, Simone, 13, 33
Death
  care home setting, 7, 11, 13, 26
  cause of, 7, 13, 48, 121
  event of, 2, 5–7, 13, 27, 89, 107, 160, 182, 183

---

[1] Note: Page numbers followed by 'n' refer to notes.

Death (*cont.*)
  home setting, 5–7, 9, 79, 92, 97, 128, 142
  hospice setting, 8, 11, 79
  hospital setting, 27
  norms, 9, 12, 13, 17, 18, 183
  type of – good, bad, timely, 8–12, 15, 16, 19, 95, 96, 122
Death studies, v, vii, 1–4, 19, 52, 130, 155, 156, 161
Deathways, 4
Decision-making, 8, 52, 187
Dignity, 9, 42, 50, 80
Disclosure, 11, 33, 181
Disposal
  ashes, 69, 77, 86, 192, 193
  burial, vii, 7, 43, 137, 138, 140
  cemetery, 132, 139, 142, 190, 193
  coffin, 7, 42, 43, 74–76, 92, 127, 132, 133, 190
  crematorium, 76, 77, 127
Dreams, 35, 41, 42, 72, 74, 102, 104, 130, 155–175, 189
Dying
  awareness, 8, 12, 33, 116
  diagnosis, 6, 10, 36, 37, 45, 69, 84, 93, 126, 184
  disclosure, 11, 33
  end-of-life care, 3, 6–8, 10–12, 33, 47, 81, 86, 94, 95, 183
  illness, 6, 21, 22, 38, 40, 44, 45, 53, 55, 66, 78, 115, 136, 146, 178, 184, 185, 187, 190, 191
  pain, 3, 10, 24, 36–38, 58, 81, 92, 94, 117
  pain and symptom management, 36
  palliative care, 10, 20, 86, 97, 122, 126–128
  quality of, 8–12
  trajectory, 2, 6, 27, 34, 37

E

Emotions, 2, 13, 19, 23, 25, 27, 71, 83, 84, 102, 103, 105, 115, 117, 143, 150, 156, 157, 178, 182, 190, 191
Exley, Catherine, 137, 140, 147
Experiential knowledge, 20, 180

F

Family
  expectations, vii, 9, 10, 133, 190
  obligations, 14, 190
  responsibilities, 36, 190
  roles, 190
  transitions, 13, 15, 18
Foucault, Michel, 9, 20, 21
Friedman, Sam, 149, 150
Funerals
  rituals, vii, 16
  service, 49, 138

G

Gender, v, vii, 4, 18, 25, 88, 131, 133, 138, 146, 183
Generation, 14, 18, 103, 108, 109, 127, 191, 193
Giddens, Anthony, 24

Glaser, Barney G., 6, 12, 33
Goffman, Erving, 11, 24, 52, 185
Green, James, 10
Grief, 2–4, 12, 13, 15, 17, 19, 24, 33, 43, 49, 79–98, 101–103, 106, 108, 113, 115, 116, 121–123, 128, 131, 133, 142, 147, 156, 179, 181, 182, 189, 190

H

Hanley, Lindsay, 142, 143
Higher education, 109, 191
Home
    hometown, 135, 191, 192
    parental, v–vii, 1, 5, 14, 16, 18, 26, 62, 191
Hooks, bell, 22, 24–26
Howarth, Glennys, 5, 8, 9, 67, 148

I

Identity
    as bereaved person, 181, 189
    as daughter, vi, 40, 47, 49, 53, 69, 79–98, 110, 111, 125, 159, 183, 184, 186
    fluid, 68, 149
    as professional, v–vii, 1, 2, 5, 7, 10, 19, 23, 27, 85, 130, 131, 141, 156, 178, 182, 183
    as son, 40, 55, 69, 73, 102–104, 107–109, 111, 113, 117, 136, 139, 141–143, 147, 148, 159, 183
    spoiled, 52, 103, 185
Illich, Ivan, 7, 13

Inheritance, 10, 18, 188, 192
Intimacy, vi, 2, 12, 33, 70, 71, 74

K

Kellehear, Allan, 5–8, 10
Kesson, Jessie, 146
Klass, Dennis, 18
Kubler-Ross, Elisabeth, 94
Kuhn, Annette, 18, 22, 148

L

Leder, Drew, 185
Legacy, 18, 101–117, 189
Letherby, Gayle, 130, 131
Lévi-Strauss, Claude, 157

M

McNamara, Barbara, 8, 9, 11, 12
Meaning, v, vii, 3, 5, 8, 10, 13, 15, 20, 22, 24, 80, 92, 130, 148, 179, 182, 189
Medicalisation, 4, 6, 8, 13
Memory, v, 17, 18, 21–23, 26, 27, 36, 39–43, 49, 72, 76, 85, 87, 89, 93, 97, 103–105, 107, 108, 110, 111, 113, 114, 117, 121, 122, 128, 130, 133, 139, 150, 155, 157, 158, 177, 184, 187
Modernity, 131, 137, 191
Mol, Hans, 67, 167, 169, 170, 172, 174
Moss, Miriam, vii, 13, 14, 16
Moss, Sidney, vii, 13, 14, 16

O

Opacity, 27, 155, 156
Orr, Deborah, 130

P

Personhood, 27, 155, 156, 188
Post Traumatic Stress Disorder (PTSD), 121
Power, 11, 81, 182
Privacy, vi, 86
Private, vi, 2, 5, 7, 24, 25, 51, 52, 80, 110, 134, 156, 160, 178
Professionalisation, 4, 7, 19

R

Recovery, vi, 3, 12, 23, 25, 38, 64, 110, 159, 179
Reflection, 1, 15, 27, 34, 46, 51, 83, 129, 136, 138, 140, 143, 155, 183, 185
Reflexivity, 150, 151
Regret, vi, 2, 6, 9, 11, 12, 102, 106, 116, 126–128, 142
Relational, 16, 17, 21, 130, 149, 150, 188
Relationships
  brother, 11, 52, 72, 82, 85, 88, 110–112, 121, 123–126, 133–136, 144, 159, 192
  daughter, 111, 186
  family, vi, vii, 2–4, 7, 9–11, 14, 16–19, 24, 26, 27, 36, 37, 40, 44, 46, 50, 52, 63, 64, 70, 72, 75, 77, 82–86, 88–90, 92, 95–98, 102–104, 106, 107, 111, 112, 114–117, 121, 123, 124, 126, 127, 133–135, 141–143, 146, 149, 158–161, 181, 185, 189–193
  parental, v–viii, 1, 4, 5, 12–16, 18, 26, 27, 59, 62, 157–160, 177–179, 182–184, 189, 191, 192
  siblings, vii, 11, 16, 44, 53, 82, 84, 88, 89, 95–98, 98n1
  sister, 7, 11, 19, 35, 37, 42, 44, 47, 49, 79, 82, 85, 96, 104–114, 126, 147, 159, 184–187, 189, 192, 193
  son, 40, 55, 69, 73, 102–104, 108, 109, 111–113, 117, 139, 141–143, 147, 148, 159, 183
Ribbens McCarthy, Jane, 15, 93
Rose, Nikolas, 130, 131, 149

S

Scarre, Geoffrey, 25, 26
Scott, Joan W., 21
Scott, Sara, 18
Scott, Sue, 18
Secrecy (sacred), vi, 155–175, 179
Secrets, 17, 18, 24, 26, 180
Sequestration, 4, 19
Silence, vi, 12, 17, 18, 24–26, 63, 70, 91, 157, 179–181
Silva, Elisabeth B., 149, 150
Simmel, Georg, 166, 167, 174
Skeggs, Beverley, 138, 148, 149
Smart, Carol, 17

Social class, 16, 18, 27, 131, 143–150, 170, 183
Social change, 8, 16, 17, 129, 143
Stanley, Liz, 21, 22
Status, 122, 139, 182, 190
Stories, 17, 18, 23–26, 74, 85, 88, 108–112, 116, 121, 130, 132, 146, 157, 158, 177–181, 183
Strauss, Anselm L., 6, 12, 33
Subjectivity, 20, 148, 150, 189

T

Time, vi, vii, 5, 7–9, 13, 14, 18, 19, 23, 25–27, 35–43, 45, 46, 48–50, 52, 59–62, 64, 65, 67–71, 73, 74, 76, 77, 80–91, 93–95, 97, 98, 101–102, 104–116, 120–122, 124–127, 130–134, 136–147, 149, 157, 158, 160, 177–179, 184, 186, 187, 189–193
Timeliness, 12, 13, 37

V

van Gennep, Arthur, 14

W

Walter, Tony, 12, 17, 147
War
  First World War, 4, 52
  Second World War, 4, 35, 52, 87, 93
Woodthorpe, Kate, 10, 16, 20, 129

GPSR Compliance

The European Union's (EU) General Product Safety Regulation (GPSR) is a set of rules that requires consumer products to be safe and our obligations to ensure this.

If you have any concerns about our products, you can contact us on

ProductSafety@springernature.com

In case Publisher is established outside the EU, the EU authorized representative is:

Springer Nature Customer Service Center GmbH
Europaplatz 3
69115 Heidelberg, Germany